Smithsonian Institution Press   Washington and London

by Dicky Wells

as told to Stanley Dance

The Night People

The Jazz Life of Dicky Wells

Editor: Kathryn Ryan Stafford
Production Editor: Duke Johns
Designer: Alan Carter

Library of Congress Cataloging-in-Publication Data

Wells, Dicky, 1910–
    The night people : the jazz life of Dicky Wells /
    by Dicky Wells as told to Stanley Dance. —
    Rev. ed.
        p.   cm.
    Discography: p.
    Includes index.
    ISBN 1-56098-067-2
    1. Wells, Dicky, 1910–   . 2. Jazz musicians—
United States—Biography. I. Dance, Stanley. II.
Title.
ML419.W44A3   1991
788.9′3165′092—dc20
    [B]   90-24916

British Library Cataloguing-in-Publication Data is
available

Manufactured in the United States of America
98 97 96 95 94 93 92 91   5 4 3 2 1

⊗ The paper used in this publication meets the
minimum requirements of the American National
Standard for Permanence of Paper for Printed
Library Materials Z39.48-1984

. . . . . . *contents*

. . . . *foreword*

It was a real surprise to me to find that Dicky Wells was doubling on typewriter, but what comes out of it is as much of a kick as his music. If you look for them, you can find translations here of some of those talking phrases he specializes in.

I don't know if they're making trombone players of the same stuff now, but he sounds as good to me today as when I first heard him, and I'm not going to say when that was!

Of course, he makes "the Road" come to life, and even a little too real at times, because it never was any bed of roses. In fact, here you have the authentic jazz world—onstage, backstage, and in the bus.

Count Basie
1971

. . . . *preface*

In telling his story here, Dicky Wells has a great deal to say about the world in which he has lived and worked as a jazz musician. He deals frankly with its occupational hazards, its joys and sorrows, and he is generously appreciative of the talents and triumphs of others. About his own successes, however, and about his own artistic contribution to the history of jazz, he is not particularly expansive.

An individualist, and one of the great trombone soloists, he might well be described as inimitable. Nearly every major creator in jazz has had his easily recognizable disciples and imitators, but this has not been so in the case of Dicky Wells. He perfected such an intensely personal style that, though it was widely admired, it was never imitated, successfully or unsuccessfully.

He became a pacesetter in his profession during the era of the big bands, and his ability as a musician is made evident by considering a partial list of the leaders for whom he worked: Benny Carter, Charlie Johnson, Fletcher Henderson, Teddy Hill, Count Basie, Sy Oliver, Earl Hines, and Ray Charles. In their highly competitive world, he maintained himself for many years, both as an exceptional soloist and as an able member of their trombone sections.

The viewpoint from which the jazz world is seen here is, therefore, that of one who has been a member of many great bands. The problems and virtues of leaders are considered and discussed, but it is a sideman, not a leader, who describes the night people and their ethos.

Reminiscences about such a long and varied career are inevitably incomplete. Essentially, this is the jazz life as Dicky Wells saw and remembered it in the 1960s. Sincere apologies are offered in advance for such factual errors and oversights as may have been made.

He has, for instance, no recollection of having worked with Luis Russell, although his employment by this leader is cited in several books. Biographies of jazz musicians are often based on discographies, but the fact that Dicky Wells recorded with Russell in 1931 does not mean that he was regularly a part of Russell's band. He believes that either J. C. Higginbotham or Jimmy Archey was indisposed, and that he was called in merely for the session.

The sequence of his early engagements, once he was established on the New York scene, is not, unfortunately, entirely clear. There are obscurantist memories of many jobs of short duration, but the order of the longer ones is almost certainly as presented here.

The examples of conversation on band buses, in dressing rooms, and at rehearsal are condensations intended to illumine a part of what might almost be called "big-band folklore." The selection of deceitful messages from Man's Best Friend, alias Ol' Man Ignorant Oil, will, it is hoped, also serve as a warning to those of the jazz audience who are guilty of the sin of intemperance.

There have been many books about jazz, but I believe the material collected here will shed new light on certain areas of the subject, and also show, as his music has long implied, that Dicky Wells is a unique and colorful personality.

Stanley Dance
1971

.... *introduction*

This new edition of *The Night People* should bring Dicky Wells's exceptional book the recognition it deserves. *The Night People* is exceptional not only because it is the biographical statement of an outstanding soloist of what we usually call "the swing era," and one who had illustrious associations, but because stylistically it virtually stands alone in jazz literature. Wisely, Dicky Wells and Stanley Dance decided to use—unapologetically—the eminently expressive colloquial language of Wells and his associates, with only enough change as might be needed for clarity.

True, there is a fine informality of language in Count Basie's *Good Morning Blues*, done with Albert Murray, and there is language in that important book that catches the genial terseness of Basie's own distillate piano. There are also Hampton Hawes's *Raise Up Off Me*, done with Don Asher, and Art Pepper's *Straight Life*, but those men belonged to another generation, and their particular stories are as much concerned with their struggles with drug addiction as they are with their lives as musicians.

From Wells's generation there is Milt Hinton's *Bass Line*, done with David A. Berger, but *Bass Line* is as much a collection of Hinton's fine photographs as it is his story, and the narrative, told with all the informal warmth and enthusiasm of Milt Hinton, is almost as careful in its language as are its author's bass lines in their choice of notes.

Dicky Wells on the page speaks as Wells and for Wells, and for his fellow riders in the band bus. He gets down, without ever getting dirty. Surely there is no more authentic record of how it felt to be a sideman in a great orchestra than this, or of how it felt to tour the segregated American South in the 1930s and 1940s, carrying the music to people who needed its message to give meaning to their lives.

There are also two wonderful, virtually self-contained episodes here: the "Bus Talk" chapter and the rehearsal in chapter 9. There is an interesting rehearsal in Artie Shaw's *The Trouble with Cinderella*, but that was a different sort of session, and the telling does not come from inside the band like this one.

Throughout it all, there is Dicky Wells, the conscientious center of *Night People*, proud, but not prideful, of his abilities; dedicated to his craft and art, but never pretentious about it or about himself. This must be what it was really like, he convinces us.

For this edition, Stanley Dance has provided *The Night People* with new introductory material for each chapter that clarifies the chronology of Wells's career. There is a new discography contributed by Chris Sheridan. And also included is the pioneering critical appreciation of Wells by André Hodeir from *Jazz: Its Evolution and Essence*.

Martin Williams
1991

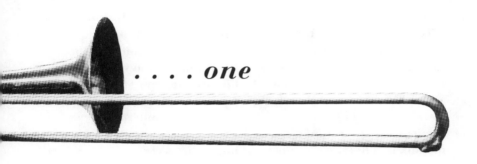

. . . . one

From Louisville

This first chapter offers a somewhat unusual picture of jazz developing in the twenties outside the main centers of New Orleans, Chicago, New York, and Kansas City. It is significant how many names later to become famous in jazz history are here encountered in what might be regarded as the hinterlands—Tennessee, Kentucky, West Virginia, and Ohio. There is, for example, a singular picture of Jimmy Harrison, one of the most important jazz trombonists, playing in a hotel with only a pianist to accompany him. Hess Grundy, today little more than a name in discographies, is another trombone player tellingly described, as is the legendary Sylvester Briscoe of the Jenkins Orphanage Band from Charleston. The importance of such charitable institutions as the latter and, indeed, of Louisville's Booker T. Washington Center, in whose Sunday school band Dicky Wells, Jonah Jones, Bill Beason, and Helen Humes received their early training, is implied but not perhaps adequately stressed. The young musicians were not, of course, taught jazz there—that and its ways they had to find for them-

selves—but they were given sound, rudimentary instruction on their instruments, and they were taught to read. Not all aspiring black players were so fortunate.

While Harrison was clearly Wells's main inspiration on trombone, the early friendships he made with Doc Cheatham, Bill Coleman, and Frank Newton, and the great impression made on him by Fletcher Henderson's trumpets—Joe Smith, Louis Armstrong, and Tommy Ladnier—inevitably had bearing on his style at a time when trumpet was the dominant jazz instrument.

Although he was to become a hip New Yorker, Wells speaks with undisguised affection of his country origins. He always retained something of the countryman's distrust of city values, and this was expressed in his blues playing. But then it is well to remember that New York itself produced surprisingly few outstanding jazz musicians in the twenties and thirties, most of them coming from other cities and towns across the country, and even from rural communities like Centerville, where Wells was born 10 June 1907.

S.D.

Centerville, Tennessee, was my birthplace. My pop's name was George Washington Wells, and I guess that's why he told me never to tell a lie. Now who can do that? Well, I tried.

My mother's name was Florence. Mom was the greatest. She told me some things I didn't dig till 'way late. She told me to respect all people; to use "Mr." or "Mrs." to all adults; to have respect for a woman whether she was a schoolteacher or a sporting woman; to believe in God above all, always; to love the ones that love you, but never to love anyone too much (even her), because that can cause you to lose your self-respect, and when that's gone so are you.

I had a brother, Charlie, and three sisters, Tenny, Leona, and Georgia. As for relatives, we had a whole mountainside of hillbillies, cousins, uncles, as well as jennies, mules, and whatnot. Centerville was a very small place, eighty miles from Nashville, a town nobody today probably heard of much. It was all farming and moonshine whiskey around there. My father was a farmer.

I had a good time, although my parents nearly lost me. That was in a little incident I had with my brother, when he was cutting wood. I was jiving around with him, backing under the ax and jumping away—but once I forgot to jump away. That took thirteen stitches, on my bottom. I didn't know if he was jiving, if he was trying to cut me a brand new one. As if I didn't already have one! No, I didn't know if he was kidding, but to show me he was really down, the very next day he split his toe in half with the ax. After that they called him the Ax-man.

That country life! "Barnyard Blues" was more than a song. It was happening. Have you ever hidden behind a barn? Well, some of the things I used to see would make "Tobacco Road" look like a bed-time story. Those cats would tackle anything breathing and call it fun! I was too young for their parties. All I could do was make it up the ladder to the hayloft.

We found a swimming hole, or at least we thought we had found it. We went back there one evening to find that some pink-toes had nailed a sign on a tree that said, "No Niggers Allowed." So we put one up that said, "No White Niggers Allowed." In our books, the word had no color. But the pink-toe that owned the farm took both signs down and put his own up, and it said, "Swimming to All." So we all had a ball and lived happily thereafter. Maybe there was a small uprising once in a while on the way to school, but next day we would bring along the gang's bully, and he would bring his shooting iron and fire up in the air. So that would cool the situation.

I had a cousin called Curly, who liked his ignorant oil. He was one of those real bowlegged cats, and he used to charge fifty cents to break a horse. If you didn't have the money, just get him high, and he would break the wildest stud in town. I never forgot how often people would ride by to tell us where to find him. A horse would have thrown him a country mile.

My other cousin, Ed, came to New York to visit soon after I got there. I heard that rascal getting up around five o'clock in the morning and asked him what was going on. He said he was going to feed the chickens!

After some years in Centerville, we moved up to Nashville for a time. I can remember there my mother ran across a fellow who had me sitting in a bar. She just turned that bar inside out, because he was feeding me whiskey. Later on, she told me to start drinking early, like wine, so I would *stop* early. But God bless her, though she doesn't know it, it took me a long time. I only stopped about five or six years ago. I woke up one morning in Paris and would have sworn Jo Jones and Buddy Rich were having a jam session around my heart. Wow! That cognac, that did it!

We moved to Louisville, Kentucky, when I was about ten years old. There, I remember, the cats used to hang out under the corner light talking big trash, and the kittens used to hide in listening distance. If the big cats saw you, they would catch you, and winter or summer, dunk you in the water trough where people watered their horses. They got me a couple of times, but then Mama would come out and clear the corner. She was small but fiery. Now if those fellows wanted to trick you, they would pretend not to see you and talk some jive, like what to do in case, etc. So one night they were talking some jive that I thought would help my troubles. One cat said, "Man, I got the cure for that. I put plenty of Jack Johnson liniment all around the area." So I eased away thinking I was straight. The next day I slipped out in the yard to the outhouse and closed the door, only to break through it in a few seconds and rush around the house, yelling like mad, and putting on speed every step. Mama told us to bring our troubles to her, so that I afterwards did, and that cured me of snooping around the corner.

My mother used to travel with my stepfather, so my sister Leona had charge of Charlie and me—mostly me, because Charlie was just about on his own. She saw to it we did the best we could, as my mother would have had it, like going to church Sundays, which I still do when I have time and am not working too late Saturdays. Yes, Leona did a good job, but one thing happened I never did figure out. I had some loot that I had hustled selling bottles, bones, rags, etc., and I had made a hole and buried it, but to this day I haven't found it. I am accusing no one, but there was only me, her, and the dog at home, and she still says she didn't dig it.

My parents died within a year of one another. When my mother passed, I slept on the floor of the room where she was laid out.

In Louisville, we joined the Sunday school band of the Booker T. Washington Community Center. We had about sixty pieces. Jonah Jones and Bill Beason were in it. So was Buddy Lee, who later played with McKinney's Cotton Pickers. And Helen Humes was singing. She was one of our schoolmates. She took up trumpet for a few months and later played piano and sang with the band. Her father was pretty well off. He was a lawyer. We were all her pals because they had a brand new car about once a year and used to drive us round town and to dances. She would drive us to the boat when we were going on a boat outing. We also used to go on hayrides, on large wagons covered with straw, and head for the open spaces. Some fun.

This Sunday school band was sponsored by a Miss Bessie Allen. She provided the instruments. We would travel in a truck and play country fairs, and the pay was three dollars and a half a week. That just about covered soft drinks—and girls. We slept in dormitories as a rule, but one time I remember we were playing a fair and were scattered about in different homes. We didn't see the fellow who owned the pad we were staying in, so we went to rehearsal with about everything decent that he owned. He wasn't too hard on us because one of the kids had on his mother's ring that he had been looking for for years. When we were ready to leave the next morning, I woke up late as usual. There was no one in the house, so I began to worry until I looked out the back. There were about ten suitcases lying under apple, peach and what-have-you trees, and all I could see was fruit falling like mad. We never made it back there again.

I started on baritone horn and later went to trombone because I slipped and broke the baritone, and we couldn't afford another. There were about six trombones, twelve trumpets—sixty pieces or more altogether. Lockwood Lewis was the conductor, and he taught us. He was a wonderful fellow, and he treated us as though we were his own kids.

Hank Duncan's younger brother was the virtuoso of the band. He played baritone horn, and no music stuck him. He got shot while playing in the rehearsal hall. It was a sad incident. Some fellow found a pistol in one of the lodge rooms and thought it wasn't loaded.

Then we organized a little seven-piece jazz band. That was how I got started at dances. Jonah wasn't in it. He seemed to be one of the slowest guys in the band. We called him Peanut Head! You wouldn't have thought it possible then, but eventually he wound up being a top man, which he is today.

We played funerals, parades, and all sorts of things like that, too, and we traveled all through Kentucky. The big band played in the day, and the jazz band at night. My brother Charlie became a drum major. I remember we were going up Walnut Street in Louisville once, and Charlie was prancing along by himself for about six blocks. The band had turned off at Tenth Street, but he was still going! He later put it down and went to Detroit, but we had a lot of fun with that band.

At the same time, I was working on an ice wagon for another

three dollars and a half a week. The fellow finally fired me because I would be asleep up there on top of the ice. I would be lying up there taking it easy on the cover. So he cut me loose, but being home, money didn't matter too much.

The band went to Chicago once, and those E Flat Capones really kept us country boys in line. Those cats wouldn't let us get five feet from the Y.M.C.A. Like real peckers, they'd say, "If I had you down South . . . " Well, if we had them down South it would have been a horse of another feather, but they had us up North. What started it all was one of our cutie pies out doing the town. He tried the wrong chick.

Up there, we played against forty-eight bands, and we came out second. I shall never forget that Kansas City Monarch Band. They had a trumpet player with a fine, strong tone. He was all over the park. I learned he was the great Bob Williams, one of the outstanding brass-band leaders and very famous at that time. George "Mitch" Mitchell was a friend of his.

The kid band in Chicago was the Chicago Defender Band. We hung them musically, but they were too sharp. They had two gold-lacquered tubas. This was 1925. Being a trombonist in a good band sure was kicks, because you were front-line material, and those rascals sure could swing those horns around. That Briscoe with the Jenkins Orphanage Band was the king strutter. He would have a bigger audience than the drum major. Of course, we had a boy drum major, but later, after coming to New York and digging some of those drum majorettes, I realized Briscoe would have had to eat it and keep it clean (I mean the trombone) to take the show.

The Jenkins Orphanage Band came from Charleston, South Carolina, and I first saw and heard it in Louisville. Jabbo Smith and Gus Aiken were in it. Briscoe was a short, tubby, left-handed guy, and he used to throw his horn around and play louder than the whole band. All the kids followed him. When he played dances he would sometimes put his right hand behind him, hold his horn with this left, then bend over and go along pushing and skidding the slide on the floor. I broke up some of Miss Allen's bones trying to dig that trick. Briscoe would also take the horn apart and play with just the mouthpiece, then assemble it bit by bit until he had it all together again, playing all the while—a one-man show. He'd play with his foot in the slide, too. Jimmy Harrison did some of those things, but he didn't dance around.

There were some other trombone players around Louisville who maybe have never been heard of. The first time I heard a guy play the plunger effect, I liked the sound, but it was kind of bitter to take. His name was Hess Grundy, and he drank a lot. He sounded good from the outside, from where I was dancing in the next room. So I went in to see him, and he was sitting there and grabbing the cuspidor or anything that came to hand as a mute. First he would chew tobacco, then spit in the cuspidor, and then grab it up and start growling in his horn. He couldn't do that anywhere, but it sure sounded good.

I would hear guys like him at house parties, Saturday nights, before I was playing. People who were short would run the parties to get extra dough. When they got 'em going, they might charge only a quarter to go in, and that way they would keep the gang together like a little club. They would have three, maybe four, pieces sitting in a corner with the lights turned down low, and there'd always be one of those older musicians sitting there playing. You could sit in or dance. They would have food that they would serve in the kitchen—maybe ten cents a sandwich.

There was a fellow called Morley Davis. He never left Louisville, but he was much admired by all good trombone players. He had a sweet, swinging style and a very good tone. He played with a guy by the name of Winston.

Jimmy Harrison used to play at a place called Ebb's Hotel in Louisville, with just a piano. He never liked anyone else to play with him then. He'd get angry if another musician came. He just liked to play by himself. He'd cross his legs and, boy, would he play! It was hard for me to get in the place because I was under age, and they wouldn't let me hang out there. There'd be gambling in the back and drinking in this little room. I suppose because I heard him so much, and liked his playing, and tried to play a lot of his things, that that was the reason why when I went to New York I began to get jobs behind him. Big Green, incidentally, was another who liked to play by himself. It seemed to give you something, something close to the voice.

Then there was Miff Mole, the J. J. Johnson of that day. I call J. J. "Mr. Clean," and Miff Mole was "Mr. Clean" then. I used to hear him on Red Nichols records, and his was one of the first,

8

fine, technical trombones I heard. He was definitely a big influence on trombone players. Jimmy Harrison was too, of course, and at the same time, but he was more of a swingster. He wouldn't play too fast, but he swung. Miff Mole was top man technically, but he didn't swing, wasn't as smutty as Jimmy. Jimmy was clean, but kind of low, too. On some records Miff got a valve effect similar to J. J. And imagine what would happen if you altered the chord construction, as they do today, on such tunes as "Nervous Charley" by Red Nichols or "Singin' the Blues" by Bix Beiderbecke. There would be very little difference.

Miff's wasn't Tommy Dorsey's style either. Tommy became an influence a little later. Tommy was with Goldkette, and it was Claude Jones with McKinney's Cotton Pickers, also in Detroit, who used to rave about this fellow playing such a fine trombone. Yes, there were quite a few guys then, and they were all different, not like today.

But I'm jumping ahead . . .

Most of the younger guys in the brass bands wanted to pull out and swing, but the older guys used to prefer to stay with the marches. They didn't earn too much, and they don't today. Parades for the Masons and Elks today pay scale and just about keep the guys on their horns, but in those days guys who were musicians usually didn't have other jobs. And music was classified as it is today. There weren't so many fine names for jazz. All we did was try to make a better arrangement than the next band had. We played as we felt; so some nights it was good, and some nights bad. There were no set solos.

I never heard that New Orleans "tailgate" style around Louisville. I guess that just wasn't the section for it. There were small bands around, but we were mostly after ten or twelve pieces, with showmanship on a kind of Lunceford kick. They would have two five-piece bands at the big white hotels, but these smaller groups—maybe trumpet, trombone, clarinet or sax, and rhythm—wouldn't play Dixieland. Somebody'd make little head arrangements, or they'd buy stocks and play solos as they felt, play what was inside them. Guys liked to play a lot of chords then, like Louis. A whole lot could be done with the chords: They could be turned so many ways.

In those days we played blues, but we played a lot of pop numbers, too. Those guys could get off on tunes like that. That's the reason Jimmy Harrison and some of the older musicians liked playing as entertainers, because those tunes would take you through so many different keys, and you'd learn so much. Like Vic Dickenson now. He knows about a million numbers, and he always likes to play melodies. He will play around with them by himself. Big Green, too, and all those people—they didn't stay in a blues vein. They could play just about anything, in whatever key you wanted, but they played it like they felt it. They would play a lot with singers. Imagine if you were playing trombone with some girl singer: you and her for several years, no other wind instrument, she singing and you playing behind her, often without even a piano. You got to get some kind of soul out of it from just listening to her. So I think there would be something kind of interwoven inside you from just being around singers so much. Even today, a trombone teacher—and he can be the best teacher in the world—will tell you that for melody you should grab a record by your favorite singer.

Louisville really was a place where most of the guys just played what they felt on their horns, but some of the older fellows had had no lessons and couldn't read. So they just grabbed their horns and made it the best way they could. We may have heard King Oliver's trumpet style, but I never heard that tailgate. I don't think I heard Dixieland until I went to New York. You might say the style around Louisville was kind of swing even when it came to a waltz. I believe it's like Basie said: "Nothing's too fast or too slow to swing!" Although Louisville is on the river and is called "the Gateway to the South," I don't think we ever got that real southern thing. There weren't many of those riverboats coming in there. I know one used to come in once in a while, but those cats out of St. Louis weren't playing Dixieland when I heard them. Those bands like Fate Marable's were playing music. And we used to hear the bands of Alphonso Trent, Lois Deppe, Arnold Johnson, and Jean Goldkette. Deppe's band was like McKinney's in that people used to go to hear him sing. In McKinney's case it was Fathead—George Thomas, that was. Deppe used to come on the riverboat from St. Louis, and he and Fate Marable covered more or less the same territory.

But our idols were Fletcher Henderson and Duke. We'd get the records and go in the house and copy those arrangements over two or three weeks, but I don't remember one Dixieland record then. They played the blues and just called them "the blues" and didn't have names for them like "rock 'n roll." We played a lot of white ballrooms, but we played more or less a swing style. We were arrangement crazy.

My first real band job was with Lucius Brown. We played at the Eight Mile House. It was the kind of place where you had your little cup, or your derby, sitting on the piano, and the people came and filled it up and requested their tunes. (Incidentally, it's rather like that in Canada now, where you play by request, and if you play what they ask for, it keeps you busy all night, and you don't have to play anything else.) I was supposed to be making twenty-five dollars, but Lucius was kind of slick, and he was giving me twelve and a half, until my friend Fletcher Allen told me:

"Man, you're supposed to be making more than that!"

So I asked Luke about it, and he said:

"Well, son, I'm learning you how to play, and you should pay me!"

Eventually he gave me the other twelve and a half.

Doc Cheatham was playing at a second road house near there, in Ferman Tapp's band, I think it was. Everyone wondered where he came from. He was such a nice trumpet player—beautiful tone, and all that. He was from Nashville, Tennessee, and he's one of the few guys still around who worked in those bands then. Tapp's still around, too, around New York, out on Long Island some place—a guitar player. In those days he played banjo and sang.

I worked with Luke until the train wreck. It happened at night. We were sitting in front. Although it was supposed to be segregated in Kentucky, we didn't have much trouble. It was an interurban car, a big car with a motorman. Some white couples came along at the next stop, and the motorman asked us to sit at the back, because we might be cursing and talking loud. We sat back at the back and about ten minutes later heard this explosion. An oil truck with about a dozen cars had come across the track. Nobody to this day knows how it happened, but they brought this motorman through the car with both his legs cut off, and put us all in an ambulance, and carried us off to hospital, and taped us up and whatnot. My chest was supposed to have been crushed. They only thing that really hurt me was when they tore that adhesive off—about a foot wide. Hair and skin and every-thing went. There was a fellow, a headwaiter, who lost his teeth in that wreck. Nobody knew he had false teeth, but they flew out, and somehow he got two or three thousand dollars of insurance. He had a lawyer work on it for him. One of the girls got hurt, too. You could hear her saying "Don't tell mama!" They were teenagers who had slipped out and didn't want their mothers to know they'd been to a dance.

We had to lay up after that. I was staying with a fellow called Les Carr in Mudtown, Louisville. It was called Mudtown because it was down the end of town and so muddy there. Then we had a Smoketown, further uptown, with a lot of factories, and smoky like. Cabbage Patch was another section, where they raised cabbages. Bill Beason, the drummer, lived there. They were the nicknames for some of the suburbs. They'd chase you all out of that part of town if they caught you after the girls, but they'd give us a break because we were musicians. We would parade through there with funerals, and after the funeral we would come back swinging. So the cats were kind of in our corner.

Next I went to Huntington, West Virginia, to join Jordan Emery. We rehearsed for just about a month there. I'll never forget the first gig we had. This guy Jordan used to work in a pawnshop. He had to work there to get the instruments and things he wanted, but the owner wouldn't let him have the instruments until he had some way of paying. It turned out that when we had finished that first gig we had cleared about twenty-seven cents. Luckily, there was a lady called Mrs. Stewart who liked musicians—her young son was a musician—and we lived in her house. We ate so many beans I was ashamed to look a bean in the face! Nothing happened there, so I had to go back to Louisville.

I went with this Ferman Tapp at the roadhouse, with Doc Cheatham, and I knocked around Louisville for a while, doing this and that, until Lloyd and Cecil Scott came through Kentucky to this Lyon's Garden dancehall. They used to have marvelous bands there—Erskine Tate, Alphonso Trent, Lois Deppe, and Fletcher Henderson. I remember when Joe Smith and Tommy Ladnier were there with Fletcher. They used to be kind of erratic because of their automobiles, and sometimes the band would be only six or seven pieces, but they were such great musicians you wouldn't miss the others. They did such terrific

12

blowing. Those were cats of distinction. You would run twenty-five, thirty miles to hear guys like that, because they had so much that was different to offer. Imagine hearing Louis Armstrong and Joe Smith side by side! I first heard Louis with Fletcher at the Lyon's Garden. There were so many things happening then that you would never have thought Louis was going to be so great. He was playing smooth and nice, and swinging. He was outstanding. After that, he put out almost too many hit records at once, like "Cornet Shop Suey" and all those things far back. You just wondered where a guy like that had come from.

Lloyd Scott first heard me at that Lyon's Garden, and he got me to go to Springfield to join his band. We played there a while—Lloyd and Cecil, Bill Coleman, Frank Newton, and Don Frye. It was a wonderful novelty band. We did all kinds of imitations—train effects, and so on. Oh, we had the gimmicks! But we didn't have any music! We would rehearse at Lloyd's house. They'd put on a pot, and it would maybe take us all day to get one head arrangement straight. We liked Duke's band for "Birmingham Breakdown" and that sort of number. That jungle thing he had had a decent sound and attracted attention. We had quite a repertoire, but if a guy was ill we couldn't hire anyone else because they wouldn't know how to play it. So we knocked around Springfield, had a good time at night, running around and carrying on. Lloyd Scott's Bright Boys—that was us! It was a cooperative band. Everybody owned a part of it. Some nights we'd make fifty dollars; maybe next night nothing. If it rained, we would all be watching the door. But we had fun.

We'd go to Cincinnati, to Bill Coleman's daddy's house. He made this home brew. We'd be knocking on his door at eight o'clock in the morning, crying "Home brew for breakfast!" He called us all his kids. We drink that home brew, and it kept us going. We had a little treasure going, too. We worked it up to about three hundred dollars, until somebody broke into the room—and we still don't know who it was—and took all our bread. That band was really a family thing. We used to live in the Sterling Hotel, Cincinnati, and it became our headquarters, because we liked the big city better than Springfield.

I was about twenty years old when we went to Pittsburgh. Buchanan of the Savoy Ballroom heard us at a little place on Wiley Avenue and took us to New York, to the Savoy. Besides those I've mentioned before, we had "Hoagie" Walker, Johnny Williams, and Harold McFarren on saxophones, "Meathead" or Mack Walker (Hoagie's brother) on bass, and Hubert Mann on banjo. Cecil Scott was called "Butterball." He had a big high hat, danced, did splits, did right well. We would give the big bands a run for their money on account of the novelties.

Cats like Fletcher and Duke used to come down when we were playing the Capitol Palace, a hole across from the Savoy. (I believe Luis Russell was the last to work there.) Everybody used to come down there from the big bands and stand around and listen to our little novelty band, because we would copy their arrangements to the best of our ability. After working around New York for a time, I went back to Kentucky. Cliff Jackson sent for me in June. He still kids me about it, because I arrived at Christmas to play at a place called the Swanee Club down under the RKO Theatre. He had about ten pieces and this trumpet player, Cuban Bennett, cousin to Benny Carter. He taught Benny to play trumpet. He played changes like I've never heard. He would play four or five entirely different choruses and try to end on a high note. If he couldn't make it, he would play four or five more choruses until he finally got it. Then he would cream. People like Hawk [Coleman Hawkins], Roy [Eldridge], Benny [Carter], and Don [Redman] always talked about him. He was a wonderful guy, the last word, and I don't know why he dropped out of the scene. At one time he was playing downtown in a taxi dance hall where Bingie Madison had a big band with arrangements. He used to hang out at a place called Greasy's, and he was drinking quite a bit, but he never really cared to play in an organized band. He just liked to hang around and blow in the joints, and the joints finally gave out. Later, I understand, he was on a farm his people left him.

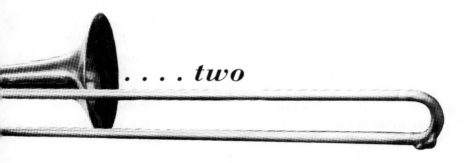

. . . . two

Harlem Heyday

Dicky Wells was barely twenty when he arrived in New York with Lloyd Scott's Bright Boys, but he was already a musician of considerable experience. His timing was good, the Savoy Ballroom in Harlem having opened a short time previously on 12 March 1926. As this chapter makes clear, the Swing Era had really begun long before 1935 and the rise of Benny Goodman. And the Savoy was the focal point. Harlem itself was an area where competition between the leading black bands was intense. Like their white counterparts downtown, they mostly played for dancing, but with a difference. The uptown dancers wanted more than music to which they *could* dance; they increasingly demanded music that would inspire or "send" them. Pop songs of the day continued to form a larger part of repertoires, but bands were more and more identified by the original work of their distinctive arrangements and soloists. The music was held to be "hot" when it was rhythmically and tonally exciting, but very early in 1932 Duke Ellington's composition, "It Don't Mean a Thing if It Ain't Got That Swing," indicated a vital element more specifically and provided a signpost to the future.

Dicky Wells was in the middle of all this instrumental ferment. His talent was quickly recognized and, often following in Jimmy Harrison's footsteps, he played in top bands led by Billy Fowler, Benny Carter, Charlie Johnson, Elmer Snowden, Fletcher Henderson, and Teddy Hill.

S.D.

The next band I remember playing with was Billy Fowler's. It was a big band, and he had such guys as Prince Robinson, Benny Carter, and Jimmy Harrison. It seems that I followed Jimmy into a lot of spots, because I went into Charlie Johnson's band behind him, too. Ward Pinkett, Freddie Johnson, and Walter Johnson were with Fowler as well. There were ten or twelve pieces, and all these guys could sight read, which I had learned to do in the kid's band. Benny Carter was a youngster, but he was really writing. He would bring these special arrangements in, and they would put them up and just read 'em down—never rehearse. "Cuttin' it," they called it. It was just a shame if you couldn't read. They wouldn't have you around. But they weren't particular about the drummer reading. They said he got too fly if he could read! A lot of times they would ask a drummer if he could read, but if he said "Yeah," they then wouldn't hire him, because it seemed as though he would always get too flashy. It's a good thing those leaders aren't active today, because it would be murder every night!

Billy Fowler played the Savoy and went to the Nest on 133rd Street, where the Rhythm Club is today. There were seven or eight bands in Harlem when I first came, and there was quite a shortage of musicians. You couldn't get a musician on the street, there were so few. There was the Plantation, the Cotton Club, the Savoy, Smalls', and several more places like that, all with big bands. There were bands coming from Chicago and everywhere to these places. There wasn't so much loose gigging then. You were always playing in an organized band, a full band, sometimes for two or three years. You might stay at the Savoy for maybe six months.

Fess Williams was the mainstay at the Savoy then; he had the house band, a big band. (Fess is some kind of official down at the union now.) He had a clarinet gimmick, and he was a pretty slick guy. He might play a waltz for an encore, and the people would applaud for ten minutes, but he would walk off the stand and say, "Always keep them wanting a bit more!" He had been a schoolteacher before that, from Winchester, Kentucky.

After Fess, Chick Webb had the house band. He had the joint pretty well wrapped up, and he used to cut everybody that went in there. I remember playing a week with Chick once when Big Green was ill. It was at the Lafayette Theatre. All the bands used to go in there. Well, I was down in front, and the people were applauding, and I was bowing and thinking it pretty nice, when something struck me to turn around, and there was Chick really breaking the joint up. He could break up a show any time he wanted. He'd start hunching his shoulders, and throwing his sticks, and really playing!

Big Green sent word he heard I got a few hands, but that they were really for the nerve I had sitting in his chair! He was one of the grandest fellows ever. There was no way of making him angry. In fact, that went for a whole lot of the cats. If you tried to shake up the likes of Benny Carter, Hawk, Don Redman, or Buster Bailey, they would just goof you off, and *you* wound up angry, not them. Big Green went out like some of the greatest— wear and tear of the game.

When Billy Fowler disbanded, I worked a while with Benny Carter, maybe six months. I think that was the second of Benny's bands. Walter Johnson told me the first one—six pieces—had played at the Colonnades downtown. Benny now took over some of Fowler's guys and had about twelve pieces, including Ward Pinkett, Prince Robinson, Joe Garland, Freddy Johnson, and Walter Johnson. We played the Savoy and later went to the Empire downtown. His arrangements at that time sounded a bit like Don Redman's, whom he idolized. Before Fletcher Henderson, the music and arrangements I most enjoyed were Benny's. I liked him so much as a person, too, and, like everyone else, I loved to hear him blow. His bands used to sound so good because of the

18

book. All he would ask you to do was to play the notes—nothing extra. If you accidentally played a wrong note, he'd stop the band and ask you what note you played. "The one on the paper," you'd answer. "You'd better look again," he'd say.

He was very well liked because he knew how to rub his men down, get what he wanted out of them, and leave them smiling. It was very rare for anyone to be late, because the guys liked playing his music so much. The band always came first with him, and if ever there was any trouble where we were playing, the proprietor had to speak to him about it, *not* to the guys in the band. We didn't make much money, but we had a lot of fun.

Benny played very nice trumpet as well as saxophone. Ward Pinkett, who looked like a Mexican, was a very tasteful trumpet player, too, although he hadn't a great range.

I was in another of Benny's bands in 1932, when he had Wayman Carver, Chu Berry, and Big Sid Catlett. We rehearsed, and we went out on the road, but the band broke up. It was too large for the times. Or too swinging. Or it had too much finesse. I don't know which. With a few changes, it was this band which made the records with Spike Hughes in 1933.

After my first experience of working with Benny, I think I must have gone to Charlie Johnson, following George Washington. George had good tone and control, like Jack Teagarden. Charlie had a wonderful drummer named George Stafford. He had a special beat that we called "shovelin' coal." He died of TB. Then there were Sidney De Paris and Leonard Davis, trumpets; Bobby Johnson on banjo and Billy Taylor on bass; Ben Whittet, Ben Waters, and Edgar Sampson were the saxes, and they were soon joined by Benny Carter. Charlie played piano, but the band often had to work without him.

Charlie had the job at Smalls', and it was a good job for pay. Charlie used to be like Chick. He liked to stick his chest out and tell how much he was paying you, and all that. He liked to pay you as much as he possibly could. Chick went hungry a lot just to keep his band in music. He would live on hamburgers so he could buy arrangements. It just began to pay off for him when— God bless him!—he had to leave.

We used to call Charlie "Fess" (for Professor). If a guy didn't know music, he was the more likely to be called "Fess." (You dig why Benny Carter was called "King"?) Well, Charlie loved to leave the piano and come out front to start his band, so much so that if only one cat had arrived he would still come out front and start him off, smiling as if the entire band were there. He was the most down-to-earth leader—nothing fancy, just a plain man— like my favorite bandleader, the one that's older than water! And both of them were King Cursers. What words! But only in a joking way. Anyway, Fess would count, stomp his feet, and use arm motions all at once to start the band. One time he was out front trying to start it when Bobby Johnson suddenly yelled, "Fess, you got the introduction!" And that was on the air, too.

Charlie's was one of the funniest bands I was ever in. Billy Taylor, the bass player, had a big alarm clock. I saw it sitting there when I joined the band. He'd have it set for twelve o'clock, his supper time. The band would be playing, and this alarm clock would go off! That was the time he wanted to eat! Smalls' usually never noticed these things, but one night it went off when he happened to be standing by the bandstand.

"What the hell's going on here?" he wanted to know.

So Charlie explained. He didn't worry. He didn't care. We just went on playing, but flies were beginning to gather in the corner where Billy was eating his sardines. "Girls," he called them.

"I got a can of 'girls' back here, Charlie," he'd say. "Lend me your opener." (That was like when I was traveling with Buddy Tate in Europe in 1959. We might be staying in the most elaborate joint, like a king's suite, but he'd be opening his "girls" at night, and I'd be going around wiping oil off the floor! He even learned how to order "girls" in German, and he'd eat them with crackers or anything.)

I remember when Clyde Beatty's "Bring 'Em Back Alive" show came out, and the guys would argue about which was the most vicious animal in the jungle. George Stafford said the tiger was the worst, the most vicious killer, and Billy would say the lion was. So the band would be playing one of these fast numbers, and George would stop playing and pull out a great, big placard he'd got from Madison Square Garden, right on the bandstand.

"Look at that, man," he'd say, pointing at a tiger, "there ain't no way in the world a lion can whip this rascal!"

All the time, the band would be playing. Another night they would be arguing about prizefighters, and a guy would quit right in the middle of his solo to get in the argument.

20

Now, Sidney De Paris and Leonard Davis, two trumpet players, weren't speaking. There seemed to be something like there was with Lester [Young] and Herschel [Evans] in Basie's band. The guys liked each other, but there seemed to be a little something that made them want to play more than the other. These two guys were both terrific, but though they were sitting side by side for several years, they wouldn't speak. They were good friends, though, deep down under.

Benny Carter would have the waiter bring his lunch around one o'clock in the morning. He'd have on a pair of dark glasses that he'd put up high on his forehead when he was playing. Charlie Johnson gambled a lot, and he'd often be upstairs gambling, maybe winning four or five thousand dollars one night and losing it all the next. So Benny would have the waiter come, and he would set this big tray down, and Benny would pull the glasses down over his eyes and start eating. Then he'd get drowsy and fall asleep—all this on the stand. Sometimes Charlie would come back and catch him and say:

"Wake up over there—eating on my job!"

"It won't happen again, Fess," Benny would say. "You have my word of honor. I respect you, and I wouldn't do a thing like this on your job. I don't know what came over me, Charlie."

The next night the same thing—here comes this waiter!

One night, the tenor player didn't show up, and that was when you couldn't get musicians easily. So Charlie sent Leonard Davis to the Rhythm Club to bring a tenor player back. When Leonard came back he had got a drummer.

"Man, I can't play no saxophone," this cat was saying.

"Oh, come on, man," Leonard was saying, "Just sit there and hold the horn and make the money. Charlie ain't going to be here. He'll be upstairs gambling."

Well, we were broadcasting, and this guy was sitting down to "play." Then, later, the show comes on, and Leonard says to him:

"Look, at this spot here, when the boy comes out to dance, to do this African thing, that's when you go out and take the drums and shout 'Ooh-wa-wa-wa-wa!'"

So we see this cat coming through the brass section, and we say,

"Where in the hell is he going?"

And he's standing by the gate where the show comes on when Charlie sees him.

"What's that guy doing out there, man?" he asks.

"I don't know," says Leonard.

The boy is looking around, all anxious. He don't know what to do. He comes back with the drums and waves to us from the door. He didn't want that job for any money. Oh, it was a crazy house!

Charlie himself was a swell guy. Pay night, there'd be a line around the booth, and Charlie would sometimes be high and pay you twice.

"I see you guys ducking back, getting in the back of the line," he'd say. "What's happening here?"

Sometimes a guy would hold out his hand with his head turned away and maybe get an extra envelope. And that didn't just happen when Charlie had won at gambling. The place was terrific, and it had a high payroll. At one time, I think Charlie was getting around fifteen hundred for himself. Bobby Johnson was kind of his right-hand man, and later he started paying off.

One night, Charlie told us: "Mr. Smalls is going to have a meeting. He wants all you guys in the office."

So we go to the office, and I was worrying, because I had just got there, and the money was pretty good, and I wondered whether I was going to be fired.

"There ain't enough cars upstairs," he said. "I want cars outside to make this place really look like something. Anybody want anything, see Sampson, the secretary."

The guys got cars. I think Sidney got a Cadillac. Jimmy Harrison had had a Dodge just before I got there. That was the kind of job it was. So the next night the people couldn't get in for the cars sitting around outside.

"How we going to pay you back, boss?" the guys asked.

"Any way you want," Ed said, "twenty-five, fifteen, ten dollars a week."

Then I remember Billy Taylor buying his son a train. We'd hit at ten o'clock, and come twelve o'clock there'd still be no Billy. He'd be at home playing with his train.

"Charlie, I don't feel good," another guy would say.

"Well, go home," Charlie would say.

George Stafford would go home and get his chick, come back

and take a ringside seat, and just sit a-looking, and us with no drummer. That sort of thing went on for a year and a half, I know, but I got there a little late, although from what I heard it had been going on all the time.

Smalls' did terrific business. They reserved the seats by the year. You'd see a party come in every Friday or Saturday to the same table. You couldn't get room down to the place weekends. And all the waiters danced with their trays, and they put on a little show all by themselves. There were ten of them, and two of them sang. Some of them own the Rhythm Club now.

Charlie's band used to swing. It used to hang Duke every time they caught him. Duke had only about seven pieces then, but he had more finesse, of course. Charlie's was a little like Fletcher's band. The cats didn't know they had a boss, but they could pull it out when they had to. Fletcher [Henderson] didn't actually want to be a boss. He was something like Buck Clayton on my third trip to Europe. Buck didn't want to be a boss, but he expected everybody to act right. Those guys of Charlie's, they did everything, and Smalls' was like home.

When we played a theater like the Lafayette, Charlie would always figure out some different way of presentation. Once we had a chocolate box, a great, big chocolate box on stage, and the band was inside it. When we played the opening, the lid would lift up, and there we'd be, inside, playing. We were called Chocolate Dandies, and I know sometimes we nearly melted away, it was so hot in there.

I played at Smalls' again later, in Elmer Snowden's band, with Roy Eldridge. Roy and I knocked around in two or three bands together. Elmer's was a good band, too. Big Sid was there. Boy, did we get our kicks! Otto Hardwick was there, too, and Duke used to come down and try to get him back. Snowden was a good guy and a wonderful leader, but it seems as though the bands that played Smalls' once they came out, didn't go. It was sometimes the same way at the Savoy; once you came out, nobody had heard of you.

Sidney Catlett was very instrumental in the success of Snowden's band. He was always pushing the guys. He was a musician's drummer. He would ask you:

"What kind of rhythm should I play for you? What do you want?"

That was as soon as you came in the band, and after you had told him, you would get the same thing every night, unless you told him to change it. He was a lovable guy. All he had to say was, "Let's go jam," and he had a mob following him. Everyone loved him for the way he would push you.

Then I played with Vernon Andrade around at the Renaissance for about six months. It was the house band at that ballroom. The boss there gave Jimmie Lunceford an early break and, regardless of what he was doing, Jimmie would come in to play there every Christmas. Later on, the Savoy washed them away, and they would have dances only once a week.

Charlie Dixon used to write for Vernon Andrade. (He also played banjo and guitar with Fletcher Henderson.) He would bring an arrangement to the ballroom, start it off, and then go and hide. When it began to get difficult for the cats, he would just about die laughing. He would put all the notes he could find in the damn thing, and then he would be laughing and saying, "I see the flyspecks blinded you cats!"

Now there was this Hoofer's Club on 132nd and Seventh, downstairs, "down in the hole" we called it. They sent out these cards—"You Are Invited to a Trombone Supper"—regular invitations like you get to a wedding. They would have these sessions, and you would be invited to a cutting contest, to bring your ax. Another night there would be invitations to a Trumpet Supper, or a Saxophone Supper. The Hoofer's Club was below Big John's bar, in an empty hall he rented for these sessions, mostly at weekends. Anyone could go, but mostly performers went, mostly musicians. There was no admission charge, and we weren't paid. No money was involved at all.

All the musicians would be sitting around the walls, all around the dance floor. Maybe there would be forty guys sitting around there. The floor was for dancers only, and they would be cutting each other, too, while we were cutting each other on the instruments. Everybody would be blowing—maybe six trombones. Now Hawk [Coleman Hawkins] would always come by the session, whether it was a Saxophone Supper or not.

"I just happened to stop by and had my horn," he would say.

You knew he'd come in to carve somebody.

Everybody would be blowing away, changing keys and going on, everything happening. You'd stomp your foot or hold up your hand if you wanted another chorus. When nobody stomped a foot, and the piano was just vamping, Joe Smith might be in a corner, and he would break in with his plunger. You didn't know he was there, but he'd play "Show Me the Way to Go Home" and break up the whole show, bring tears to your eyes. The next time it would be Hawk who would run everybody out.

Joe Smith and Johnny Dunn had a fight on a corner when I first came to New York, about who first started using the plunger. We wondered what was happening, but they shook hands after that. Before the plunger, guys were using ordinary water glasses for mutes. Joe used a plunger, but he didn't growl at all. I think the closest today is Dud Bascomb. He's an individualist and hasn't lost anything. He plays a good, stable style, a second-chair style, so that at times he sounds a bit like Bill Coleman or Bobby Stark. He's still gigging around. On an open horn, Harry James sometimes sounds like Joe did with a plunger. Joe was so smooth. It seemed the plunger was part of him and the horn. He had it so perfect that when he wanted to swell a note or bring it in, it was just like a human voice. He had a beautiful tone. His brother Russell said he didn't know where he got his ideas from. Tyree Glenn, now, he can play smooth with a plunger like that, and Shorty Baker has a similar soft tone, but when Harry James wants to play real sweet, he really gets it sometimes. Joe really could make you think it was somebody singing. He had it so even. There was a boy named Harry Cooper who had it down good, too, but the last was Howard Scott—"Scotty" we called him. Last I heard, he was working in the post office. He had it down and played for Benny Carter for a while, and Benny liked him because he sounded like Joe. I guess he was the last to imitate Joe. Frank Newton had a special sound, too, but Frank was very inventive, and I never knew where he got his ideas from. All trumpet players respected Frank for his ideas. He always believed in giving the people something different.

To go back to the Hoofer's Club . . . While I'm blowing, the next trombone player would go in back, where Big John would be serving bean soup free. Maybe you would have a little taste upstairs, but when you got your gauge up and your stomach full, you'd go back and blow some more. That would go on until seven or eight in the morning.

Everyone loved Big John. His nickname was Meatball. If you

had a buck, okay; if you didn't, okay. Horace Henderson wrote that swinging tune, "Big John's Special," and dedicated it to him. Horace was, and still is, a top arranger. He brought a wild band to the Savoy from Wilberforce University and had the town talking.

We'd be playing a show at Smalls' with Charlie Johnson—a two-hour or an hour-and-a-half show—and ofays would come from downtown, like Tommy and Jimmy Dorsey (Jimmy with his clarinet in his pocket), Benny Goodman, and Jack Teagarden, and those guys, and sometimes they'd play our dance sets for maybe a couple of hours. Just sit and jam. And we'd go to Hoofer's and have a little session, or go to a place called Ed Wynn's and get some chili, hot-dogs or hamburgers. Then we'd go back and play the show and then maybe walk around the street again. It was really a wonderful thing. Musicians from out of town all used to want to come to Harlem and go to Smalls'. That was after he moved from Fifth Avenue, and most of the guys used to come there to hear Charlie Johnson and see the big shows. Ethel Waters was there before I came. Smalls' moved over to Seventh about a year after I arrived in New York.

Of course, when we went to Buffalo, we would have another kind of supper, a Buffalo Supper, at a cabaret Ann Montgomery had. There would be Jonah Jones, Willie Smith, and the Lunceford alumni waiting to carve you. Ed Inge, the clarinet player who later on worked with Don Redman, was there, too. They'd keep you out to seven or eight in the morning. They'd be waiting to work you over, and when they came to New York, we'd be waiting for them. That was the thing in those days. When you got through in a strange town, you went out and jammed. The bands were so organized that you wouldn't even ask a guy to let you sit in. You would rather hear the music the way it ought to be played. The best thing, if there was a guy sitting up there you wanted to carve, you'd tell him you'd be waiting outside, and then you'd take him off. There was a little more finesse in those days. You wouldn't ask a guy, "Man, let me blow the next set!" Because the music was a lot of "heads," and if it wasn't, some of Benny Carter's music was pretty rough, and you couldn't play it. Guys like that really fooled with keys in arrangements. Now, everything is probably F or B-flat, but then B-natural, C-minor, and everything went. So you go to Buffalo, and you'd get pretty well shook up there, and you'd be waiting for that cat when he hit New York. Waiting to hang him, see?

I remember going to the Lafayette with the Big Four once—Benny Carter, Hawk, Jimmy Harrison, and Prince Robinson. I couldn't understand what was happening until later on. They were having bets between themselves to see what key the band in the movie was playing in. That was how they sharpened their ears, with the band in the movie, not the one on the stage. About the live musicians on the stage, they said:

"You don't have to tell me that. I can see what finger he's putting down. I know what valve. I know what position."

So one would always be saying:

"Let's go to the movies tonight."

"Okay," the others would say, "meet you at seven o'clock."

And they'd be passing the bets along in the dark, a dollar, a quarter, or whatnot, and people wouldn't know what was happening. Benny Carter was the big guy. He had a perfect ear and could always tell you what key it was, so he acted as a kind of referee. If he wasn't there, he'd maybe make it the next night, and then the next show you met at they would tell you:

"Well, you lost that bet. It was A-flat."

Those guys were really nice, and they had a ball. Jimmy had all Bert Williams's records and liked to copy him. One of his favorites was "The Preacher and the Bear." He was quite a comedian, and he would have you dying with laughter. He didn't like to record though. Hawk used to make some swell arrangements to feature Jimmy. I remember that "Singin' in the Rain" was great, and Hawk arranged "Hard-to-get Gertie" and Smack's [Fletcher Henderson's] theme song.

I remember I went down to hear Fletcher's band at Roseland once, and Jimmy was on one end of the stand and Hawk on the other. When Hawk was playing, Jimmy would turn his back. Now Jimmy had a funny expression. "Pew-wee," he would say. So after Hawk got through about four choruses, he said:

"Pew-wee! What is that young boy trying to do over there? That's the worst I ever heard in my life."

When Hawk finished his solo, he shouted:

"Take it, Tom!" (He called Jimmy "Tom.")

"I don't feel right tonight," Jimmy answered. "I am a man who plays with feeling, and I don't feel so good tonight."

So the next night Jimmy would come down and stomp his foot and take ten or twelve choruses.

"Tom, you were blowing there," Smack would say.

"Yes, Smack, I play with a feeling, I felt all right tonight."

Meantime, he might ask what Hawk had done over there, and he could come to you and say.

"That boy sure was blowing his horn, wasn't he? But I don't let him know it!"

One time Hawk told Jimmy:

"I won't be here tomorrow at the matinee. I'm sick of this stuff, coming down here and blowing—for what?"

"You're not coming?" Jimmy asked.

"No," says Hawk.

So next day Jimmy went down about ten minutes before the matinee ended, with some kind of story all ready to tell Smack. As he went in, he heard a tenor that sounded real good, and sure enough Hawk had been there all the time. So when he spoke to Hawk, Hawk said:

"Don't pay me no mind, man. I was just kidding."

Hawk and Jimmy were two grand pals. They really made it together. They joked like that something awful, but there was never any ill feeling.

Fletcher had a way of writing so that the notes just seemed to float along casually. You just had to play the notes and the arrangement was swinging. Both Benny Carter and Don Redman had great respect for Fletcher's writing. There was something he seemed to have inside there. "Can You Take It?," "Shanghai Shuffle," "Wrappin' It up," and "Down South Camp Meeting" were Fletcher's. Don wrote more technical things like "Whiteman Stomp," and then "Chant of the Weed" with all those flatted fifths that were 'way ahead of their time. The guys in the band used to bring arrangements, and they seemed to know just what Fletcher wanted.

Fletcher himself didn't write too high—there wasn't any screaming—so that the music seemed to roll along. It was good dance music. Like Buddy Tate's little band today—when you've got all those people popping their fingers and jumping around, it's got to give you inspiration. Of course, you've got to have a drummer with a beat. Fletcher's Walter Johnson used to lay there, and play a simple kind of drums, and let the musicians go for themselves. But today it's pretty rough, and sometimes you can't tell whose solo it is—yours or the drummer's.

And those rhythm sections used to rehearse. Sometimes they'd get there an hour ahead of time. It's like running an automobile. If the motor's no good, what happens? You don't go. Those rhythm sections were the motors, and they wanted everything to be solid, but today it's often every man for himself. A guy would just about shoot you today if you asked him to rehearse with a rhythm section.

The reason I got the gig with Fletcher I'll never forget. The band was playing the Hollywood Beer Gardens, the Fourth of July. That was a place Smack used to play every summer, a beautiful place on the ocean. Up the road, about five miles, was a place Jimmy and Tommy Dorsey used to play every summer, too. The Casa Loma and all the big bands used to play up there, and this night PeeWee Hunt of the Casa Loma came visiting. He was a friend of Sandy Williams, and he gave Sandy a firecracker. It was a great band for dares, and somebody dared Sandy, and he lit it, down under the ballroom. This thing went off and scared everybody to death up above.

"I didn't know that thing was so loud, man!" Sandy was saying.

PeeWee laughed and was gone. But Fletcher told Sandy *he* had to go, so that was how I got the gig, for about two years.

I got another gig behind Higginbotham when he was playing with Benny Carter. Higgie threw a hand grenade at the boss's wife. (A hand grenade is a note saying, "I want to see you," or "I got eyes for you.") That was at the Empire Ballroom, down opposite Roseland. So she carried this note to her husband, and he told Benny Carter about this happening to his old lady. Oh, hand grenades have got a lot of guys out of work, and Higgie had to go! It's always bad to write.

For a short period I played with Fats Waller at Connie's Inn. Frankie Newton was in that band, and Big Sidney, and Red Allen. They had this long organ in the corner, full size, for Fats to play. Jesse Crawford was the organist down at the Paramount Theatre then, and the talk of New York, but he used to live in the joint. We're supposed to finish at four o'clock, but Fats would put his derby on the piano after the second show and tell us to go home. They'd fill his derby up with money, and he'd be singing and composing songs, and we'd be on the street, or down the Hoofer's Club, or some place. That happened two or three times a week. The bosses were nice, treated us wonderful, and paid us our money just the same. When Fats left there, Crawford would take him down to his house, and Fats would stay there all night. Next night, same thing. All the people would gang around the piano and we'd quit about two o'clock. I got a kick out of playing with Fats, and the bosses were crazy about him.

One night, Frank Newton was playing a solo, and Fats started to stride and overshadow him. So Frank stopped playing and asked Fats how much he wanted to cool it. Fats smiled and said, "Half a buck." Frank gave it to him and started blowing again—no hard feelings.

They had a great show at Connie's. Snake Hips Tucker and the Mills Brothers were there, and Louise Cook, a shake dancer, Bill Bailey, Jackie Mabley, and Paul Myers. We had a line of girls *and* fags. The fags were so sharp that some of the male customers would tip back and try to make dates—until they found the difference. Sometimes, maybe, the difference didn't matter. I think that was the last place to have a line of girl impersonators in New York.

Very often in those days we would play at theaters like the Lafayette or the Apollo with the entire show out of a cabaret—if you had a good one—because people couldn't all afford those stiff cabaret prices. The theaters very seldom had house bands they way they do now, but further back they did. In Louisville, Kentucky, they used to play every act, which came back at the Apollo with Reuben Phillips. In '36 and '37, there would be a different band every week at the Apollo or the Lafayette. They would be featured on the stage as a band *and* accompanying the acts. They very seldom played in the pit, because there was a question of different rates, and the union would have stepped in.

I remember seeing Lew Leslie's "Blackbirds" earlier on, and I don't think that show has ever been equaled. Pike Davis was leader of the pit band, and he was a wonderful trumpet player with brilliant tone and attack. The band had the largest collection of classic Oxford Greys I've ever seen. There was nothing short in that show. It had the great Bojangles, and Jo Baker was a chorus girl. There was Snake Hips Tucker and many, many more. It was a great spectacle to see.

When I joined Teddy Hill at the Savoy in 1935, the job paid thirty-five bucks, and I lived as good then as I do today, if not a little better. It was a wonderful band, and Teddy was a swell guy. He didn't do anything he didn't want you to do. He never drank too much on the job, and he was quite a gentleman around. Male and female, everybody respected him. Some of the fellows in the band were Roy Eldridge, Chu Berry (the one and only), Bob Carroll after Chu, Russ Procope, Howard Johnson, Bill Beason, Dick Fullbright (the bass player), Sam Allen (pianist), Bill Dillard, and Shad Collins. We worked at the Savoy quite a while. Then we got a lift and went to Connie's Inn—fifty dollars, big deal! That was downstairs next to the Lafayette Theater, and it was operated by the same people who owned the Cotton Club. It had a show, about twelve girls, and everything. At that time, Harlem drew the ofays in droves because then it had something different. Now the guys like Sammy Davis and Billy Daniels work downtown. Billy was here then in a little, small place. They used to burn candles in the joint. It was so dark you wouldn't even know anyone was there. We had pretty late hours in Harlem then—ten to four, two shows a night, and dance music.

There were three or four places going like that. Competition, but nobody paid it any mind, nobody suffered, and all the joints were doing good business. At Connie's, they would give us a fifth of whiskey, sometimes two a night, on the bandstand, and the guys would sometimes leave it there till the next night. Saturdays sometimes, we had eight or ten fifths of whiskey on the stand, and nobody bothered, because you'd be going out to the joints and taking a taste at intermission. Those mobs were pretty good people to work for in those days. They always treated us well and never bothered us. Of course, we never interfered with their business. We had better sense.

The clubs in Harlem were run by big-time mobs, not tramps. But if they wanted to close up competition for some special reason, they'd send and wreck the place, break up the piano, and whatnot. When Prohibition ended, they were owning the clubs, and they carried them on with entertainment. The underworld really ran the cabarets, and they had a way of running them better than anyone else. They never owed you money. You always got it, two or three weeks before, if you needed it. The clubs could be a front for other activities, but they had good producers and put on tight shows. It was never as rough as Chicago. It seemed to run smoother here. Everybody may like to see the underworld disposed of, but it sure did hurt show business, nightclubs, and whatnot, because guys used to come in and spend three or four hundred or even a thousand dollars and tip the band fifty or a hundred.

Later, nightlife spread out. It was like a landslide—a talentslide downtown. The scene changed when the Cotton Club moved downtown. Then Connie's followed. There are no chorus lines at the Apollo now. Let's face it; the only cabaret here is the Baby Grand. They have four girls, a little jive, and for a long time a comedian who told all those fine jokes—Nipsey Russell. He's real good. But that's the only place up here now with girls. If Birdland had been uptown it would have been a little different. As for all those guys who used to like to go slumming . . . the projects are cleaning it up nice, and it isn't slumming in Harlem anymore. But they still have lines in Vegas, like they used to have here. And gambling is legal there.

Greasy's, down on 129th and Seventh, was another place we used to go weekends. It was a real barrelhouse place. Greasy was the name of the bartender, and he would let you tab. A lot of chorus girls used to go there, and there were quite a lot of dancing schools in Harlem then, so you'd get hostesses, too. And the musicians! Most of the musicians would get off around three o'clock and show up about four. You'd meet all the Cotton Club crowd there. All the gang would be there, getting high at the bar. The Hoofer's Club was where we went to jam, but this was where we went to get high. And this was a place where the chicks would come. It stayed open until seven or eight o'clock. It was a regular rendezvous.

Then there was a place near the Savoy uptown, called the Brandy House. Like you would run out with a gang at intermission and get this brandy for twenty-five cents a half pint. It was peach brandy. It was light, and it didn't get you drunk. You'd go up there and get your chicks and split, cut out, maybe have a little ball, and make it. That joint catered mostly to the Savoy crowd. They also had what they called Top-and-Bottom, which was wine and gin. That would make your top come off if you drank enough, and you'd stay high for three or four days.

One time, when Roy Eldridge and I were with Teddy Hill at

the Savoy, we peeped through the little loop they pushed the food through and dug the Chinese cook. He looked to be feeling good, so Roy says:

"Ling, what's happening, what're you drinking back there?"

"Oh, you no like," Ling says.

"What do you mean, we no like?" Roy asks. "You like, we like."

The band was off at the time, so we told him to give us a taste. He had this cup, but there wasn't enough in it. You could barely see it, there was so little.

"What is this?" we said.

"You need no more," he said.

"Oh, man, pour something in there!"

So he poured about half of this little cup and, don't you know, Roy and I drank that and went back to the band floating on air! We don't know how we got there, but we still were there, and we stayed high for about six hours. Chinese something it was. We got the prescription, but we had to put Ling down. The next night, Roy said,

"Man, you got him! I'm going back to the Brandy House."

I forget the name of it, but it was the equivalent of our corn whiskey, only you don't have to have about a tablespoon of it. We asked the guys in the band:

"How did we act?"

"The way you always do!" they said.

So we didn't know.

In those days, they mostly sold beer and sherry at the Savoy. Later, they got a liquor license. They had a little trouble and lost it, but they got it back again.

Then there was the 101 Club on 138th Street, down in a hole, where Frankie Newton and everybody used to go. That was about the last of the downstairs places. They had good bands there, and cats used to go and jam a lot. That lasted up to around '38 or '39. Then there was the Brittwood, another hole, near the Savoy. They used to jam a lot there, too, the Savoy gang. But it would be most of the lightweights around in those joints, because the heavies were going to Hoofer's, cats like Hawk and Jimmy Harrison. Those *bad* cats, they all went down there. You had to graduate to get down there. I think Hoofer's ran from about 1930 to 1937.

Among the other places cats used to dig was Campbell's egg-nog joint up over an undertaker's parlor. Some location! Then there was the Cave, a spooky joint! There were all kinds of skeletons around the walls. It was a pot joint, and if you carried a chick she had to be real pure in heart, or she would want to cut out. It was real dark in there. Another place we got great kicks had a dog which used to get high. Everybody would dig him. When he smelled the stuff, he would scratch on the door. They would blow the jive in the dog's face, and he would start jumping straight up in the air. When he started to come down, he would slow up until he fell out. Then everybody would say, "Ole Spot is out!"

Bert Hall's Rhythm Club was on 132nd and Seventh, a part of a whole block the Williams Church had bought that includes where the Hoofer's Club and Big John's used to be. Bert's was strictly a musicians' club. I've seen fellows go to Bert when their cards had to be paid up, and he would gladly help them. Everybody dug him. After his death, George Rose and a few of those terrific waiters from Ed Smalls's kept it going. Today, it has moved to 169 West 133rd St. and is called the Wilrose Social Club or Rhythm Club. That gang consists of Will Rose [Georgia Rose], Willis [Chink], and Junior [Junie].

The Harlem Opera House, one of the oldest theaters in Harlem, used to be a segregated house—no colored allowed—and now they're opening it as a bowling alley. They wouldn't allow colored in the Cotton Club, not until later on, unless it was some guy who had become world famous. They had a stiff cover charge, too, which kept a lot of people out. A lot of places uptown relied on downtown tourists in the early thirties. The Opera House was segregated when they had opera, but not when they turned to vaudeville, and then movies. For a time it was between the Apollo and the Lafayette. They had bands there. There was the Alhambra Theatre, too, but it wasn't open long. The Alhambra Ballroom was on the top floor. You had to take the elevator. We used to gig there from Charlie Johnson's band—Sunday matinees. The Alhambra Grill was on the corner, but it was never very popular with musicians, although they had sessions in a little place in the back. It never made it. The ballroom mostly ran weekends or for matinees, but it didn't go long either. The Savoy was too much, and the Renaissance. The Savoy was well run and had just about everything you could want. The bouncers made it safe for a girl to go by herself, and a lot of out-of-town girls used to come to the Savoy, from all around, on their days off. They didn't want to go to dives where they couldn't be protected like at the Savoy. When the Savoy closed, it took a lot of heart out of Harlem. A whole lot of cats didn't know where to go. They tried to get the Savoy gang at the Celebrity Club, but they didn't follow through.

After the big band thing, I don't think they made so much money at the Savoy. Sometimes, if you went there on a Monday night, there wouldn't be fifty or seventy-five people. The social clubs, too, that went in there, didn't pay off, not when you had about thirty people on the payroll. A lot of people used to come from Jersey and Brooklyn, but now they've got their own ball-rooms to go to. And they sit at home with TV. They don't come out in masses anymore, and the Savoy was the cheapest form of entertainment aside from movies. The bouncers used to keep the place straight, and Charles Buchanan was the man who kept the door open so long.

I've seen some terrific happenings in the Savoy. I remember Duke was in there once, with Tricky Sam and Lawrence Brown. That floor was built to vibrate, but I didn't know it. I was stand-ing by the bandstand, and it started to vibrate, that floor was loaded so. I came out of there and didn't find out about it being a sprung floor until a year later. Yeah, I vibrated on out the door! Duke was playing "St. Louis Blues," and he had on a big, brown plaid suit, and it looked like the blocks on the plaid were sitting out, 'way out. Lawrence was blowing away, and Tricky was coming down to growl his part, and Barney was wailing. It was a beautiful thing! They must have had eight or nine thousand people in there. I think Duke should be appreciated more than he is today, because he's had it rough. Imagine if there hadn't been a Duke Ellington, what would we be listening to without "Mood Indigo" and all those fine tunes? There might be some-thing else—who knows?—but that man really brought the world something.

Thinking of Tricky Sam, too, I remember when all the real elite used to hang out at Pod's and Jerry's on 133rd Street. Willie the Lion used to play there, and it was another favorite place for musicians and chicks. I went in there one night, and there was

Tricky Sam with all his mutes, plunger, etc., spread out—and Duke at the piano. They were waiting for us to come from the Savoy. Tricky said:

"Okay, come on, let me hear what you can do! I've been hearing about you around here, shooting off your horn!"

It would have been sudden death. That man could say as much as a human voice on his horn. So I didn't mess with him. He was some guy. It threw a lot of people when he passed. Like Jimmy Harrison, he was a king.

Sometimes we used to chip in to get a jug. Tricky would say, "Chip in for me somebody, until later." Before the session broke up, he would take off a shoe and pull out a hundred-dollar bill, and say, "Change that." Of course, no one could, so back in the shoe it went.

I don't remember the Audobon in the thirties. A lot of those halls were ofay places then. The Audobon is pretty old, and there are quite a few places like it in the Bronx. All those neighborhoods were entirely ofay thirty years ago. They were there, those places, but we didn't care, because we had the Savoy to go to. You wouldn't think of going anywhere else to dance. You'd go two or three times a week, because they had the bands, the main thing, but business began to fall off when the bands began to fall off. Trios and whatnot couldn't fill that place. They even had Erroll Garner in there once, but they decided a trio was too small.

In more recent years, there was the Golden Gate. Some other outfit opened it, but I think the Savoy crowd bought it. It didn't last long. Then there was the Rockland Palace for special occasions, but the Savoy and the Renaissance were the only two ballrooms going every night. Cabarets were the thing then. There were more of them going, and they employed bands steadily, year in and year out.

They used to have these bands of twelve or more pieces in small rooms. When Basie came on the scene, he told me he had learned his lesson in Pittsburgh. He was kind of loud there. He came to the Famous Door in New York, and that was real small. People would come in, and the waiter would seat 'em by the band.

"No, we're sorry, we don't want that table," they'd say.

36

"Well, sit there," the waiter would say, "and if you're disturbed you'll get your money back."

And the people, when they came again, would want that same table. Because Basie would sometimes make us blow at the floor and keep those mutes in. The guys could play high notes, but we did that so much that after a time we found we could play soft without the mutes. Harry James and those guys would sit right by the saxophones, and the room couldn't hold over two hundred people without being crowded, but they had that turnover every night, and the owner made money.

I know Chick Webb had a band in a room in Boston no bigger than a box, but he had such marvelous control over the band that it could sound no louder than four pieces. If you went down to Birdland and heard Basie, the whole band would be playing, but it wasn't too loud. After a while, they'd blast out and then back down. It can be done. Then you might have five or six pieces in the same room, and they'd run you crazy, playing so loud. And then there's the organ and the drums. The organist can deafen you whenever he wants, but a drummer today will as a rule carry six pieces like he would carry twelve or fourteen, with the same volume. He couldn't play any louder with twelve pieces.

It's a funny thing how that band thing faded out. The kids go to school now and study arranging, go over to Columbia and take Schillinger and all those things and learn beautiful music, but what are you going to do with them? Because they can't bring it to the people. Guys like Benny [Carter] and Don—Don Redman is just about tops—they don't get to arrange their kind of music much, but they can prove it with a big band—anytime.

Back in the days I've been talking of, everybody was trying to play something like Louis Armstrong. His records influenced all jazz musicians, not only trumpet players. But something of their own would come out, even with the guys who got nearest, like Jonah Jones. Jonah had a really Negro feeling coming through his horn. Almost all of them had a good broad tone, which you don't hear much today. They might drift away in their style, but they'd keep that good, fat tone. The ones I look at as the limbs of the Armstrong tree were George Mitchell, Red Allen, Joe Thomas, Cootie Williams, Taft Jordan, Emmett Berry, and that extreme swinger, Lips Page. The next kind, those who drifted away from it, would be Bill Coleman, Buck Clayton, Frank Galbraith, Peanuts Holland, Johnny Letman, and Walter Fuller. Then you get the personally inventive kind—and they didn't all go to the same teachers—like Joe Smith, Rex Stewart, Tommy Ladnier, Johnny Dunn, Shorty Baker, Bobby Stark, Cuban Bennett, Roy Eldridge, Bubber Miley, Red Nichols, Bix Beiderbecke, Frank Newton, and Harry James.

And Jimmy Harrison—the reason he was swinging so much was because Louis was his ideal. He copied Louis on the trombone the way J. J. has copied Dizzy today. He was actually playing a lot of Louis's solos on trombone, and you'd say, "Gee! I've never heard anything like that from a trombone before!" It would be swinging, but he'd also play melody, because in those days trombone players had to play melody, or it wouldn't be trombone. But well as Jimmie knew "Cornet Shop Suey" and "Beaukoo Jack," the slide and his way of phrasing always caused that little sweet difference.

Then Jimmy influenced Jack Teagarden, I'm more than sure, because Jack used to come into Smalls's and listen to him quite a bit. But he had lots of his own, too. He always did have control of his horn, and to my mind he was a wonderful trombone player. He was one of the few really down cats who knew that horn bottom side up, and he really poured his feeling through it. Like Jimmy used to say, "He's a man who plays with a feeling." And when a guy didn't feel good then, he'd go away and come back the next night. You *had* to play with soul then. There wasn't anything false, anything mechanical, because with the mechanical thing you can just about do today the way you'll do it tomorrow. Actually, a lot of soul has been lost out of the music the last ten or fifteen years, and it has something to do with dancing.

It's always inspiring to have people dancing in front of you. There's a beat there which gives you a lift. The drummer digs those people dancing, and he tries to keep them happy. Or there may be a cat over in a corner, clowning, and the drummer is watching him, going along with him with a good beat, and you got to feel it. When the people are dancing on the beat, you got to feel it. It's a kind of imaginary thing when there are no people dancing.

When we'd play a show at the Lafayette, those girls might take seven or eight encores, and the band would be sitting riffing behind them with their derbies and whatnot. So that would go on for a week, and after you'd played the show for that time you would have it all pretty well in your mind. Then we get a gig— maybe at the Savoy—and the girls would come up, laughing and saying they'd come to hear their favorite band. So we'd be playing the things we'd played for them in the show, and they'd say:

"Give us our music, or we'll take you to the union! You know you're playing our music."

We wouldn't have played that music the way we did if we hadn't got the spirit of things from watching those girls dance. And the drummer, too, would have got it, and one like Big Sid would be pushing you.

A lot of battles and carving contests went on at the Savoy, and Chick Webb would just lay for other bands to come there. And he'd rather they came on Fridays, Saturdays, or Sundays, because then the place would be packed with dancers, and they'd say:

"Play that number you played last Tuesday, Chick. We can dance by that."

He'd play it, and the house would start rocking. Lots of times the dancers more or less dictated what the bands played.

Chick used to sit back looking out the window while his band played early in the evening, but when the visiting band would get rough—here he would come, and that was it! When you told him that he had his ax out, he would say, "What did you say, man? What did you say, man?" And all the time he would be hitting or smacking you.

Every time Fletcher [Henderson] came to the Savoy, Chick would ask him,

"Well, who do you want this time?"

Chick's band was Smack's grab bag, and it knocked Chick out, because he knew if Fletcher came to get someone he had the best to pick from.

The Savoy Sultans were another band that was a living headache to everyone. They could swing and make most bands happy to play "Home Sweet Home." When a band like that's on your tail, the night seems to never end. They didn't seem to know the meaning of letting up.

Jimmy Rushing later had a band like that. So did Bob Merrill.

Once in a while that kind of band comes along, but as soon as one man is changed it seems to do something to the whole outfit. But at the Savoy, if you didn't swing, you weren't there long.

There was a little band from Florida that came in there once. Roy Johnson's Happy Pals they were called, and they all looked like "mismatches," as Chick Webb used to say. No two guys looked alike. There were skinny guys, fat guys, all sorts. "Skinny" Trent was very fat and used to play with his banjo resting on his stomach. They looked like a collection of antiques, but when they finished swinging they'd have swung us out of the joint. And we'd have been rehearsing all day.

In a dance hall, you're not as self-conscious, and you do a whole lot of things on the horn you wouldn't do at a concert—a whole lot of relaxed things. For the dancer, you know what will please him. It has got to be something that will fit around him and with his step. When you see a dancer take his girl and then drop her hands and walk off, something isn't right. Most likely the rhythm's wrong. But when you get that beat, he is right there, saying, "Play that again!"

If you've got two or three thousand people in front of you at a concert, it's hard to imagine what they like, what rhythm they like. But when you've got people out on the dance floor and dancing, you know what they like—you got 'em! Tommy Dorsey told me he could pretty well tell when he had a hit, because that floor stayed packed, and because that music sounded good to them there it would sell on a record. I've always thought that if they could screen the bandstand with glass or something at a place like the Savoy, and record while the band could still see those dancers, they'd get a wonderful effect. It would help the musicians a lot. Just like at the Hoofer's Club, while we were battling, they were dancing out there. So the two have to go together. Without them, and you just sitting up there playing a concert, it's pretty cold. There was more soul when jazz and dancing went together. It's a case of lost soul now!

Of course, vocalists helped take the spotlight off the bands. A band became a show in itself. Take Andy Kirk: he had Pha Terrell, June Richmond, and Henry Wells. Every good band had one or two vocalists and different styles of arrangements. Put the band on the stage, let the curtain go up, and you had a whole lot of entertainment already there. Then the singers began to leave the bands and go out on their own, and everything got to be vocalized as it is now.

That didn't apply so much to bands in the early days like Charlie Johnson's, Duke's, and Fletcher's. They played hardcore music, but each of them had a different thing, so that you didn't know what to expect, whereas with a house band you always know what is going to happen.

The entertainment used to be in the music itself, and you would hear people saying they liked that arrangement by Benny Carter, or that they were going next week to hear Fletcher's "Sugar Foot," and so on. There wasn't much hokum with bands of that kind. You didn't have to jump around. The audiences were real hip. They went for the overall musical picture without picking too much on the individual, although they might like you as a soloist. Jimmie Lunceford's band was liked as a band, and for Sy Oliver's arrangements, rather than for his soloists. Of course, he had singing and entertaining, too, so that his band was a double treat and an exception—novelty *and* beautiful arrangement. It's Duke who has had the hard way to go. He's just been going on music alone, and that man's wonderful to keep those ideas coming for forty years, because he's never relied on clowning or anything like that.

People in those days really were more arrangement conscious and less concerned with vocalists. Nowadays you hear a person say, "Man, I dig what that cat is doing!" But the cat doesn't always dig what he's doing himself, because the passage is so rapid and everything that they don't know. Then it's not often you can sing a man's solo today, but you used to hear a whole lot of people whistling a tune when they were leaving a big-band show. You don't hear it today. The bands were playing more melodies, and the people were digging the melodies.

Gerald Wilson brought a band to the Apollo once and got applause for just the arrangements. It can be done. Gerald had such pretty things just swinging along that he got good hands. Suppose the kids had heard more of that sort of thing. Or take Basie's band now: he has a whole lot of fine arrangements, and the kids dig them. You cannot do the same thing with five or six pieces. You go to a bar, and you hear something; you go to the next bar, you hear the same thing. But carry seven or more pieces to a man's bar, he acts as though you've got a symphony band. He wants to throw you out!

When you hear some of Fletcher's old records, there may be just one jammed chorus, but on the job there'd be a lot more. They called it "stretching it out." I think it should be reversed today. We should have more good big-band arrangements and leave the solos go for a while, because just about everything has been heard. Yes, play some good, pretty, swinging music. Basie could always play two or three good arrangements without solos, because he has the instrument there to do it. Mind you, it mustn't be too clean and stylized. There's an expression Claude Jones used to use: "It's got to be a little fuzzy."

"Yeah, that was a pretty solo you played," Claude would say, "but there wasn't enough fuzz. Everything was too exact. Don't try to play like I play. I play too clean, and I'll never be nothing."

But his time came. He just didn't stay with it long enough. They figure now the cleaner you are the better you are. Everything's mechanical. That's why I used to like to hear a little band Jay McShann had. Boy, they had a lot of fuzz hanging around! In fact, they had so much that Basie told the agents, "Don't book us with those cats!"

I really believe you can get too clean. Everything now is being woven into one style, and everybody knows that the ofay's playing is clean. Let's put it where it is. He's been the cleanest on his instrument. He's been taught longer. No other way he knew. And deep down in, he's the master when it comes to cutting something, when you put the music up there. The Oxford Grey was noted for his fuzz and just swinging, and he knew it, and everybody knew it, but now it's all coming right in with this cleanness, so where's the other part of it, where's the fuzz? Nobody's fuzzy and smutty. So both races have come right together, cleaning up and getting mechanical, and there's no variety. Now a cat would say to Benny Carter when he was organizing his bands:

"Hey, Benny, how about so-and-so?"

"No, I don't want him, he plays like so-and-so," Benny would say.

He wouldn't have two guys who played alike, although they both might be real good musicians. There was a trumpet player talking to me about a record the other day, one they made with four trumpets.

"Man, that's a killer, isn't it?" he said.

"Yes," I said, "It sounds good."

"You can't tell us apart, can you?"

"That's the trouble, for me," I said, "I *can't* tell you apart!"

He seemed to be under the impression it was great they all sounded alike.

The difference between these schools and colleges today and how it was with us is like this: When you drum into a class of ten people, what's right and what's wrong, you're drumming the same thing to all; but when you get ten people turned loose in the world and told to learn how to do this, they're not coming back the same way. Like the band I was in when I was a kid. They gave you those instruments, but the teachers weren't the best. So you go home and learn wrong, but while you're learning wrong you strike up on something, and it seemed then as though it was best to be different, to get what you could and *then* brush it up. Too much attention to polish in the first place can stop what is really yours from coming out. You're going to say to yourself:

"This isn't right. I wasn't taught like this."

Like Louis and all those guys, and even Charlie Parker—they're practically self-taught. Later on they polished it up. The new kids are often too full of theory. Where do they go from here? I heard a case of one of them saying:

"Man, I'm going to get funky now!"

What they call "funky" is still too clean. They're trying to put back what should have been there in the first place.

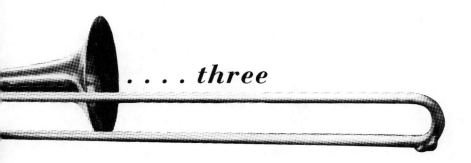

. . . . *three*

The Hazardous Road

Jazz took to the road very early as ballrooms mushroomed around the country. Some bands, like those of Duke Ellington, Fletcher Henderson, Earl Hines, and Chick Webb, were lucky to secure long engagements in venues where their reputations were considerably enhanced, often as a result of regular broadcasts. Others, less fortunate, had to travel from city to city to keep working. The broadcasts, however, created such a demand for in-person appearances that even the more securely established had to hit the road for part of the year. As bands multiplied and competition sharpened, so distances between one-nighters tended to increase. First in automobiles, then in buses and trains, jazz musicians endured an arduous existence on the road for many years, usually with fortitude and sardonic humor. Ultimately, of course, the "road" was extended into the skies, and planes made one-nighters possible in different countries as well as in different states!

The hazards were many. Auto accidents took the lives of numerous good men, and the strenuous life ruined the health of others. Racial prejudice in what Dicky Wells casually refers to as "down home" led to bitterness, just as prolonged absence from home led to broken marriages. But the creeping nemesis of all too many was whiskey, alias Ol' Man Ignorant Oil.

S.D.

We used to travel the best way we could in the early days. When we were with Cecil Scott we had an old, twelve-cylinder Packard. We used to fill that thing up with gas paid for out of our own pockets. The tank would be leaking. About twenty miles—it would be empty again! We would be going up the Cotton Top Mountain, seven miles, right out of Ohio on the way to Pittsburgh, and we'd have to push the rascal halfway up that mountain and then ride down the other side. We'd all sleep in the car and everything—about ten of us. We had a bass player called Mike who used to drink a lot. He would put his fiddle case up on top of the car. We left Springfield once, got to Pittsburgh, opened up, and no fiddle! Mike was high and had left it in Springfield. All he had was the case.

We very seldom went by train, because we couldn't ride on tab. We took this raggedy old Packard up to the car lot once and asked the man how much he would give us, because we had eyes for a bus—about three-thousand dollars. The man said:

"I'll give you about fifteen seconds to get out of here!"

We had that idea because the cats who rode in a bus then were something. Few had buses. Nearly all the bands traveled in private cars.

We had a Ford for traveling when we played with Tapp, an old-time Ford with these little window blinds. We had about six pieces. So we were going from Terre Haute, Indiana, back to Louisville, and the roads were covered with ice, and the windshield frosted up so we couldn't drive. This same bass player, who drank a lot, always kept his whiskey sticking out of his pocket, and he was asleep. So we had to take his whiskey and pour it on the windshield.

"For God's sake, don't tell him!" one of the guys said.

It was a wonder it didn't break the windshield. It was that bad corn. But when this cat woke up, we had to chain him. He called everybody everything.

We played a dance with Ferman Tapp when Bill Beason was in the band, about twenty-five miles out of Knoxville—the first time I ever had any trouble. So a guy brought us some corn whiskey, a gallon. He came back after a while and said:

"Everybody drinking the whiskey? I'll bring you another one."

"Okay," the cats say.

So he comes back with another gallon. An hour later, here he comes again, and we hadn't finished the whiskey.

"Drink up this whiskey," he says.

He was under the impression you could play louder or something when you were drunk, and we weren't drinking fast enough for him.

"Why, you black b—— s——."

The usual thing to make you angry. I looked back, and Bill Beason had picked up a chair, to hit this man in the head, and us at nothing but an ofay dance, and we're twenty-five miles from Knoxville, Tennessee. A couple of cats had their rods then, but they couldn't pull them out, for what were you going to do at a dance with six hundred people? Bill's hotheadedness almost got us messed up there. We went to Knoxville, and they said we better stay in the house in case they came down and wanted to make trouble.

We found that only one man, Mr. Johns, kept night people there, so we made it to his joint. Pops Johns was about fifty and had just married a chick about eighteen. He had a spare room and charged three of us a buck each to sleep in the bed and the other three fifty cents each to sit by the fire all night. He also sat up with us, with one eye open, and a double-barrel shotgun in his lap. He said on account of us being strangers he had to be careful, but on the way back to Louisville, we came to the conclusion Pops was guarding his eighteen-year-old lollipop. Anyway, he wasn't a square, because if he had closed that eye for one second, he would have been a dead duck. I often wonder how long he lived after that marriage. I guess maybe he went out like another oldtimer down in Centerville. He was 117 when he got hitched to a filly of twenty-two. After a week of married life, they said it took the undertaker a couple of days to wipe the smile off his face. Pops went down swinging, eh?

Working in a unit with a leader like Tapp, it wasn't like it is now with big offices. He would wire ahead to a promoter, who would put the placards out. They'd split the take sixty-forty— we'd take sixty and the promoter forty. The leader would take out expenses for promotion and transportation and then split the rest between us. It was that way all over. The leader would usually be fair, because we'd know what he was making. There weren't any big agencies then, and very few white bands played those territories. It was very seldom white bands played colored ballrooms, although we used to play white ballrooms. The big white bands didn't play one-nighters much in those days. The Swing Era didn't open up ballrooms for colored bands, because they were already playing them. They were playing for white audiences even in the Deep South. You played there then, but not now. No, the Swing Era didn't open up any new ground for colored bands. The ballrooms all through the South always did hire them, but not as much now as they did then. The bands themselves were segregated. They were units of one race or the other. The present style of playing is pretty well played by the ofays, so in the South they figure why bring in Oxford Greys? But long before, all those little bands I played in in Kentucky, we played for white crowds.

In those days, when we were traveling in the South, most cats had firearms somewhere, somehow. Because you used to run up against a lot of frightful people, drunken people, and whatnot. The ofays would try to frighten you if somebody got out of line and want to beat up the band or shoot somebody. If you pull a gun, there's two chances to one the cat is going to cool down. It's a fool who's going to keep messing with you after he sees this gun. As a rule, all the bands, white and colored, used to have a stash someplace, because there'd always be some crank who wanted to mess with you. Somebody always seems to think a musician on a bandstand is woman's man, and he just hates you for that, so the best you can do is rub him down or fan him. You don't have time to make love to everybody! Or maybe you're a friendly guy, just going around shaking hands, trying to look

neat and your best, as the public wants you to. You'd be surprised how a lot of guys figure you're acting cute and trying to
be something else.

There was that incident in Florida some years ago. It happened to a band called, I think, the Whispering Serenaders of
Gold, out of Columbus, Ohio. It was when the Charleston first
came out. They had a drummer, a very nice-looking fellow with
long black hair. They went to Miami, and some girls there wanted
to learn to dance, and they asked their partners, and these ofays
said to the band:

"Okay, go ahead. Learn 'em how to do this dance."

So they danced around, and the drummer tried to learn them
how to do it, although he probably didn't want to. But nobody
bothered them.

Afterwards, some cars came to take them all to a party, and
they asked for this drummer in particular:

"We're going to have a party and some drinks for you guys."

They carried them out, and they cut him up, that drummer,
castrated him, and he swelled up and died in the hospital. We
heard about that in Louisville, and that's one of the reasons the
cats started to carry firearms, because if we were traveling
around and ran into something like that, we'd all have to die for
nothing.

Later, when I was with Fletcher Henderson, I found he never
approved of it, but the guys would say:

"We're going South, man! We've got to have our artillery."

Now, Fletcher had good transportation—five or six cars, new
ones mostly. They had a lot of wrecks, too, but Big Green was
telling me something before he died that was funny.

"Man, you don't have fun like we used to," he said. "We'd be
coming to a small town with all these big cars, and outside of
town we'd start speeding up to around seventy, eighty miles an
hour and start shooting at chickens, cats, and dogs as we went
through town—anything but people! The chickens would be
flying and running, dogs barking, and people screaming—it was
like the Wild West!"

That's one of the things they actually used to do. The cars
were high powered then, mostly convertibles, and they'd be riding with the top down. They had a ball. Often there would be
just two cats in a car. Hawk and Jimmy always liked to ride

together. Hawk always did like a big automobile, and he always had a fine one. And Fletcher was car crazy. When John Kirby joined, he got a car. Pops [Russell Smith] had a car.

Pops had his little Dodge, but the rest of them had these big automobiles. They'd pull up, and after a time here'd come Pops streaming up, with Red Allen, Bobby Stark, and me in it. He'd say:

"Well, we're here!"

"We thought you weren't going to make it," the others would say.

"You may have been here a few minutes, but you bet I'll always make it!"

It seems like the older a car gets, the higher it gets, so Red Allen would always be kidding him:

"Pops, your car is getting awful high!"

"If it gets as high as the Empire State," Pops would say, "I'm still going to keep it."

Pops would have his head back, his hat on crooked, going down the highway. . . . He used to tell us we didn't know how to drink. . . . He'd make a half-pint last a week, and he always sounded beautiful.

We went out West from Memphis once, must have been going two days, and pulled up at this little place about eight o'clock for the dance at nine or ten o'clock. No lights. We began to get that feeling. There was a man inside sweeping the hall.

"What time's the dance?" we asked.

"Dance," he said. "Oh, yes, we had one last month."

"No," we said. "When's the next one?"

"About a month from now."

Boy, that was a dismal day. It must have been six hundred miles. The cats said:

"What! You brought us 'way out here!"

"Have another drink," Sandy Williams says to the cats.

That corn whiskey! Then we were riding again. We soon forgot things like that. That was the kind of spirit the cats had. They weren't always worrying about money. In Fletcher's band, once you started playing, once you hit the first note of those good arrangements, all that was forgotten. It was something the music would do for you, and I think that's the reason Duke keeps a lot of guys. They go for that big sound.

In Baltimore, there was a Chinese restaurant next door to the hotel, and there was a Chinaman peeling potatoes at an open window. So someone bet Bobby Stark he couldn't shoot the dish out of this fellow's hands.

"Wham!"

The potatoes flew in the air, and the Chinaman split down the street yelling and carrying on. He got a cop and came back searching everybody.

Bobby did something like that to me in Kansas City. We had been drinking and were lying around in the hotel.

"Come on Wells-O," he said. "Let's get up and go to the show."

"Bobby, I don't want to see no show," I said. "I'm supposed to see a chick tonight."

"Man, if I shoot you in your ass you'll get up and go to the show!"

"You'll shoot what, man?"

"I will. I'll shoot you, you ———."

"Oh, go on, man," and I turned over in the bed.

Bam!

He missed me, but he hit the bed railing about an inch away. He ran out the door to hide the gun or something, and I was dressed and waiting for him to go to the show in nothing flat. Well, he had been drinking, but I didn't know whether he was a hell of a marksman or not.

The next day, a couple of big cats came over from the Cherry Blossom, where Basie was playing, and they said:

"We hear you've got a bad man over here with a gun. We'd like to see him."

"We ain't got nobody around here with a gun."

"Yes, you have. His name is Bobby Stark."

So they came on up to see Bobby.

"We've come to take you for a ride," they say. "We don't allow anything like that in our territory."

Bobby was getting all sincere and frightened—the only time I ever saw him frightened. Then the guys—a colored fellow and a white fellow—winked and said:

"Okay, watch it around here. Don't let anybody catch you with that thing."

So that cooled it, but it was a pretty close call for me.

Apart from shooting up the towns, Smack's guys used to drive fast. They would do that so much, the cops would be looking for them, and they would have to go other routes. Hawk got so that if he wanted to go to Philadelphia, he couldn't go through Princeton, that way, but had to go damn near to Boston. All the cops knew him, but they couldn't catch him. He had that Imperial, and he used to like to drive fast.

We used to go to Philly—ninety miles about—and the dance would start at ten. These guys would say:

"We'll leave at eight-thirty. It's only ninety miles—that's ninety minutes."

And they'd damned near be there—if they didn't have an accident!

I think Joe Smith hit a guy when he was driving once and killed him, and that kind of stuck with him. Then a chick shook him up pretty well in Kansas City. Pops [Smith] begged Fletcher to go get him, to kind of straighten him up. So they went and got him, but coming back on the bus he was talking to himself, talkin' way out and everything, and they knew there wasn't any hope. He was too far gone. His mind was slipping. It was a shame, too.

Well, there were all those one-nighters and long distances, and you were tired, but you still got to play, and you need a lift. Whiskey could be a big help. I don't think many musicians just naturally loved whiskey. Some people, you see, just naturally love it. It makes them say things and do things and gives them nerve they wouldn't have without it. I know with musicians that wasn't usually their reason.

You may play a beautiful ballroom in Alabama or Mississippi, and maybe you've traveled four or five hundred miles getting there, and people are crazy about you while you are on the bandstand. There's a big restaurant next door, but when you've finished playing they won't serve you. But they'll give you whiskey, all the whiskey you want. So then you've got to go maybe another five hundred miles, and you're coming through a territory that's segregated. You stop at a grocery. They'll always serve you something, and you start eating cheese and crackers and whatnot. Then there are liquor stores. You can always get whiskey and moonshine. That had a lot to do with musicians drinking. I know it had. And once a guy starts drinking, it's hard to pull off. Day in and day out, your system begins to ask for it, and whiskey will tell you—which is one of the damnedest lies—that it's a food, and you don't need nothing to eat. You go ahead and believe it. That was my trouble, because when I was drinking I didn't want to eat. I remember Big Green told me that, after you get far on, when you're a real alcoholic, if you ask people to give you a quarter to get something to eat, they won't do it, but they'll spend two dollars buying you a drink. So there you are, still drinking!

Lots of people figure once you start, you've got to keep drinking to play your horn. Probably you may play the same thing, but your nerves won't be so stable. That's another of the reasons—and it's a terrible thing—although there's as much whiskey drinking outside musical circles. But we're spotlighted. People can see us where we can't see them.

If you had enough to help you make this gig when you're tired, and afterwards you could get a big meal and forget it, it would be a big help, but then you often couldn't get it because people wouldn't serve you, or the places were closed. You'd be surprised how you can ride five or six hundred miles through the South and West without hitting a place where you can eat. Sandwiches, maybe.

Being away from your loved ones can entice you into drinking a lot of whiskey, too. A guy gets to thinking of his wife, his kids, or something and says, "Well, give me a little taste!" He may be away from home a long time, too. One of the bad things is when you start drinking early in the morning. Time to play, you're still drinking.

Then the guys would be wondering about their wives, wondering what they were doing.

"Shorty George," like they'd say, "must be in your house now."

Cats would be yelling from one end of the bus to the other. Maybe this guy is weak and sitting in the middle, and another gets up at one end of the bus and shouts:

"Hey, man, wonder if Shorty George is in your house now?"

Maybe they're just bugging the guy, but he starts thinking about it. "Shorty George" was the name for the Invisible Man, anybody. I know Lucky Millinder and different guys began using it around here, but you never know where things like that begin. If you were drinking, they'd say:

"Keep drinking all that juice, man, you won't be here long. Shorty George'll be wearing all your togs."

"That's why I kept a lot of clothes," the cat might answer. "I don't want my wife walking around with Shorty George looking bad."

Now, in the South they had another name for Shorty George—"Darby Hicks." Darby Hicks and Shorty were the same. If you were about five hundred miles from home, a cat would say:

"Man, I dreamed last night Darby Hicks was trying to get his key in your door."

Shorty George, or Darby Hicks, was the other man, and he was also the other she-male. When you saw a masculine-type chick, with a crew haircut, walking like a man, you'd say, "There goes Shorty!"

Fletcher Henderson had an expression when he saw us getting sharp after the gig. We'd be all dressed up, maybe coming through the lobby of the hotel, and he'd say:

"Well, where's your traps?"

"What traps, man?"

"I see you're going bear trapping again tonight."

He knew we were going after chicks. He meant that we had no shame and would bring anything back.

Then there was an expression one of Basie's most famous cats would use. You'd see him going out all dressed up and you'd say:

"How're you doin'? I see you're gonna make it, eh?"

"Horse, hawg, or dawg," he'd say, meaning that anything goes.

Somebody else had an expression about chicks that I never forgot. He didn't care whether a girl had eyes for him or even what she looked like. All he would ask was, "Is she breathing?"

Another expression began, as far as I know, at the Hoofers' Club. If a guy was feeling good, he would stomp his foot at the end of a chorus and take another, and maybe stomp his foot again, and keep right on. Eventually, that got to happen in bands. Like you'd be playing "Sweet Georgia Brown," and if you didn't hear somebody stomp his feet, you'd still have it, or it would go back to the piano. Or you might point at another guy, meaning, "Why don't you take one?" If he didn't want to blow, he'd say "Want none!"

Next thing you know, when a chick comes by the bandstand who looks kind of weird, you hear a cat saying:

"Want none, want none!"

Then a fine one comes by, and he says:

"Want some, want some!"

Basie's fellows had another expression for sad chicks, and they'd say, "That's a wayback!" Another ways of saying "Want none!"

You have to consider the mental and physical wear and tear on us musical salesmen out on a tour of one-nighters. But we'd be worrying, too, about what went on back home. We've lost wives and sweethearts, homes and horns, cars and clothes, and even lives, all through the wear and tear of the road and night life. I've often heard day people say, "I wish I could travel like you guys. You have all the fun." Okay, but here's what they don't know!

There may be days and nights when you won't see even a bed or a sofa. Why? Because the whole band may be suffering from all forms of the shorts and miss-a-meal cramps—no loot, no love, no food. The high cost of living has taken the fun out of travel, anyway. Now you travel for loot, period. In fact, the best gray musicians won't go on the road now, because of radio, TV, recording, and whatnot. They won't bother. Nobody's going much now. They seem to have a kind of gimmick going of $150, which is what they give you on these rock 'n' roll things. They just won't give you more, and it's kind of rough when they're grossing maybe $30,000 a night. You do extra shows, and you have hell trying to get that extra money. Your hotels can run you $60, and then there's food, so what have you got left? It doesn't seem right. The musicians seem to be the last to be considered, but they've got to have you so far as dances and shows are concerned.

But night people don't lose their pretty so easily as day people. After meeting so many ups and downs, they get to make jokes about the worst happenings. They even make jokes about death. Big Green said to me, "Looks like I'm going to join the band downstairs." (There were two bands: St. Peter's sweet band upstairs and Satan's hot band downstairs.)

When I look back, I know traveling had a lot to do with some of the great ones going out early. The problems of where to stay and where to eat didn't help either.

When we hit town in the old days, the leader would say, "Hold it fellows. Let me go out first and try to find us a place to stay." If we had been on good terms with the rooming house and restaurant the last time, he wouldn't be gone long, but if he had to rub them down (or "fan" them, as Buddy Tate would say), he would be gone just about all day. On the other hand, the boarding house down the street might have gone out of business, like Pop's in Cincinnati and Pop's in Philly. The wrecking crew got both of them. Then there was the Henderson crew, which would upset Father Divine's, must less a small eatery. I don't think there have ever been three greater destroyers at dining-room tables than Mr. Don Redman, Mr. Benny Carter, and Mr. Coleman Hawkins. Boy, what a team they were! After everything was gone, one would say, "I wasn't feeling so hungry today." Another would remark, "That little snack will hold me until suppertime!" I think before Pop's in Philly went or was forced out of business, he had barred the crew from his joint. But it was too late. They had already hung him!

Well, here comes our leader back. The people we stayed with last time are still in town and still in business. The sax player the old man was going to shoot need not worry, because the old man died and his daughter got married. Her mother is running the house, so we stay there and eat down at the Dewdrop Inn, like before.

If you own a boarding house, you have to be on the ball to prevent your family being larger after the band leaves or your household wares being much fewer. Of course, if the cat involved is a leader or well-fixed loot-wise, they may be happy to give their daughter a shove and diminish the home front. Then, too, one cat may rent the pad, and when the day people are in dream city he will open the window, and after a while it's like some of the bars around town—two for one, or more. Such a cat will open his bag of tricks and start his tearjerking lies around feed time, like being a million miles from home, etc. Sometimes it works, but if the landlady tells her old man, and he's a down cat, then the whole gang may be dumped. Her old man may lose some sleep from watching doors, windows, and porches, from keeping his ears to the doors listening for female voices (or if it's a girl band, for he-male voices). I've known some to lie awake listening for the voice of a daughter, a wife, mother, or sister. They may be in one of a million other places, of course, but the old eye is on us, poor us, the night people.

In any big band, when you hear "Come 'n' get it!" you'd better be as near the table as possible to avoid the stampede, and if they use the platter system, you'd better be down with the Boarding House Reach. As one of five children, I was in the groove. If I hadn't known about the Reach, everyone would have cried shame on me. When I was a kid, my mind might have been going along with Mama and Papa saying grace, with no idea the other four minds were on the nearest platter, but by and by I latched on. I had no idea the Reach would come to be such a major factor in my musical life. I sure was lucky to have been schooled early, because without it, when I made it to Basie's band, I would have been a dead duck. The only eyes closed while grace was being said belonged to whoever said it, but when his or her eyes came open, all the plates were full, and the heads bowed and eyes closed. That's called the Magic Touch. I had seen it done by one or two cats in a band, but not by a whole outfit—valets, girl singer, manager, leader, all had the Magic Touch.

One trumpet player, a very good one, would ask for the cat eyes (biscuits), and when he reached he would come up with one between each finger (four) and, at the same time, one or two would be in the palm of his hand. Walter Page told him he had hands like an octopus. He said, "Baby, those cat eyes must have glue on them— they just got stuck to my hands!"

In most of the hip joints, they would use the plate system and bring the food from the kitchen straight to you. Now, whatever you had to do (like going to the outhouse), you had to be sure you did it before you ordered, because if you had to leave the table after your plate arrived you might as well have kept going, or you had to be ready to hang someone, or get hung. But most likely you would get the old treatment of the three monkeys— hear nothing, see nothing, know nothing.

There was another trick they liked to pull. You get out of the bus at a small restaurant in the South that could only accommo- date a few people, and the cats that were most hungry would rush to get their orders in first. Suppose you had ordered pork chops or something, and they had only one order of it left, the cat sitting next to you would go out back and tell the waitress:

"Don't give him any meat, miss. Meat of any sort gives him fits."

He'd sit down near the back, and when she asked him what he wanted he'd say:

"Well, since you've got the order ready, I'll take the pork chops."

You'd be sitting there waiting, and then you'd start to raise the devil about it, and a couple of days later it would all come out.

They had other ways of easing you out of chicks, too, especially in the Fletcher Henderson band. If a fellow knew you had eyes for a certain chick—and he had, too—he would say:

"Man, see that chick?"

"Yeah," you would say.

"It's a damn shame about her," he would go on, "but she goes to my doc, and he says there ain't nothin' she hasn't got. She is all burned up."

So naturally you cut out, and who do you see her with afterwards but him! You tell him you don't dig him. He says he felt sorry for her and carried her home to give her some fatherly advice.

Another gimmick they had when you were with a chick was to come up and say:

"Your wife just called, man. She wants you to bring some milk home for the kids."

Or they might come and say, "Say, man, your wife is outside." So you would split.

The traveling scene is much better down home since my blood brothers came up with some modern hotels, motels, swimming pools, etc. Once upon a time, too, when lushies and junkies were fewer—say one or two at most to a band—rooms weren't such a problem. In fact, when word spread that the band was in port, doors flew open. Now they fly shut—wham, wham!—twice, so they will stay closed. Often, when you're short of sleep, the next jump is over the hump, a real long distance, so when you arrive it's too late to get a pad. (I heard that one of our famous tenor men, who now lives in Europe, once got full of Red Eye and slept from Key West, Florida, to Bangor, Maine.) Or you can't get accommodation for various other reasons. In Europe, it's quite different. The only thing is that the little dolls can't crash the hotels after eleven or midnight, which is darn near as drastic as not being able to crash any ofay joint below the Mason-Dixon line. Not all are okay above the Mason-Dixon either!

Then I musn't forget that we have some rough ones, and there are fights sometimes. Someone may borrow something and forget to return it, things like ties, socks, suits, wives, daughters.

However, I do think that through the ups and downs of life, there's no greater bunch of big, fat-hearted people on God's earth, because I know of no other profession that requires the expression of happiness at all times, whether it comes from the horn, mouth, eyes, or feet, and regardless of what's happened to you and who you lost. I don't think there's any other business outside show business and music where you can crowd so much fun and pleasure into a life's span. But talking of big, fat hearts, it sure was a drag to see show girls leave the picture. They used to be the biggest lift to musicians, because we thought alike. About lending money, if you were broke—bam, bam! They'd lend you money, those chorus girls, just like that, as a friend, and that's something else missing now.

But it's easy to see how anyone can take the wrong path in our game. Just don't look at us as if we started the war. We are showcased. By that I mean everyone can dig us on stage, but it's dark Out There.

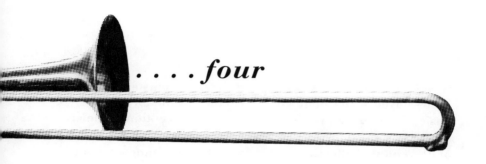

. . . . four

Basie Days

Hired for six weeks, Dicky Wells stayed with Count Basie's band eleven years. There was an enduring bond of deep mutual affection between the two men, and Basie undoubtedly understood and appreciated better than most the meaning of those "talking phrases" with which his star trombonist accompanied Jimmy Rushing's blues.

This chapter provides an insider's view of the Basie band during what most knowledgeable listeners consider its greatest period. Besides the outstanding rhythm section, it always featured exceptional soloists, and of these Wells ranked with Lester Young among the most original. The emphasis he places on Basie's way with arrangements should be noted by those who underestimate the importance of that leader's role, as well as his belief that "Basie is always listening, and he's the one who gives the band its character."

S.D.

Basie sent for me in 1938 and told me to come by his house, because Herschel [Evans], Lester [Young], and some of the fellows in the band liked my blowing with Teddy Hill.

"Okay," I said, "but how about you?"

"Well," Basie said, "so long as they like you, you must be okay."

We went to play in a country club in Plainsfield, New Jersey. It was a small room.

"Come on," Basie said, "take your ax out and sit down and blow with the cats. See if you like it."

"Where's my music?" I asked.

"Sit in and see what happens," he said.

I took Ed Durham's place, and they had only the two trombone parts for Dan Minor and Benny Morton.

"Grab a derby and start fannin'!" Basie called.

I was so busy getting my kicks, because Billie Holiday was there, and Jimmy Rushing, and Herschel Evans, as well as Pres (Lester Young). Herschel and Pres had their battle going, and it was the swingingest band I had been in since Fletcher's. Basie would start out and vamp a little, set a tempo, and call out, "That's it!" He'd set a rhythm for the saxes first and Earle Warren would pick that up and lead the saxes. Then he'd set one for the bones, and we'd pick that up. Now it's our rhythm against theirs. The third rhythm would be for the trumpets, and they'd start fanning with their derbies. (Derbies were very effective with brass sections then, and it's too bad they're so little used

63

now. Derby men like Lips Page, Sidney De Paris, and Harry Edison could always make your insides dance.) The solos would fall in between the ensembles, but that's how the piece would begin, and that's how Basie put his tunes together. He had a big band, but he handled it as though it were six pieces.

When we got through, Basie asked me how I liked the band. I told him I was crazy about it.

"Am I hired?" I asked him.

"I didn't fire you, did I?" was his answer.

It took me quite a while to pick up on some of the psychology he used. He was the first leader I ran into who used jokes as hints, along with nicety, to whip you back into line—maybe damned near too late! I found out afterwards that his motto was: "I'm not going to fire you—you're going to fire yourself." Just about the only way I had seen cats whipped back in line in Louisville was when others whipped out their shooting irons or blades. The leader I first worked with, the one who was pocketing the other half of my weekly pay, carried the longest rod in the world. It should have had wheels on it. He said he had it for pink-toes, but he must have been color blind, because I've seen him pull it on some pretty dark pink-toes. Anyway, give me Basie's style as a leader, and I can make it.

It was a happy band. Even when Herschel and Lester weren't speaking, they were the best of friends! There was so much humor in that band. It was like being part of a family. And all kinds of people liked Basie. Sometimes there were so many millionaires on the bus there wasn't room for the guys to sit down. Walter Page was very popular, too. Carloads of people used to come long distances just to hang out with him. I'll tell you another thing. We were a clean band. When we played hotels, we didn't leave the stand littered up with cigaret butts and chewing gum. They used to be so surprised. They'd say, "Hey, didn't you guys work here last night?"

Soon after I joined, we went into the Famous Door. It seemed that everything they had then turned out to be a hit, like "Jumpin' at the Woodside," and "One O'Clock Jump," and "Doggin' Around." And Jimmy Rushing had his hit songs, too, like "Good Morning Blues," "Sent for You Yesterday," and "Don't You Miss Your Baby." Billie didn't stay long, but she had her songs going as well. This was about the time she began to make a name for herself on records.

We were supposed to be in the Famous Door six weeks, but we stayed three months. Basie and I had a little spat there one night, and he told me to go home until he sent for me. I thought he would never send for me, but he did. So I went back after a couple of days and was there until the job ended, when I was supposed to quit. He asked me if I wanted to stay a bit longer and go on the road. The band was swinging, so I said yes.

The bus left from outside the Woodside Hotel. Herschel was sitting in the front, and he started cursing me out right away:

"You knew you weren't going to leave in the first place, and here you come dragging back! Get the hell in the back of the bus and set your red ass down."

He made me kind of angry, but the other guys said not to pay him any mind, and soon we were all smiles. He turned out to be one of my best friends, and they used to call him, Buck [Clayton], and myself brothers, because we were about the same height and color. I soon seemed to settle in in that band, although the only guy I'd known before was Benny Morton. I remember him coming to Louisville with Fletcher, and everybody marveling about how well he played.

So we went out, and that was the beginning of my eleven years with Basie—what was supposed to have been six weeks. We went touring, mostly in the South, because Basie didn't cover the wide area he does now. In fact, he almost never goes South now.

The band gradually took on a lot of arrangements as well as the heads. Don Kirkpatrick, the pianist, used to bring in arrangements while we were at the Famous Door. He was a wonderful writer. Now, Herschel was a slow kind of reader and didn't care about reading at all. So after we had spent about three hours rehearsing, Basie would call out that night:

"Get out that number Kirkpatrick made!"

"I can't find my part," Herschel would say.

We'd all be down, looking under the stands, and Basie would be looking through the piano music. Herschel would be real busy helping Basie look for it, but after the gig he'd tell me:

"Man, I tore that damn thing up and sent it down the drain— all them sharps and things. I didn't feel like fooling with that."

That happened three or four times, until Basie got wise. He said:

"I believe that rascal's tearing up our music."

But I don't think he ever actually *knew*. Herschel would wait until after rehearsal and tear it up, six or seven sheets for saxophone. Well, he read slow, but that was one of the reasons why he swung so much. I asked Fletcher Henderson once why he wrote so much in those keys like B-natural and C-sharp, and he said he'd been doing it so long because it meant less notes and the band would swing more. Sandy Williams verified that later on. He said when he left Fletcher he couldn't read fast in flat or natural keys.

Basie really began to get a book together when Ed Durham was in the band. Basie and Ed would lock up in a room with a little jug, and Basie would play the ideas, and Ed would voice them. Durham could write real well then, as he did later for the Glenn Miller band. After Durham left, Basie began to buy different arrangements from outside. Even so, Basie always played a big part, because he would cut out what he didn't like, what wasn't Western style, just as he does today, until he got it swinging. He always said you could swing a piece no matter how fast or slow it was. He always believed in making people's feet pat, which is one reason he still has a swinging band. And he had that feeling for tempo. He'd start the band off, maybe fool around with the rhythm section for thirty-two bars, until he got it right, and then it would stay that way right through.

I don't think the Basie band had anything *new* except the idea of the two tenors. After all, Fletcher had swung just about everything that could be swung. Maybe Fletcher's things were a bit more polished, but Basie had those tempos like Bennie Moten had. Bennie's brother used to play accordion, and I believe it helped to groove the band. If you were standing in a corner, you'd hear it coming through with the rhythm. Ed Durham contributed a lot, too. He didn't write too complicated, and he voiced so open, like Jimmy Mundy, and I think it caught the dancers better. Now Don Redman and Benny Carter wrote tough parts for trumpets, but their style couldn't be better for trombones. Benny's writing for saxes was something else, and there was no limit to what Don would write if he could pick his men.

Basie's two battling tenors were two of the best, and the crowd went for them. I heard them going like that at the Cherry Blossom when I was in Kansas City with Fletcher Henderson. Plenty of bands had two trumpet soloists or two trombones, but not two tenors. I noticed their effect for the first time when we played the Paradise Theatre in Detroit, a place like the Apollo. As soon as Herschel stood up, before he ever went down front, the people would start yelling. The same when Lester stood up. I think that started the tenor sax duet within a band. Before that it had been drums and trumpets. The flute's popular now, but I think it's more of a novelty. It has more of a symphonic sound, but that's the way it's gone lately, as though everyone wants to see how technical he can get. So they've tried to squeeze the older sounds under the rug. The older people you used to see, you may see now in a ballroom, dancing to a band like Buddy Tate's. That they can understand. The more Buddy swings, the sooner he fills the floor. And the blues still fills it up. I always remember Buchanan at the Savoy saying, "The best band is the one that keeps the floor filled."

Herschel had a kind of first tenor sound that made a real contrast with Lester's, and Herschel was playing that way before he ever heard Hawk in person. When Buddy Tate, Lucky Thompson, Don Byas, and Paul Gonsalves were in the band, though they were tops, there was never the same contrast. It's pretty hard to duplicate the original, especially when the original is perfect—and that it was. Wow, what a team! I think, though, that if any of the fine fellows with real tenor tone, like Don, Paul, Lucky, Jacquet, or Buddy, had been on the scene *at first*, it would have been pretty much the same. Don, Lucky, and Paul were supreme technicians. Illinois Jacquet was an all-round man with something of Herschel's style. Buddy was tops for gutbucket, and he has a lot of Herschel in his playing, too. Those three, Herschel, Buddy, and Illinois, all came from Texas, and they have that big Texas sound.

Buddy came in when Herschel left, and Basie liked him because he had a quality like Herschel's. So had Illinois, but there was never again quite the same effect, although Basie always had a contrast going. He wouldn't put Don Byas and Lucky Thompson together, or Don and Paul Gonsalves. He aimed for two different sounds and styles. He had fine tenor players, but it was as though he was really lucky the first time. He could never get that flavor after Lester left, but at least the first two gave him a pattern. He came closest to it when he had Paul Quinichette.

Basie is always listening, and he's the one who gives the band its character. Like if I had a band, and he and I bought the same arrangement and rehearsed it with different bands, when we came to play it most people wouldn't know it was the same arrangement. He'd have whittled it down, maybe only kept the introduction, though he'd have paid good money for it. So it was Basie music! As great as Don Redman was, he'd rearrange his arrangements, too. Basie told me once about one of mine:

"That's good, but you've got enough there for fifty arrangements."

When he'd finished tearing it up, I didn't know it, but it was swinging.

Andy Gibson wrote things for the band like "Tickle Toe" and "Beau Brummel." He knew about Basie's way with arrangements, so one night he brought one in written on a bit of paper about the size of a postcard.

"Turn it over when you get to Letter B," he said.

Basie had gone to the phone. When he came back he heard us playing this number, said it was swinging, and wanted to know what it was. When he saw the size of it, he said:

"This one must be on the house, man!"

So I think the real difference between the Basie band and most others was in the way they broke down arrangements the way they wanted them. Sometimes, Benny Carter's bands sounded almost too perfect. That's the funny thing about jazz. You may rehearse until you're hitting everything on the head, and here come a band like the Savoy Sultans, raggedy, fuzzy sounding, and they upset everything. "What am I doing here?" you wonder. But that's the way it is. That's jazz. If you get too clean, too precise, you don't swing sometimes, and the fun goes out of the music. Like Fletcher's arrangements—they'd make you feel bright inside. You were having fun just riding along. You could almost compare it to a lot of kids playing in the mud, having a big time. When the mother calls one to wash his hands, he gets clean, but he has to stand and just look while the others are having a ball. *He's too clean, and he can't go back.* Same way when you clean up on that horn and the arrangements are too clean: You get on another level. You're looking down on those guys, but they're all having a good, free-going time.

Basie's book was probably more varied in the old days than it is today. Buck Clayton used to know just what to write for the guys, and Basie would often suggest the number he wanted. Besides Andy Gibson's things, Don Redman wrote some good ones like "Old Manuscript" and "Down, Down, Down." I wrote "Stay Cool" and "After Theatre Jump." He used to play my "Kansas City Stride" and every night, too, the one we recorded on V-Disc. One of the last the band recorded was "Just a Minute." "Dickie's Dream" was Lester's tune. He made it up in the studio. We hadn't got a title for it, so John Hammond said, "Let's call it 'Dickie's Dream'." I sometimes get a request for it, but until recently I had forgotten how it went.

When the band first came to New York, it was pretty rough, but the time at the Famous Door ironed out quite a bit of that. Each section used to iron out its own problems. And then we used to have different guys for different chairs, sometimes maybe two first men. Like in Smack's band: Joe Smith wouldn't play first, nor would Louis. Today, everybody wants to be so great on their horns technically that they can say, "I play first." I once heard Sy Oliver say, "If a man can't play first, I don't want him." That's all right, but if everybody can play first, you end up with a similarity of sound in solos. When you had definite first, second, and third chairs, I believe you got more of an individual flavor in the different solos. I go along with each playing *some* first, but there should be a key man. If everyone plays first, what about cats like Louis Armstrong, Buck Clayton, Emmett Berry, Bill Coleman, Bobby Stark, Bix Beiderbecke, Red Allen, Jonah Jones, Bobby Hackett, Miles Davis, Dizzy Gillespie, and Harry Edison, all of whom I consider great? There are many more, not to mention saxes and bones, who have a beautiful color (musically), who are also great and don't play first or care to do so.

Now, Arthur Pryor, who had a band like Sousa's and started lip vibrato for trombone, was one of the greatest trombone soloists, but he always kept one or two of the best first bone men in his band. He used to demonstrate trombones for Conn, and he gave me lessons about 1936, when I was with Teddy Hill. Keg Johnson and Claude Jones went to him, too. He was one of the best artists, but when he was teaching you just had to watch and listen. He was so very fast, you had to tell him to slow down. There was nothing stiff about his playing; he was very flexible.

Basie was one of the best to work for. He takes quite a bit, and then he may get mad and explode. Could be that you're on the way out and don't know why. Well, it's a poor guy who doesn't know he has done wrong and keeps doing it. Basie's pretty easygoing, but he still lets you know who's boss. He doesn't want you to drink too much on the job. That is, he wants you to be careful. I think Pres was about the only man he let have a taste on the stand, and he always hid it and wouldn't make it obvious.

I don't think Basie plays enough piano solos today. One guy in the band used to kid him and say:

"Man, I hear you reaching 'way back'!"

He acted as though he were kidding, but he meant it, and that was no good, because Basie is kind of shy and sincere about his work.

Whether it's old-fashioned or not—and I don't think it is—the real question is: Is it good? A lot of new-fashioned things are no good. That's what I like about European audiences. They don't just want the newest; they want the best. The Basie rhythm section could still be featured by itself like it used to be, because it's still a good rhythm section.

When we were at the Lincoln Hotel in New York, the owner, Mrs. Kramer, was fond of swing, and she'd pull up a table near the stand. She especially liked the rhythm section, and sometimes they'd play alone for maybe an hour, and Basie would tell us we could leave for a while, and we'd be in the bars around, drinking.

One of the things that keeps tension down in a band is a drummer who plays for the band and for the soloists, rather than for himself. Basie's rhythm section used to be so light and so strong, that it was a real inspiration. My idea of a rhythm section is one you feel or sense, one that doesn't disturb you. In the forties, some of the drummers got so technical they spoiled everything. Before he died, Shadow Wilson told me that before he went with Basie he had one way of playing in mind—the latest thing, that was it! Then he got hungry and found out, and began playing with a beat to satisfy the band. He was very versatile and a good drummer, and he played for the musicians on the order of Big Sid. At its best, the Basie rhythm section was nothing less than a Cadillac with the force of a Mack truck. They more or less gave you a *push*, or a *ride*, and they played no favorites, whether you were an E-flat, or B-flat soloist.

It was at the Lincoln that Pres got his little bell. If somebody missed a note, or you were a new guy and goofed, you'd hear this bell going—"Dingdong!" If Pres was blowing and goofed, somebody would reach over and ring his bell on him.

"Why, you———," he'd say when he finished.

Jo Jones had another way of saying the same thing. *Bing-bing-bing* he'd go on his cymbal rod. When you first joined, you would take it kind of rough, but later you'd be in stitches with the rest and take it as a joke. They'd ring a bell on Basie, too. And if Pres saw someone getting angry, he'd blow the first bar of "Runnin' Wild."

Harry Edison named himself "Sweets" because he was so rough, always kidding, hiding your hat, and things like that. Sweets, because it was the opposite of what he knew he was. He and Pres just about named everybody, and when Pres named anybody the name stuck.

Basie was "the Holy Main." That meant "tops" in the way you'd apply it to someone you greatly admired. Buck Clayton was "Cat Eye," and Snooky Young was "Rabbit." Ed Lewis was "Big D." George Matthews was "Truce," and Benny Morton was "Mr. Bones." After Benny left, I became "Mr. Bones," but before that I had been "Gas Belly" on account of my troublesome stomach. Freddie Green was "Pep." Walter Page was "Big 'Un" or "Horse." Jo Jones was "Samson." Buddy Tate was "Moon," and Herschel was "Tex." Rush was "Honey Bunny Boo" or "Little Jim." Earle Warren was "Smiley," and Jack Washington was "Weasel." Emmett Berry was "Rev.," and Eli Robinson was "Mr. Eli." Jimmy Powell was "Neat," and Helen Humes "Homey." It was Pres who named Snodgrass, the manager, "Lady Snar." Everybody had one of those names.

Herschel worked up to the day before he died. I think it was dropsy. He swelled up so he couldn't get his hat on. It could have been cured if he had gone to the doctor earlier. Everybody loved him.

Helen Humes did well as Billie's successor, and her blues style fitted the band. Even her pop songs had a blues flavor. She and Jimmy Rushing used to get along well, telling tall tales and keeping the bus in an uproar all the time.

Jimmy used to come aboard the bus with a bag of food, chicken or something. We'd be leaving around two o'clock, and he would wait until everybody was asleep, snoring, and then open his chicken bag. I was sitting behind him one time, hungry, and saw his jaws working, so I touched him on the shoulder.

"Ah, man, I thought you were asleep! Here, fool, eat this and go to sleep."

He passed me a very small bit of chicken. I'd wait a couple of nights and then touch him up again.

Rush is a big man, but he's real light on his feet and can move fast. The only time that I saw Rush depressed was when his wife or mother was sick. He's something like Earl Hines. Earl may have troubles, but he doesn't let you know it. Earl told one of his guys once, "You may have holes in your shoes, but don't let people out front know it. Shine the tops." And Rush never forgets anything. He can tell you exactly what happened twenty, thirty years ago.

Basie kept going all through the difficult period when most other big bands broke up. Somehow, he always managed to get good transport and accommodation during the war. But then conditions caught up with him, too. It began to get rough some time before he cut down to six pieces. The band wasn't drawing, things were rough all over, and guys were coming in and out of the band fast. He asked me if I wanted to stay, and I appreciated it, but by that time I had had enough of the road, so I told him I thought I ought to stay home for a while.

Before that I had been out of the band for a while. I had my tonsils removed, because they kept swelling, and I also had stomach disorders. That was because I was drinking quite a bit, trying to stay together. I guess anyone but Basie would have fired me long before. He didn't want to have you on the bandstand if you felt bad, and I'd lay off a week or two, and he'd tell Lady Snodgrass to bring me my money! After I'd had my tonsils out, Lester's burst on him. That was in Chicago. They got the house doctor in the hotel, and Pres said afterwards:

"Where the hell did you get that cat from? He must have been a horse doctor, cutting away at all the wrong places in my throat!"

He got better, but he took it pretty hard when he had to go in the Army.

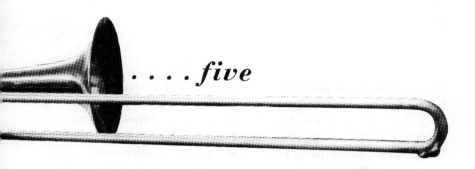

. . . . five

Bus Talk

Much of this book derived from tape-recorded talks, but a considerable part was typed by Dicky Wells on an old typewriter given him by his good friend Bill Coleman. At first, the written material tended to have much more formality than the spoken, but when he realized that his frequent use of musician's slang was a cause of much amusement, he loosened up on the typewriter, too.

A lot of jazz slang originated during the long hours the musicians spent on buses. The joking and ribbing that went on was enhanced when carried out in "jive" language. The sample that follows is obviously concentrated, but there is no doubt about its authenticity as to subjects—gambling and women.

S.D.

All performers in show business seem to have their own kind of talk, their own language. Musicians use slang among themselves, and I know that with us a lot of it was done just for amusement, particularly on those long bus rides. Each band had its own expressions, and they became a part of you, but outside your little circle they might not mean too much.

I'll try to give some samples of the expressions in use when I was out touring, as well as of the kind of conversation that went on in band buses. Some of the expressions have since gone out and been replaced, but this was more or less how it was.

"Say, ol' man, where the hell have you been? You've held the bus up one solid hour."

"I'm sorry Boss. I had to go to the doctor."

"For what?"

"Don't you dig my hand all bandaged up?

"I know you got it caught in a door."

"Well, I'll tell you how it was a door was involved. I was trying to knock one down, to the ground."

"Why?"

"You remember that chick came in the bus just before we left Durham last Saturday?"

"Uh-huh."

"Well, she told me to go by and see her girlfriend when we got back to the city. So I dropped by her pad and blew her horn."

"Shake me, daddy. I'm not with you."

"I mean, rang her bell."

"Now we're cooking. Carry on."

"Well, man, she came to the door with nothing on but the radio. She must have thunk I was her holy main. Wham, bam, slam! Right in my face."

"Hahaha!"

"Shut up, fool, back there!"

"As I was saying before I was so rudely interrupted—I mean the door was in my face now. So I started banging."

"I knew you were a weird cat all the time," says the same voice from the back.

"Shut up, d.a.!"

"Well, go on."

"Did she open up? Did she open the door?"

"No."

"What did she say?"

"She told me through the door that though my eyes might water and my teeth might grit, none of her lovin' would I git. But like the rooster told the hen in the old chicken shack, 'Don't worry, baby. I'll be back.' Wow! What a sight to remember!"

"You ain't lying," says a cat across the aisle, "and since I'm your roomie I guess I'll have to get a jug and sit up all night. Where you going?"

"Excuse me, while I go back here and talk to the guy who was heckling me."

"Okay. Later."

"Say, man, ain't I as nice to you as I can be? Why the hell are you always messing with me? I never told the gang about you-all's mumbling to yourself while you're playing. After all, I'm sitting right next to your ol' buns. Just what is it you're saying under your bad breath every time you see a real bad chick?"

"I say, 'Dear Lord, I see what I want, but I'll be thankful for anything I can git. Amen.'"

"Say, that new boy has been asleep for two days. What goes?"

"I'll tell you. When we went South before, you do remember that shy little bundle that was standing by the stand when we played Chittlin' Switch, Georgia?"

"Uh-huh."

Well, I happened to walk by the two of them at intermission and heard him say, 'Baby, all I want is four bars after the gig.'"

"So? What shook?"

78

"Man, he hadn't been South before. These aren't those Chicago, New York, or Detroit scotch-and-soda barflies. These broads drink corn. I tried to hip him. He asked for four bars, and she composed a whole tune. So ever since he's been trying to get his health back."

"Speaking of getting your health back. I think I'd better turn in. I see my roomie has fallen asleep after that night-to-remember lie. Later."

"Okay, later."

"Say, wake up, man, and turn over on your side. What the hell kind of juice have you been drinking? Smells like you've been inhaling train smoke or chewing old socks. All I need sitting next to you is a chaser, and I'll be as high as you are."

"Man, shut up. Your breath don't smell like no bed of roses either. You're always as high as a Georgia pine. Anyway, since you're so down, why do you blow for a living?"

"Well, I'll tell you. In case you haven't heard, tricks ain't walking no more."

"No?"

"I saw a little wayback hit on you. In fact, she told me she had eyes for you."

"Oh, her. I told here I was a natural beggar, so she told me she could give me a fin a day to keep the wolf away. I said, 'Sweetie, a fin a day wouldn't keep me in hay, and what's more, Dick Tracy will throw your ol' buns in the house of many slams, bams, bumps, and bruises for selling love!' Dig? Now turn in, fool."

"Okay, but I still think you should have dug that little chick."

"Nix, she was 'way out in field."

"Like what?"

"She wanted to shack up."

"Yeah? Maybe that's just what you need."

"Are you kidding? Hell, I don't need no one to help me starve. Don't try to make a home: make a hit and then split. That's my motto. Anyway, I dig the highway."

"Me, too, daddy."

"Say, man, go talk trash with the bus driver, because you've heard your last words from me for quite a while."

It gets real quiet in the bus, until up the aisle from the rear roll the two blind mice and a voice:

"Pitch till you win!"

Soon the game is in session. It may be domino or cards, but no matter what the game, there's always a city slicker around. He may say:

"Wide open spaces!"

That means a high-sitting woman. You all look out the window, and when you look back there is the most disgusting seven or eleven you have ever seen.

"Man, shake those damn dice the next time!"

This cat is called the Slider. Now dig the Jumper. He always makes it his business to be on the left side of the shooter.

"Say, man, stay in your place!"

The toughest cat is the Beggar. His prey is the new brother in the band. Each payday he heads for Western Union or gives his loot to someone like Herschel or Rush. I saw the Beggar take a quarter and run it up to sixty-five dollars. But the old members wouldn't fade his jive bets.

"Man, get away from here with those peanuts."

Sometimes he would get hot and go in his private stash, but very seldom, because this cat is so tight he squeaks between the legs when he walks.

Then there's the Squeezer. He squeezes his pockets and hits on the new brothers for a loan. Then it took me a long time to dig one cat who was a good friend. He was dipping in my E-flat bag and, come to find out, he had more loot in his pocket than the whole band had. Know what he told me?

"Man, your money is lucky to me!"

You can hear more different kinds of lies in a crap game than anywhere else on earth.

Now there's the voice of the Holy Main:

"Better watch your cues back there! There's no draw day this week."

"Now he tells us," say the losers.

"I'm glad you're winners."

"Why?"

"Well, ain't I your man?"

"Yeah, when I'm winners."

"Lights out! The driver can't see."

"Ain't that a bit———?"

"What makes a broke man sleep so sound?"

"I don't know. Why?"

"'Cause he didn't have nothing when he first laid down!'"

"Say, Stiget, how about a coke?"

Stiget was one of the valets. He had an icebox in the back of the bus, and he also had a lock and key to it.

When all the domino boys are asleep, Basie heads for Truce [George Matthews].

"How about a little tonk?"

"Base, you saw me get busted in the crap game."

"Yeah? So bust one of those Lucky Millinder or Chick Webb dollars!"

"Man, I'm tired. Go get some rest like I'm going to do."

"Well, I'll tell you. You can play some tonk or be fired."

So it's tonk all through the night. At the same time, Rush has his man, Weasel, in one of his favorite games, pinochle or black-jack.

Sometimes you would swear you were in Monte Carlo. The thirteen straight craps I threw, and the hanging Smiley and Rabbit gave me later, cooled me. Russ Procope cooled my black-jack playing when we were with Teddy Hill, and I think his cooling was the most brutal. That cat took my whole week's salary in just four hands, and just by one point each hand. He added fuel to the fire with seven words: "Let that be a lesson to you!" I don't remember his ever saying good night. Maybe he did. I couldn't have heard him because I was as hot as a bad girl's dream. Come to think of it, he didn't say good night because he was busy getting out of the Ubangi Club before I borrowed some of my money back.

Next morning, the same conversation. Chicks. What else?

"I told him not to keep messing around with that little E-flat chick. Anytime you want to get wasted, just latch on to one of those bashful babes. I don't know what happened, but the next night you would have had to have sat on that cat's shoulder to hear him blow. There wasn't enough of him left to make a sick man a bowl of soup."

"Give me a double B-flat chick every time, especially in the winter. I want my love to keep me warm."

"You aren't kidding. You should have rented a Mack truck the other night, when I saw you heading for the show, instead of trying to squeeze her into that poor man's taxicab."

"Cool it, daddy, I don't want to go upside your head!"

"Look, man, it ain't no iron fence around yours!"

Another brother is heard from. He likes them tall.

"Say, what about a nice, tall, cool mama?"

"You mean a six o'clock chick?"

"How's that?"

"Straight up."

"Oh, they're crazy in the summer time!"

"Anytime, man. If she's neat, she's a treat."

"Well, listen, ol' man. Come what may, you can send them all my way. Short, tall, fat, or small, I dig them all!"

"My ears was open, and I would like to put my little two cents in, which is to say: When the horn blow, they all go. And what's more, if you cannot be seen and can dig one of those she-male club meetings, it's something else. That's the only time you will hear Shorty's name called, unless it's from the lowest, a cat that's hitting real hard on your holy main and trying to make a name for himself."

This shoe fits another brother, and he comes on:

"Well, there's one thing about me. I never fool with my friends' wives, sisters, or daughters!"

"Say, man, your ears were open. How about your eyes? How do you dig the babes?"

"You don't know how to dig the chicks?"

"What kind should I dig?"

"Well, one who has it and doesn't know it—she really has it! But don't ever tell her so or you'll be in Hung City."

"Say, Sweet Willie, they tell me you have slid under more beds than Jackie Robinson has slid in home plates."

"I made a few in the South, but these big-city pads are too close to the floor. I don't dig them."

"Well, how do you make it now?"

"I'm not a gay blade no more, you see, but I can still make a first- or second-story window. Nothing any higher. I remember once I dug a barfly, and like they all say when their wigs are tight, she said, 'I'm the only one who has a key to my house.' They never tell you who pays the rent! But my wig had also begun to tighten, so we took off to the pad. We were balling like mad until—knock, knock, knock! By the second knock she was shaking like Basie's whole brass section. 'Oh, oh! There's my ol' man. Step out on the ledge.' So I looked out and said, 'Fool, we're on the thirteenth floor.' What did she say? 'Man, this ain't no time to be superstitious. Get on out there!'"

Two more guys wake up.

"Say, ol' man, what's your excuse for livin'?"

"I don't know, but if it's what it sounds like—the Dozens!"

"My excuse for living is to hang your ol' buns."

"The last cat that tried it is in the real estate business. Now he owns six feet of land, and the groundhog is his mailman."

"Oh, yeah? Look, man, you would rather pull a lion's tooth in a telephone booth than mess with me!"

"Okay, if you're so bad, why did you keep running when you caught the Claw coming out of your back door that time?"

"You misunderstood one thing I guess."

"Well, I was kind of sleepy, so tell me again. I know I told you to throw your suitcase up against the front door and run around back, but to be sure you could handle him before you tackled him."

"Well, let me tell you, that cat had to stoop to get out of the door, and that's no E-flat door. Now, what would you have done?"

"Same as you. Kept going."

"Laying all jive aside, if you're as smart as you think you are, you should take that chick to Hollywood I saw you with Saturday."

"For what?"

"To get her a gig in pictures."

"Doing what?"

"Haunting houses."

"Very funny."

"And what became of the babe you had who looked like she was fixing to sneeze all the time?"

"She was a fine chick a year or so ago, but then rigor mortis set in."

Two more get going at the back.

"Say, now you're my ace boon-koon, I'll tell you something I couldn't tell you when I first joined the band. All the guys are calling you 'Hoggie'."

"Why, man?"

"They say you try to hog up all the solos."

"Well, man, my theory is every ass for himself!'"

"Something else I must tell you, baby. That chick you had last Friday sure did have a broad understanding! Boy, was she stacked! And that stride! She looked like a farmer chewing tobacco when she walked. As Moon would say, what a drop she had! What she hadn't got, I don't want."

"Thanks, daddy, You see, that's where you can tell the men from the boys. She's the kind that'll make a rabbit hug a hound and a preacher lay his bible down. Now you wouldn't know what to do with her if you had her."

"Well, I can dream can't I? She sure was a crazy dish. She raced my motor so you could cook an egg on my head."

"Where did you get that name 'Bird Dog'?"

"I'll tell you," says a voice up front. "Haven't you ever dug him tree a babe? He throws a beam in her eye, and she can't move."

Now the new boy gets some serious advice:

"Tell you one thing for sure, Junior. If you do get hitched, try your best to send some pieces home every payday. They like to say to their friends they just received a little check, and if you don't do your best, Shorty George is waiting. I've had so-called friends tell me about having so-and-so's old lady, and that I don't want to hear, because if they'll grin in so-and-so's face and bite his back, they'll do the same to me."

"I'll buy that."

"You might as well go back and cool it with the chick, because harmony is the greatest, and as is you're only one note. It takes two or more to make harmony."

"I haven't sent a single dime back for two weeks, so if Shorty has broken through I've only myself to blame. Why do you think I keep messing with the dice? I would have done better if I'd taken that day job like she asked me to."

"I dig you, man, but it's funny how my old lady would rather me starve than put my ax down."

"Oh, well. Women . . . When it gets too rough for me, I'm going to put it down."

"Yeah? Well, right here and now, let me tell you two of the closest friends to separate are you and your horn. The horn has broken up many families. You can believe that. It's hard to put the horn down."

"That I know."

84

"No kidding, boy, when I'm on the highway I write some letters home that would hang a queen. And know what?"

"What?"

"After I'm home ten minutes, a war breaks out. Then, after the fur starts flying, she says, 'What about all those sweet letters I got from you? Here you didn't get off the bus before you start raising hell!'"

"Is that really the happening?"

"Sure is. Next trip, same thing."

"How did you meet her?"

"From the bandstand, trying to look cute, and waving and winking like a fool. I only wanted a little taste, and then I was going to split, but she wasn't the splitting kind. Anyway, I don't regret it a bit, because you really need someone in your corner."

"How 'bout Shorty George?"

"He doesn't bother me."

"No?"

"Hell, no. I used to be Boss Shorty!"

"Yeah, I heard about you. They tell me you used to be a bitch on wheels. Got any kids?"

"Not that I know of."

"How's that?"

"'Cause ain't nothing shaking but the sheets. You any?"

"Uh-huh."

"How do you know?"

"'Cause they look like me."

"So what? Haven't you never seen anyone that looks like you? No relations?"

"Damn. I never thought of that."

"As Dusty Fletcher used to say, 'The biggest fool ever known is one who rocks somebody else's kid and thinks it's his own.'"

"Well, anyway, that's why I'm out here on the highway, and what's more I'm going to be out here."

"Can't run forever!"

"I can run till they catch me. Say, when we get to New York, will you invite me over to peck?"

"Yeah, but you'd better call first."

"Why?"

"She may be baking a cake."

"What's wrong with that?"

"Well, I'll tell you. They have a pretty good sound, but, boy, are they tough? Sometimes I have to crack 'em with a hammer. Sam, next door, takes a piece to work with him, but he has to dunk it in milk, coffee, or something. I wouldn't mind it if they didn't look so bad. Instead of carrying it to the neighbor, she should carry it to the House of Horrors. My poor stomach! But I got to go along with the action, because when I first met her I wasn't doing so good. So I would accidentally happen by on purpose, and then it would be fish and rice. I ate so much fish in those days I was afraid to look a fish in the face. Things are a little better now, but if you do make it, be sure to have some Tums, Rolaids, or soda stashed on you! What's funny is that I've fallen in love with her cooking and don't dig no one else's. Say, man, wake up!"

The cat is either sleeping like mad or playing possum now for fear of getting that invitation, but he wakes up and shouts:

"Pee stop, driver! I won't take but two bars."

"Okay."

"Thanks, daddy-o. When we get through the Tunnel, the drinks are on me. I dig you not drinking while driving, but I would like one more favor when we get through. Stop and let me kiss the ground of good ol' New York."

And I've got news for you. That's what a lot of musicians really used to do after they'd finished a tour of the South.

The Sunday school band of the Booker T. Washington Community Center in Louisville in the early 1920s. Dicky Wells is the foremost trombonist; Jonah Jones is at Dicky's left, with a peck horn; Charlie Wells is the drum major at the far left.

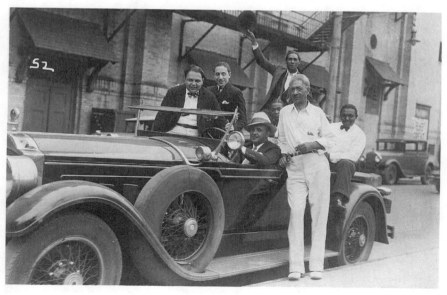

Fletcher Henderson at the wheel of his Packard in 1930. Surrounding friends are, left to right: an unknown saxophonist from The Buffalodians, composer Harold Arlen, trumpeter Bobby Stark, Lois Deppe (waving hat), composer/conductor Will Marion Cook (standing), and cornetist Rex Stewart.

Outside Ann Montgomery's Club Harlem in Buffalo in 1933. Left to right: drummer Walter Johnson, unidentified woman, Dicky Wells, and trumpeters Bobby Stark and Henry "Red" Allen.

Bill Dillard, Frank Newton, and Wells perform a vocal with the Teddy Hill band in 1936.

WILBUR DICK DILLARD
SMITTIE HOWARD

E·BIERE GRAF
PHONE

to Dickie Wells,
a Swell musicia
Hugues Panassié
22...

Top: Wells drives a horse-drawn cart while on tour in Ireland with the Teddy Hill band in 1937.

Center: Members of the Teddy Hill band in Dublin in 1937: Wilbur De Paris, trombone; John Smith, guitar; Wells; Howard Johnson, alto saxophone and clarinet; and Bill Dillard, trumpet.

At left: Recording producer and jazz critic Hugues Panassié in Paris in 1937.

Flyer for one of the many "battles of the bands" at New York's Savoy Ballroom in the late 1930s. Clockwise from top: Count Basie, singer Helen Humes, Jimmy Rushing, and Erskine Hawkins.

Flyer for one of the many "battles of the bands" at New York's Savoy Ballroom in 1937. On this occasion: Chick Webb with Ella Fitzgerald vs. Count Basie with Billie Holiday. Collection of Duncan Schiedt.

Count Basie and Billie Holiday in 1937.

Dicky Wells at right with friends at Chicago's Grand Terrace Cafe, ca. 1940.

Count Basie at the piano with his orchestra in 1941. Rear: Walter Page, bass; Buck Clayton, Ed Lewis, Al Killian, Harry "Sweets" Edison, trumpets; Robert Scott, Wells, Eli Robinson, trombones. Front: Freddie Green, guitar; Jo Jones, drums; Buddy Tate, tenor saxophone; Tab Smith, Earle Warren, alto saxophone; Jack Washington, alto and baritone saxophone; Don Byas, tenor saxophone. Courtesy Charles Wells.

Basie's reeds and trombones in 1943. Rear: Eli Robinson, Robert Scott, Wells, and Louis Taylor. Front: Jimmy Powell, Earle Warren, Buddy Tate, and Rudy Rutherford. Courtesy Duncan Butler.

Count Basie reviews a manuscript, ca. 1944. Courtesy Duncan Butler.

Dicky Wells rehearses the Count Basie reed section in 1944: Rudy
Rutherford, clarinet; Lucky Thompson, tenor saxophone; and Jimmy Powell
and Earle Warren, alto saxophone. Courtesy Duncan Butler.

Filming *Jammin' the Blues* in 1944: Norman Granz, producer; Red Callender, bass; Sidney Catlett, drums; Marlowe Morris, piano; Wells; Harry "Sweets" Edison, trumpet; and Illinois Jacquet, tenor saxophone.

Members of the Red Allen band, ca. 1944: Clarence Lemont ("Bennie") Moten, bass; Paul Barbarin, drums; J. C. Higginbotham, trombone; Wells; Red Allen, trumpet; Don Stovall, alto saxophone; and unknown pianist.

Members of the Count Basie orchestra in 1945. Rear: Freddie Green, Shadow Wilson on drums, unidentified trombonist, Ted Donnelly, Al Killian, Wells, Joe Newman, Louis Taylor, and unidentified trumpeter. Front: Buddy Tate and Rudy Rutherford. Courtesy Duncan Butler.

Trumpeter Bill Coleman, ca. 1945.

The J. C. Heard group in 1946: Al McKibbon, bass; Jimmy Jones, piano; J. C. Heard, drums; Wells; George Treadwell, trumpet; and Budd Johnson, tenor saxophone.

Brothers Dicky and Charlie Wells, ca. 1950.

Earl Hines's group rehearses in 1954: arranger Willie Maiden at the piano; Jerome Richardson, clarinet; Leroy Harris, clarinet and alto saxophone; Paul Binnings, bass; Hank Milo, drums; Gene Redd, trumpet; Hines; and Wells.

Earl Hines's group in performance in 1954: Hines, piano; Carl Pruitt, bass; Shadow Wilson, drums; Leroy Harris and Jerome Richardson, flute; Wells; and Gene Redd, trumpet.

Trombonist Trummy Young, ca. 1956.

Wells and Benny Morton in 1958.

Dicky Wells and his orchestra recording for the Felsted label in 1959: George Matthews, Benny Morton, Wells, and Vic Dickenson, trombones (front to back); Herbie Lovelle, drums; Skip Hall, organ; Harry White, arranger (standing); Everett Barksdale, electric bass; and Kenny Burrell, guitar.

Wells and singer Jimmy Rushing at a Columbia recording session in 1959.

Wells takes a swig of his favorite nonalcoholic beverage—buttermilk—ca. 1960. Courtesy Duncan Butler.

Trombonist Kid Ory with Wells, ca. 1960.

At the Celebrity Club in New York, ca. 1960: Pat Jenkins, trumpet; Wells; Buddy Tate, tenor saxophone; and Ben Richardson, alto saxophone.

Count Basie's all-star septet in 1963: Jo Jones, drums; Rodney Richardson, bass; Buddy Tate, tenor saxophone; Freddie Green, guitar; Buck Clayton, trumpet; and Wells.

Wells and his famous mute, ca. 1965. Photo by Victor Kalin.

Buddy Tate's band prepares to fly to Europe in 1968: Ben Richardson, clarinet and saxophones; Dud Bascomb, trumpet; Buddy Tate, tenor saxophone and clarinet; Billy Stewart, drums; John Williams, bass: Wells; and Skip Hall, piano.

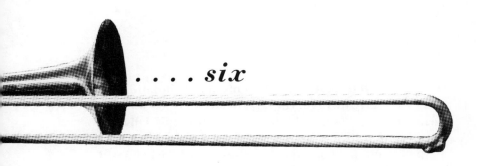

. . . . six

Changing Times

Dicky Wells left the Basie orchestra early in 1946, returned to it in 1947, and left again when it broke up in 1950. Hard living had taken its toll. He had tonsil trouble and "stomach disorders." No doubt, too, he was glad to get off the road for a while to spend more time with his wife, Cherry.

As a result of World War II and its aftermath, the big band era was coming to an end, but for a musician as gifted as Wells there was still no great problem finding employment. The kind of employment, however, often left something to be desired. Wells was in his element in Sy Oliver's excellent band and in the groups of Earl Hines, J.C. Heard, and Illinois Jacquet, where a degree of idiomatic compatibility still prevailed, as it also did in those of old friends from the Basie years like Jimmy Rushing, Buddy Tate, and Buck Clayton. But as he entered his fifties and the business continued to deteriorate, he found it necessary to learn Dixieland!

S.D.

Around 1946, after the tonsils, I was on tour with Lucky Millinder for a few weeks. Lucky was a good showman, had a good ear, and knew what he wanted. He could put a show together at the Apollo as good as any producer. He always kept a good band, and at one time it was terrific. He had Frank Newton and Charlie Shavers, and an arrangement on "Changes Made" that everyone was going up to the Savoy to hear. Most of the book was by Andy Gibson. This would be about the time, too, that Andy quit playing trumpet. The other trumpet players were so terrific, he just stepped down and went to work as an arranger full-time.

Then I was with J. C. Heard in a small band he had at Cafe Society in the Village. He's a rough hide man. He had Budd Johnson on tenor, George Treadwell on trumpet, Jimmy Jones on piano and Al McKibbon on bass. The wonderful Sassie [Sarah Vaughan] was in the show, and about this time she recorded with my band for H.R.S. She sang a tune called "We're Through," and it's still one of my favorites.

I never got the straight of the reason for our departure, but the vine had it that the boss had no eyes for J. C. doing outside gigs. It was one of the best small bands New York has had, something on the order of the Stuff Smith and John Kirby groups, only it wasn't on the scene long enough. Now that Kirby bunch was a m-o-n-e-y band, and it was such a shame they had to break up.

Then I was in the band Sy Oliver had at the Zanzibar. It was an excellent show band. We went out on one-nighters with the Oscar Moore Trio, which was hot at the time. They'd had a couple of record hits. We did some college dates, too. It must have been some kind of package deal, because I remember the Charlie Spivak band was along, too, and Charlie was getting triple the loot that Sy was. Oscar was getting good money, too. We would play those frat houses, and all the crowd would end up listening to us, but Sy could never get enough money to keep the band going. The band was well liked, and we hated to break it up. We played opposite Lunceford at Symphony Hall, Boston, when he had Al Grey in the band. That was too much of a family thing to be a battle, and the arrangements were too much the same. The concert ended with the two bands playing "Brotherly Jump" together! The real battles came when two bands had quite different books.

George Duvivier did a lot of arrangements for Sy then, but sometimes Sy would fix them up the way Basie did. George wrote in a more fiery way than Billy Moore, who did that pretty "Slow Burn."

Sy did some wonderful things at the Apollo in the Lunceford style. He'd have the whole band down front on a choral thing. It looked good on stage, and the people loved it. We did "Walkin' the Dog"—"get 'way back and snap your fingers!" Sy and I sang "Hey, Daddy-O," too. I think the band ought to have made it. It had plenty of talent, and Sy knew how to please the public, but he also liked to pay his men well, and the money didn't come in. He paid over scale on that engagement, and the management and everybody came by and told him he was crazy to pay us so much. There was quite an argument there, but he said he had promised it, and he would pay it, even if it meant breaking the band up. He went to all the downtown offices and did everything he could.

Sy's like Wilbur De Paris in one way. He knows what he wants and tries to drill it into the guys' minds. It's not so much he wants to be the boss man, but he has the idea of what he thinks will be successful, and he goes after it. He doesn't want to sound like everyone else. Wilbur had his band together for quite a few years, so you can't say that he was wrong. Sy has his music down there, and he wants it played the way it is. A lot of guys want to take liberties, of course. It was the same with Benny Carter. If you kind of changed a note, wanted to turn it a little different, he would come over and say:

"Gee, that's swell! I like the way you arrange. It sounds better than what I wrote." Then he'd add, "Play that damn music the way I got it!" And walk away.

Oh, he was something! Another time he would say:

"When you get *your* band, I'll play it like *you* write it. Okay?"

He stood beside me once when I was playing with Teddy Hill. I was thinking, "I must be playing pretty good, with his standing here and listening so carefully to me." He's my idol as an all-around musician. As far as saxophone playing and writing are concerned, he's about as far as anyone can go.

"I want to see you when you're finished," he said.

We got together after the set. Now I knew him, and he knew I knew him, but he said:

"I'm Benny Carter, you know? I'm a musician, and I appreciate what you're trying to do. That's a good idea you've got. You keep at it for about twenty-five years and maybe you'll make it." He laughed and walked away.

You couldn't get angry. I was just standing there looking. Of course, guys like him could see around corners. Set special arrangements in front of them, and they'd knock them off right away. He'd tell you things, and you'd think and think. You'd go home and get yourself together—go woodshedding. They figured it was best to tell you rather than to let you go wrong, and they had that funny way of getting around you.

After I left Basie, I was with Jimmy Rushing's good-sounding band. We had two tenors—Buddy Tate and Harry Johnson. Then there were Buck Clayton, Emmett Berry, Danny Smalls on piano, Walter Page, and Walter Johnson on drums. We stayed at the Savoy about six months. Benny Carter heard the band, liked it well, and said he wished he had it. Later, they cut it down, and Rudy Powell, Al Williams, and Herbie Lovelle came in. It was a swinging band on the order of the Savoy Sultans, but Jimmy never took it out on the road. He had a good book, too. Buck, Rudy, and I wrote the arrangements. We rearranged and played all the things Rush had done with Basie. There was plenty of competition on the next stand then, with all the different bands coming and going. And the Lindy Hoppers there made you watch your p's and q's. The dancers would come and tell you if you didn't play. They made the guys play, and they'd stand in front patting their hands until you got the right tempo.

Jimmy Rushing was and is a big man in the South and West, and he has added to his territory by adding North, East, and abroad. After working alongside him for eleven years, I can very easily see why he is so well liked. In fact, he ought to be called Mr. Sunshine. Doing those one-nighters down home, he would draw his share of the crowd every night.

I went to a few house parties with him, and although we had been together then at least five years, I had never heard him sing the blues as he did at those times. Maybe it was the right atmosphere. It would be real barrelhouse, with whiskey, wine, beer, and high-sitting women, and sometimes he would accompany himself at the piano (in the key of F). He'd get his kicks hearing such names as Big Daddy, Little Daddy, Sugar Daddy, and Sweet Papa Fine, and he would really send all those people. It didn't make any difference if they were waybacks, git-backs, jump-backs, stay-backs, slide-backs, back-backs, or creams (the cream of the crop), he treated them all the same.

He likes telling tall tales. He has a rare way of feeling out the audience and then applying the joke or tale that will really suit it. "Did you hear the one about the . . . ?" he'll ask and then hesitate and say, "Maybe I'd better not tell that one." The crowd always winds up shouting, "Ah, go on, tell it!" Anyway, the next time we hit that town again, all of those people, and more, will be there, and I'd be the first one in the band to be dressed and in Jim's room ready to head for the party. He's one of the most same-at-all-times people I've ever known, and that you can hurry up and believe.

Anyone lucky enough to sit in on a Basie-Rushing tall-tale jam should bring medals, because they would sure be in order. That Greyhound Bus Hotel was the place for them, too! The wonderful thing about people like that is that they give out a tremendous amount of relief, the kind no money can buy. I remember how they changed many dull times into laughter in a second. Sometimes they would just carry on as long as we rode, on and on through the night, and sometimes the bus driver would almost run off the road laughing. Almost, but not quite, because when it came to bus drivers we had some of the best there were, as men and as drivers. Basie saw to that. He would tell Lady Snodgrass to order the driver before he ordered the bus. That helped to make a tour a kick.

Rushing can really sing the blues, and I dig blues singers the most, because they are natural soul stirrers. If you don't believe they're the life of the party, put on the other part of the show or concert first, and then bring on the blues singer. Dig the facial expressions and the feet of the audience. They both change. The face lights up, and the feet light out. It goes for a sitting audience the same as a dancing one.

We all get the dumps some time, and then you've got the blues, nothing but, and when you start reciting your woes to yourself or to another, then you're singing the blues. Maybe the melody isn't there, but it's the blues just the same. Our outlet for misery is the twelve-bar blues, and I guess we owe some thanks to the great W. C. Handy. The Jewish people have also got some fine chants in a bluish mood, and other races have their own music for the depressed. But being of people who've suffered racial persecution, like the Jews and Negroes have, I dig our hurt the most. And it's the same old story—it doesn't hurt until it hits home— and it has been hitting the darker races for too long. So why shouldn't we have the bluest feeling and play the darnedest blues? It's an American music, but there are a lot of notes being dressed up in blues clothing. Don't let them fool you. The good old southern blues will move them all, whether they're young or old, hot or cold. Yes, the blues move you, and they seem to do something to you inside that makes your body laugh.

Blues singers I like, besides Jimmy Rushing, are Joe Turner and B. B. King. Then there's Mr. Cleanhead Vinson. He sings good blues, and in tune. Bill Broonzy, Bessie Smith, T-Bone Walker, Jimmy Witherspoon—there have been so many good singers of blues. But don't forget the blues singers without words, like Johnny Hodges, Buddy Tate, Lester Young, Red Prysock, Lips Page, Buck Clayton, Emmett Berry, Harry Edison, Frank Galbraith, Joe Smith, Jimmy Harrison, Jack Teagarden, Tricky Sam, Vic Dickenson, Earl Hines, Pete Johnson, and the bands like Basie's, Duke's, and McShann's. There are a lot of ways of singing the blues.

After Rushing, I was with Bob Merrill for a time, also at the Savoy. He had a good little band with Harry Johnson and Floyd "Horsecollar" Williams on tenors. People said it was the nearest to the Savoy Sultans. Bob sang, too—a cross between Walter Brown and Eddie Vinson—and in tune.

So I worked with quite a few bands at the Savoy until they began to cut down to the point where there wasn't room for a trombone in bands like Cootie Williams and Dick Vance had. They brought Erroll Garner's Trio in there once, and they drew a good crowd, but the management didn't think they sounded big enough for the place. It was sad to see it die after the great days when it was jammed to the rafters and had bands like Chick's, Fletcher's, Duke's, and Basie's. It was built on good music, and when the music went, it went.

Small bars, with their trios and quartets, were getting popular, but in the days of the big bands there were not so many bars with music as there are now. When the organ came in, that helped further reduce the number of musicians. The organ has really been a big knock. The first boy to popularize it up here, that I heard, was Charlie Stewart. I don't think it's a fad that will last. Right now, quite a few guys are dropping piano, because if the pianist isn't experienced, doesn't know what to do, he gets in the way. Slide Hampton's a good arranger, and he had a ten-piece group up here recently with no piano.

After those Savoy bands, I went with Earl Hines—my last regular group. For versatility, that was about the best small band I ever worked with. I replaced Benny Green, one of the greats, who had been in Earl's last big band. Jonah Jones had been playing trumpet, and it was a musician's band, but before I joined there had been a certain amount of confusion because of the progressive element, who didn't want to play Dixieland. We played a bit of everything, including Dixieland, which Earl taught us. We didn't play much of the music we recorded on that Nocturne album, because when it got down to music, most of the houses we played didn't want it. All through Canada, Earl broke records, which are still standing. He's such a tremendous showman. There'd always be a pile of requests on the piano. He'd go into a Dixieland house and say:

"Bear with us, friends, but we've got a request for so-and-so."

It would be some progressive-type number, and he'd bring the house down, although no one there had really wanted it. In a progressive room, he'd do the same thing, play "Muskrat Ramble," and maybe say, "I don't like it any more than you do." The people would accept it, and that was his way of keeping the band flexible.

We had Morris Lane on tenor then. He had a big, fat sound. We were going out to the Hangover in San Francisco, a Dixieland house, and Earl told Morris to be sure to get a clarinet.

"Yeah, Gates, I'll get it," Morris said. "Don't worry about nothin', Gates."

Opening night, he didn't have it.

"Get the clarinet next week, Morris," Earl said.

"Yeah, okay, Gates. A little short, you know, but everything will be all right."

The boss there liked Morris, and Morris was playing a couple of beautiful tenor solos. The place had been a Dixieland joint for years, with a clarinet every day of the week, but the boss said:

"That boy plays so fine, Earl. Don't bother him."

So he never did get the clarinet.

Earl liked everybody to stay neat and sharp, and he had two or three uniforms for us. He gave me the keys and told me to see they took the uniforms off before they left. I had to hang on Gene Redd to see he took his off. Then I would lock them all up. Redd had been with Bostic before. He was a fine trumpet player, but he was sold on vibes.

That was the way to keep Earl happy—to stay neat. I haven't heard him say anything to anyone yet about playing his instrument. That was *your* job, and he expected you to take care of it, but for heaven's sake, stay neat! He'd tell you it didn't cost anything to shine your shoes.

Of course, he was forever trying things. I remember he came through here with girl violinists and everything one time, and when he had big bands, new things were always being tried out. In this little band—and I remember Shadow Wilson, God bless him, was with us for a time—there was so much variety that you never got bored. Jerome Richardson would sing a couple of songs, and so would Earl.

Earl would dedicate a number to the memory of Fats Waller every night. He won't let him die. He'd play "Honeysuckle Rose" and tell how Fats wrote his songs, on a tablecloth in London, an i so on. They used to be regarded as rivals, but Earl was crazy about Fats, idolized him. He'd be talking and playing, and the crowd loved his spiel, and he'd do it to give us a rest. He'd tell us to go out for a half-hour or more and carry on working himself. Sometimes, when he knew the house, he'd look at his watch and say, "Make it an hour." We'd go out on the street, come back, and they wouldn't want him to stop. He was a hell of a showman. You listen for a while, and he could sell you Brooklyn Bridge. He'd tell us to sit down a while, and he'd be telling people about James P. Johnson, and he'd have his left hand going, and after a time he'd bring us in on a number. The time went quickly that way. It was a kick working for Gate, and he always paid us as much as he could.

Then we went out with the Harlem Globetrotters for several months. It wasn't actually the basketball players. They always had several acts to entertain in the intervals—jugglers, acrobats, trick cyclists, a singing ex-basketball star, and whatnot—and we accompanied these acts and played several numbers on our own. We went all through the West, playing at the halls where they had basketball. It was a show—no basketball at all. Abe Saperstein had got together about thirty people who had entertained with the Trotters that way, and it was his way of giving them some income in the off-season. Sometimes we might play to an almost empty house, but he didn't seem to care.

"It serves a purpose," he'd say.

We were supposed to go for six weeks, but we stayed three months, and on the whole did good business.

Earl has a way of playing that makes *you* feel like playing, but we had to prod him into doing all those numbers he was famous for. When we got on to "Piano Man," he'd remind us how it became "Drummer Man" later, with the same melody. He didn't get any royalties or even, he'd say, a "thank you." He's inspiring to work with, and I think he's at his best in a small band. A big band restricts him, although, I must say, he led some of the finest big bands through the thirties and forties.

One night at the Hangover, some cat kept calling out for "Royal Garden Blues," and Earl didn't hear him, but Carl Pruitt, the bass player, did, and Carl answered him:

"Man, you come on up here and play it if you want it. Damn it, we're going to play what we want!"

So Earl says, "What's that noise going on over there?"

"This man keeps yelling what he wants us to play," Carl says.

"Man, we've got to play what the people want," Earl says.

We found out later Carl was arguing with a man from one of

the big newspapers in 'Frisco. Afterwards, the guy met Carl, liked him, and told him:

"You don't tell me. We're supposed to tell you what we want. We pay you."

"I guess you're right," Carl admitted.

Pruitt is a good musician, very popular about his sound, and has a tremendous variety of experience with trios, small groups, big bands, and even symphony. He has worked with Earl Hines several times, and I think there's a good understanding between them.

We had a lot of fun with that band. It was a swinging group, especially when Shadow Wilson was in it. I found that Earl had quite a name in Canada. Maybe they hadn't forgotten all those broadcasts he used to do from the Grand Terrace. We played Montreal, Quebec, Toronto, London, and Vancouver. The people up there have different taste in music. They want more melodies, and they make more requests. That can be inspiring, too, because it means you play a lot of different numbers besides the regular program.

Earl doesn't like to argue. He gets upset if anyone argues about money. I guess he got tired of the road and the hassles like anyone else, and that's why he enjoyed spending more time in his own home and with his family in San Francisco. I am glad he has been recording more, because he can *really* play that piano.

After that, I did a bit of gigging around New York with Buddy Tate. He's as near as a brother, and one of several brothers I pulled out of Basie's band—Buck, Buddy, Herschel, Earle, Ed Lewis, and Basie himself. Basie was real good to me. He didn't fire me when I had my troubles. My people were always worried about me keeping my health. If they thought anything was wrong, they wanted me to go home. That's another thing that helped me quit drinking. I didn't want to hurt the people around me. Drinking, you can dog yourself, but why dog a lot of innocent people? I always feel much better when I know I'm not worrying people about me.

Buddy Tate, Buck, and Earle have been real good. They always call first on some of the cats they knew with Basie. Then I gigged with Max Kaminsky and Rex Stewart, and they were both nice. I met Rex when he was with Fletcher. I've worked with

Illinois Jacquet quite a bit, too. He's a terrific tenor player. Now he's another who brought in the tenor trend after Hawk and Pres, with his high notes. And apart from those high notes, he's a great sax man. Most musicians know he can play. He's very devoted to his brother Russell, who originally persuaded him to go out on his own—and hit the jackpot. Russell used to be on a progressive kick, but he can also play a lot like Louis if he chooses.

Then I worked with Red Prysock, more or less on a rock 'n' roll kick, for a tour down South, when we played places like Atlanta and Birmingham. We had a ball that time. Sarah Vaughan was in the show, and Al Hibbler. First, we'd have a concert, and afterwards they'd push the chairs away, and we'd play for dancing. Hibbler would come on and sing four numbers, and then Sarah would do four. They had a kind of battle of music going, and it used to make us think of the old days. It was always good to have a good vocalist with a band, but eventually the vocalists got too important and took away from the bands.

The last few years have meant all kinds of music for me. I've had a go at Dixieland, at Latin-American, at Jewish, and at rock 'n' roll. That last name did more harm than good. All the time, it was only a poor kind of swing music, fast or slow. I got involved in progressive jazz and whatnot, too. Sometimes it was a tough order to keep from going too modern. There's another name has to go, because how long can "modern" be? Monk was at Minton's Playhouse some twenty-five years ago, playing the same as now. So was Bird, out West, blowing like mad. Then I had a problem of not going too Dixie for my regular gigs with Illinois Jacquet. While with Jacquet, I was called to the Central Plaza by Jack Crystal for Fridays and Saturdays.

Believe me, the cats that blew there knew what they were doing! Cats like The Lion, Gene Sedric, Charlie Shavers, Roy Eldridge, Max Kaminsky, Dick Wellstood, Lawrence Brown, Cecil Scott, Don Frye, Wild Bill Davidson, and Eddie Barefield. I remember one night I forgot myself and flatted a few fifths. Eddie Barefield yelled in my ear, "This ain't no bop joint!"

Before that, Tyree Glenn had told Jimmy McPartland to dig me. So he did, but after a couple of nights the both of us wondered why! Because I didn't know *one* of the Dixie tunes. So I blew that gig! But after finding out that Tyree and Vic [Dickenson] had been making it with him, I didn't feel bad at all, because those two cats are rough. I headed for the music store and got some books by Henry Levine. Along with two or three weeks of work with one of my best friends, Wilbur De Paris, I began to pick up on the happening.

Don't let anyone fool you. Dixieland isn't easy to play by a long shot. After knocking around a while, I dug a similarity between the marches I used to play and some of the Dixie tunes. They require the same broad tone and punch. The rhythm sections are much more stable than in most types of jazz today.

The boss man of Dixieland trombone was old Kid Ory. He had been brought up in it, invented some of it, and knew it all—where to go, where to push, and where to lay a big foundation. I was really surprised, the last time I heard him, with how much fire he still played. He seemed to have as much energy as cats a third his age.

Doing all sorts of gigging is really enlightening, if only because it broadens your repertoire so much. Good music is good whatever the style may be. I am surprised sometimes when I think of what I've had to add since I came out of the big bands—not only the Dixieland numbers, but a whole lot of cha-chas, meringues, calypsos, and what have you.

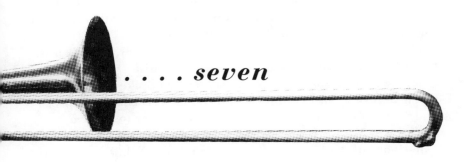

. . . . *seven*

Those Europeans

Dicky Wells was one of the stars on the records made by the British musician Spike Hughes in New York in 1933. Playing alongside such men as Benny Carter, Coleman Hawkins, Red Allen, Chu Berry, and Sidney Catlett, he acquitted himself brilliantly. Hughes was so delighted with the sessions that he forthwith quit jazz. "I have left jazz behind at the moment I was enjoying it most: the moment when all love affairs should end," he wrote years later.

This was Wells's first real experience of the European interest in jazz. Four years afterwards, he was in Paris with Teddy Hill's band when Hugues Panassié gave him the opportunity to record at two sessions for the first time under his own name. The results were sensational. At the first, backed by three trumpets and a rhythm section that included Django Reinhardt, he recorded a superb version of "Between the Devil and the Deep Blue Sea," based on an arrangement he and Roy Eldridge had devised while Eldridge was in the Teddy Hill band. On the second date, backed only by the rhythm section, he made two masterly solo statements on "Oh, Lady, Be Good" and "Dicky Wells Blues." These performances immediately established his reputation in Europe, but his next visit there, in 1953, was less successful because, as he relates, of cold weather and cognac.

Five years later, Sir Edward Lewis of British Decca, who had backed Spike Hughes's New York recording venture, sent this writer to make a series of albums of "mainstream" jazz. While in London, Count Basie had vouched for the trombonist's health and availability, so he became leader for two sessions that year and two more in 1959. The combination of four trombones and organ that he put together was unusual and generally considered successful.

Subsequently, he made and enjoyed several more tours, his appreciation of European audiences remaining unshaken.

S.D.

The first kind of contact I had with Europe was when Spike Hughes came over from England in 1933. He was the surprise of the year when he came to New York to record for Decca. No one in the outfit had the idea that he had so much hell in that valise until we started rehearsing. It was a good thing he had a gang like he had—Benny Carter, Hawk, Chu Berry, Wayman Carver, etc.—because these were cats who could see around a corner. It still shakes me to think of such swinging notes coming from England back in those days. Although some of them sounded kind of Dukish, he had so much Spike in the tunes that they stood up strictly on their own. Anyone who heard it ought to have been very enthusiastic about his wonderful music. I expected to hear some sharp, swinging music coming from our English cousins after that, but it seems as though they went on copying or buying American music. I don't dig it, because there could have been another Spike Hughes through the years, in the same way that Benny Carter shoved himself off from the likes of Don Redman. I don't think there will ever be another Duke Ellington, but Strayhorn has come through also. Don't get me wrong: There are some great arrangers in dear old England. I only have to say that somewhere through the years a cue was missed. Lately, they've been on the ball again.

When I went to England, I looked very hard to locate my man, if only to tell him that he made a lot of friends with his fine music. It was only when I was over the last time that I heard Spike's one desire had been to have his music recorded by the swingingest cats that he could get here, and that then he was ready to put it down. Well, it was a thrill for us all.

It was with Teddy Hill I went to Europe the first time. Chu Berry didn't want to go. Roy Eldridge didn't want to go. That's when Dizzy Gillespie came in the picture. Teddy had to go to Jersey to ask Dizzy's mother could he go. He was about seventeen then, and she said:

"Mr. Hill, you watch over him."

He liked to run Teddy crazy. In Paris, Teddy was trying to keep up with Dizzy, so Teddy said:

"I'm going to take this boy home. Momma can have him back."

Dizzy was a swell guy. He was playing lots like Roy then. Like this record of "King Porter" we made. You could hardly tell if it was Roy or Dizzy. Of course, Chu Berry stayed behind, and that's when Bob Carroll joined. He was a good tenor man, too. Some people have forgotten about him now. He died about 1952. We played the Cotton Club show in Paris and London. Clarence Robinson carried it over. We were only allowed to play the show in London, no dances, because of union laws. We didn't have any outstanding stars in the show. There were the Lindy Hoppers. Buddy Johnson was in the Tramp Band—all in patched suits— and Bill Bailey was dancing. Even without top performers, it was a swinging show, the kind Clarence Robinson was noted for. We didn't have acts like the Cotton Club had here, like Bojangles and Ethel Waters. They were still playing here, so ours was an addition to the big show.

We played London a month, then Manchester, and about a month and a half in Paris. We did quite well. They liked it very much.

It was a joy recording in Paris for Panassié. He gave me my first recording band, and I shall never forget him for it. We had champagne, wine, whiskey, and food in the studio. It was a ball. Of course, those girlhouses were wide open in Paris then, and it was a miracle we could hold the cats together long enough to record. It was Panassié's idea to use some of the guys from Teddy's outfit, and through his supervision the discs turned out well. Django Reinhardt helped us a great deal with his fat guitar sound. He was a swinging cat and a swell person. They don't come better.

104

My second trip to Europe was for a concert tour with Bill Coleman in 1953. Bill sent for me. It was a small group. Zutty Singleton was on drums, and Bill had a girl singing spirituals. I saw her later in *House of Flowers*, a Broadway show. Something was always going on and the tour was quite successful, but I met my Waterloo in Paris. I told the *garçon* to take the bottles out of the room. I had three sitting up there, and a whole lot more in the drawers. The heating facilities in the hotel were very bad, and I had been keeping warm with cognac. I always knew how to order cognac in French.

In the bus, Zutty and I would sit next to the exhaust pipe, but when that and two blankets were not enough, we'd take a taste of cognac. And the halls we played were so cold that I'd be ducking backstage for more of the same. It was when we went back to Paris again that I had that drum contest in my chest I mentioned earlier. I decided that wasn't for me, and that's when I started putting the bottle down.

I often wonder whether André Hodeir knew that the reason I wasn't playing at that time was because I was half–high and half–frozen. Bill Coleman told me not to be drinking so much, but it was so cold, and it was pretty difficult to get Coca Cola to mix with the stuff, and my stomach was bad anyway, and I never seemed to be able to get the poached eggs and things I was supposed to be eating. My French didn't go that far! So some years later, when Hodeir wrote his book, he first built me up and then kissed me off. I guess he didn't know the condition I was in then.

When I got back home, I was still trying to get the fumes of the cognac out of my system. They really seemed to linger, and I guess I was nervous and acting strange. Some dear friends of mine even decided I was a junkie. One night I played a gig and got home about five in the morning. There was a wagon from Harlem Hospital standing outside my place, so I stood around waiting to see who they'd bring down. So I'm standing and waiting and looking around, and after a while I think:

"Oh, to hell with this! I'm going upstairs and going to bed."

So I go upstairs, and they're waiting for *me!* I get inside, and the cop says:

"You Dicky Wells?"

"Yes," I say.

"We're supposed to take you to a rest home, you know."

"For what?"

"All you need is a little rest," they say.

I don't know to this day who actually called them, but I called my doctor and asked him if it was a crazy house I was bound for. I was getting mad now. When I told him I stopped drinking two weeks ago, he spoke to the cops, and I had to sign my own release.

It's hard when you stop drinking suddenly like that. If you could do it, you ought to ease off gradually. The doctor told me once before that, if I quit, it would be two years before all the whiskey was out of my system. It was about that time before I could go in bars and pay the whiskey no mind. Of course, when I first came to New York, when we would be drinking and carrying on, we'd sit outside until the milkman came and then drink a whole quart of milk. We were younger then and could throw it off.

Early in 1958, the record company that sent Spike Hughes over sent another guy to make some records. The bossman of that outfit, Sir Edward Lewis, deserves a lot of praise from jazz people. Anyway, I had met this cat for the first time at the Savoy in 1937, and once or twice in between, and he had been wondering what happened to me. So he asked Basie when Basie was touring England, and Basie told him I was in good shape again. He called me, when he got here, and in the end I made two albums for him under my own name, as well as half a dozen other dates.

The *Bones for the King* session had just about the warmest feeling since the good old Basie dates, those with Pres, Samson, Walter Page, Vic and Sweets giving their share of natural comedy. It used to be more like a three-hour party than a record session. This one was warm because we had Vic, Skip Hall, and Mule Holley to spark it with their jive. It was a pleasure to be blowing with my old bone cronies again, too, and they are still along with the tops. It also put together a portrait, seeing them all together on the cover, and hearing them blowing together inside. Both of the albums remind me of the great bone sessions we used to have in the big bands.

It was an ideal section, as Jo Jones said, because I've always thought that a four-piece brass section should have two first men. We had two of the best, who also had their own kind of sweet, soothing, swinging styles—"Mr. Bones" Morton and George "Truce" Matthews. The other two had to furnish some joy, wildness, and sadness, and that's where Vic "Dorian Gray" Dickenson and yours truly came in. We had swinging rhythm sections on both albums: Skip Hall, Everett Barksdale, Major Holley, and Jo Jones on the first, and Skip, Barks, Holley, Kenny Burrell, and Herbie Lovelle on the second.

I like the second of the two albums more (*Trombone Four-in-Hand*). I like the sound of the bones and organ together. It has a mellowness that seems to come from the fact that they're both voice-leading instruments. I'd like to hear more recordings of this type, because there are quite a few fellows with different styles who could sound great together. Just think what Duke had! Tricky, Tizol, and Lawrence, three *not* of a kind, making just about the most amusing section that ever happened along. You bet it was Duke's idea to put them together.

On our records, Vic and I tried to make a little joy by reminiscing about the great bands of the past, which made it a must for a certain amount of entertainment to be included in each set. Entertainment is a sure shot for reaching the public, which is very important, at the gate, bar, or wherever it is. Words will reach them where notes won't. I will admit it's very hard at times for us not to get carried away and forget who's paying the food bill. It's our job as musicians to be inventive, and it's also our job to deal with the public.

In 1959, I went on a European tour with Buck Clayton. It was the most kicks since I was in the piano player's band. You know, the one who's seven years older than water, the rascal who has worn out more young men than any bandleader in show business, and who still looks great, and is great, as a man and as a bandleader.

This gang Cat Eye took to Europe was something of a Basie band. Other than Herbie Lovelle and Al Williams, we had all played with him. Gene Ramey made it after we left. Also, at one time Cat Eye, Moon, Emmett, Al, Herbie, and myself had all been in Jimmy "Good-Living" Rushing's band at the Track.

We went to about twelve countries in seven weeks, and not one fellow was late or disorderly at any concert. I was glad, because Cat Eye is such a swell guy. We had a swinging outfit, with Mr.

Five By Five—Little Jim, that is—to take care of the vocals. And we ran across some swinging cats over there, like Bill Coleman, Jack Butler, Bennie Waters, Fatty George, Don Byas (as great as ever), Oscar Pettiford, and Wallace Bishop, not to mention a whole lot of swinging European cats.

Those Scandinavian chicks are the cutest, and the cats are great. They are very warm people. Italy is crazy, and they have just about the sharpest gang of people anywhere, but they are not as down on swing as in some other countries. You can't play the Germans cheap either, because they dig jazz in a nice, cool way.

But Paris and London are the boss towns. When we played the Olympia in Paris, Jo Baker was there, too. This was one of the highlights. She was fantastic, and it was a great show. Paris hadn't lost any of its beauty, and it's still a bad joint, but as time goes by it changes, just like London and New York. What helped us a lot was seeing some of our favorite faces, like our pals Panassié and his wonderful Madeleine, Bill Coleman and his sharp Lily, Mezzrow, Miss Baker and her husband, Curley Hamner and the Cooper brothers, and a whole lot of others. Then there was Leroy and Gaby's. What a hash joint! It was a must before and after checking into the hotel.

Speaking of hotels, this was the third time I'd been over, and this time I found I was paying New York prices—in fact, a taste more. I remember the maid charging me $3.50 for pressing two suits. "Damn Sam!" I said, but she just gave me that cute smile. Most of the big joints charged a daily tax, and my bill used to look like a map, with all the different charges for this and that. But the hotels were the greatest. They say they're okay here also, but, other than a few hotels in New York, and some other big cities, an Oxford never knows how they are, for the simple reason he never sees inside the joint, much less in the rooms. There's all the difference in the world between touring over there and here. The Swedish hotels are great. So are those in Paris and London. When you go to bed to rest, that's what you do—no noise. You really need the rest, too, because when you hit the road in one of their buses, you will have had it. Because of the narrow streets, there are no Greyhounds or Trailways, and it takes much longer to cover the same distance than it would here.

As for getting food at any time of the day—no happenings! So carry your lunch pail. When they say the kitchen's closed, they mean it. But when the kitchen *is* open, there's no better food. Those chefs take great pride in their work.

Cat Eye ordered for us most of the time, until we started buying phrase books and dictionaries. You can just about get anything there you can get here, but it wouldn't be cooked like it was at Leroy and Gaby's. Boy, can they burn! They are the prez and vice-prez of Paris—of Europe, in fact. Ol' Mezz dug the joint the most. Bill Coleman and his wife threw me a spread, and she can burn, too. Bill's one of those cats (like Cat Eye and Moon) that I can't seem to divorce—pals to the end. The Basie band left cemented marriages between quite a gang of cats. Eleven years is a long time to be snoring in a fellow's face. (One night, I was bedded down with Ed Lewis, and he had me jumping up and grabbing my horn, because I thought the band was rehearsing. "Man," he said, "that must have been someone next door. I sleep like a babe.")

I had never been in Italy before, and those beautiful churches made me wonder how it could be that so many gangsters came from such a place, especially since the people are so swell. I guess it's like when a kid has kept by the rule. When he does get loose, he's all over.

We had a great variety show. Besides our group, there were Dave Brubeck's, Dizzy Gillespie's and Vic Ash's. We got along swell. Cat Eye told us in front that every man was on his own, because he didn't want to be a leader. And he wasn't lying. If things were going right or wrong, all you would see were green eyes and dimples. I do believe he would laugh if you broke your leg. When something kind of drastic would happen in Count's band, Herschel would say, "Look at the green-eyed fool laughing his ass off!" Pres would say, "Nothing worries Lady Clayton." I dug him after he had told me he had made up his mind not to worry about anything too much, because what will be will be.

The only time the Eye would be drug was when the front line wasn't standing together on stage. As soon as we tightened the line up, he would be happy. I don't know what would have happened if we had been together longer, because someone has to crack the whip once in a while. All hell can break loose with an easygoing leader, unless there's a good gang of guys in a band. Basie had to get us into line once in a while.

We went to Sweden and Denmark before London, and it began to seem that London was not going to be it. You know how a big town is—New York, Paris, etc.—no one minds you too much, the rent must go in, and everyone is trying to make it for themselves. Well, after doing some other dates and going back to England, it was like going to heaven. Were we glad to get back to those English-speaking people, especially Max Jones and his wife, Carlo Krahmer and his wife, Dave Lee, and so many nice people. And I musn't forget those restaurants. I really went for that mad Indian curry. I found a joint back of our hotel, and I had a ball. I would order curry with eggs for breakfast, and the waiter would be standing in the corner digging me, holding his breadbasket [stomach] and frowning, because I was eating curry so early.

Those people are 'way out front of us as a whole in digging swing. They make it, regardless of age. It's nothing to see a whole family come to a concert. And I'll never get enough of the beautiful sights over there: the Changing of the Guard, Big Ben, the pretty churches, Piccadilly Circus, etc. And that Flamingo Club, jumping until six a.m. on Saturdays, is a place where you would see quite a few GIs from home. London has spread out since I was first there, in size and population.

Algiers, I think, had the most responsive audience. They were very quiet during the performance, but after the tune was over they would break the house down. They were having their troubles there at the time. We flew in on a government plane, and they carried us to a little shed on the army base. The cats were getting kind of restless sitting around there until here comes a soldier in uniform, with a machine gun loaded. Then we took off to the hotel. Before getting backstage, we were searched, cases and all. So was the entire audience before the concert began, for real hand grenades and such. We were glad to split from there.

I went back to Europe in 1961 with Cat Eye, but this time we had Sir Charles Thompson on piano and Oliver Jackson on drums, two of the best there are around today. We didn't make England, but we did make Spain, in one of the longest jumps I ever made. It was a little E Flat bus, too, but when we got there I though I would never get myself unbent. I had been to Barcelona before, with Bill Coleman, but this time we played Madrid as well. I ran into Don Byas again there. The Spanish people seemed to like our music very much.

The other big happening on this tour was the International Jazz Festival in Essen during April. It ran two days, and they had a whole lot of musicians there. We played the day they had Bud Powell and J. J. Johnson, and Johnny Dankworth's good-sounding band from England.

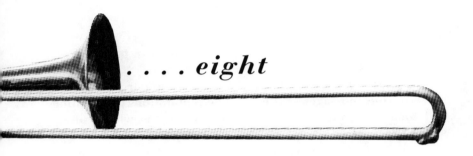

. . . . eight

Man's Best Friend!

This chapter deals with the treacherous messages sent by Ol' Man Juice, alias John Barleycorn, alias Man's Best Friend. In previous chapters, Dicky Wells has more than hinted at his own continuing battle with alcohol, the victories, the truces, and the defeats. Here are the arguments pro and (in parentheses) con, all designed as "advice to junior brothers." The temptations confronting jazz musicians, who so often work in places where the customers drink and press drinks on them, are not easily resisted.

S.D.

If I had my days all over again? I don't know. But my advice to young musicians would go something like this: Men, let 'em roll, but watch that gold.

You have to dig the loot, because, as Luke Brown my first boss told me, there comes a time when it costs twice as much or more to live. We asked him to turn us on, so this cat says:

"There'll always come a time when a man starts to fall apart at the seams, to disintegrate, and you have to start buying replacements, like hair, teeth, glasses, and young-again pills (better known as stick-widum pills). And, dig, all things won't be going, for coming your way will be corns on your toes, chilblains, aches, pains, and all sorts of doctor's bills. And soda-counter flies will turn into barflies, the scotch-and-soda kind. Dig?"

Oh, that cat could talk some fine jive! Or was it jive?

One thing for sure, you had a little change left back in those days, because things were made of much better stuff than they are today, and that applies to cars, homes, clothes, and horns. I don't know that they even make people today as good as in the older days. A lot of youngsters today have had it by the time they're twenty-one. Children a couple of years old can talk more mess than I would have dreamed of when I was ten. Talk about being down! The gang at the rear of our house would make King Kong blush. They'll be falling apart at the seams sooner than they think. I dug some youngsters doing some weird actions while I was touring with rock 'n' roll shows. The agent or manager who lured them away from home should be handcuffed to a B-29.

Of course, whiskey is the worst liar on earth. It used to tell me that it would settle everything, and in order to be a gay cat, blowing my horn, there I would go—past the lips, through the gums, look out stomach, here it comes. But at last I got a telegram from the Ol' Man Upstairs, and I decided I'd better put the bottle all the way down, before I got another telegram from the cat Downstairs. So my advice to junior brothers and all alike is: Don't let Ol' Man Juice try and sign a truce. You don't need him or the likes of him. Straight-life it from the go. It's not like that saying when you've drawn a blank with a chick—"You won't miss what you never had." When you start juicing, you'll miss what you had—health.

One thing about Ol' Man Ignorant Oil, alias Bug Juice, alias John Barleycorn, alias Lightning Water, alias Red Eye, alias Firewater—he sends you a lot of messages. He sends them after he has tightened your wig and made you think you're Mr. Big. Here are some I remember:

Tell the leader you don't dig him playing all that corn. Me 'n' you, baby. (Till he tells you to pack your horn.)

Forget the ones that stood by you when you were poor. Hell, you don't need them no more. Me 'n' you, like hand in glove. (Till you find you can't buy friendship or love.)

Jack, you're the sharpest cat in town. Go on out on the turf and talk loud and draw a crowd. Don't take low from no jive cop. I will be your friend, till the end. (Anyway, until your head starts to bend.)

All the chicks dig you. You shouldn't be married to no one woman. Man, you don't need no one but me. I am with you. (Till your wife gets hip and takes away the key.)

Why stay in the house and play the part of a goat? Come on with me and play the part of a sport. Me 'n' you. (Till she takes you to court.)

Man, you're too much for this band. You're ready for TV. You and me. (Till those early morning calls start to come in, and your hangover won't let you out of your stall.)

Don't worry about doing 150 miles an hour and falling asleep. I am with you. (Until they plant you six feet deep.)

Go on, slap that big fool in the mouth! He can't talk to you like that. Me 'n' you. (Until he starts to bend your hat.)

You're a big man now. You don't need no one but me. (Till you're broke and hungry as a flea.)

Now we're together and your head is bad, let's find a chick and take her back to your pad. Be a lover from the sign "Go." Me 'n' you. (Till your wife knocks on the door.)

Pay the doc no mind and don't listen to Dad. Keep smoking, drinking, and doing everything bad. Me 'n' you. (Till they order your permanent pad.)

Man, you must get high to blow. Go, go, go! Me 'n' you. (Till the boss says you're through.)

Go ahead, blow over the first man. That cat's too soft. Me 'n' you. (Till the notice is in your hand.)

You ain't high yet! I bet you can drink all those cats under the table. Me 'n' you. (Until you're down, out, and disabled.)

Stick with me, and you will be the greatest lover since Gable. (I'll keep you willing, but I can't make you able.)

Listen to me. I wanna teach you a little trick. Never go to the leader, but start a little clique. (Sooner or later he'll call you down front, and out of the clique you won't hear one grunt.)

When they take you to court, play it real cool. Talk to the judge as if he were a fool. (When they finish tanning your hide, I'll be waiting—outside.)

Man, you don't need to go and eat. I am food. (Believe this lie and soon your Maker you will meet.)

Stick with me every day, and soon you'll be stiff as starch. (You won't even hear them when they play the funeral march.)

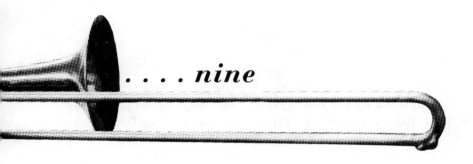

. . . . nine

Genius and the Blues

The year 1961 found Dicky Wells back on the road again, this time as a member of the Ray Charles big band. The one-nighters came harder than before, but he found the conversation of the younger musicians amusingly familiar, even though their idols were not. He includes here an enlightening account of a typical band rehearsal.

After the Ray Charles engagement, he played in a band backing B. B. King at the Apollo Theatre in Harlem. He has some sage words to say about the blues before offering a sample of dressing-room conversation.

S.D.

I went out with Ray Charles and his big band in October, 1961. It's no use saying those one-nighters came as easy for me as they once did, because they didn't. It was a real road band if there ever was one, and made some pretty big jumps. I remember the manager, Jeff Brown, telling us one time: "Fellows, we've got to eat out of the bag for the next two days. We've got to make the job, and it's a long jump."

Jeff's a fine cat, and he got tremendous cooperation from the guys and gals. When the bus stopped for us to scarf, he would yell, "Thirty minutes!" and, believe me, he meant thirty, not thirty-one. Then we'd be off and rolling down the highway again.

Ray would usually fly in his own plane. We were to leave New York for Chicago one day before eleven o'clock, but his small band was recording and it was two before we got away. We carried Ray out to the airport to pick up his plane. I was standing there admiring his five-seater when he comes out of the hangar, all by himself. He went straight to one of the gas tanks on the tip of the wing, raised the flap, and stuck his finger in the tank. "This one's okay," he said, and then went around to the other tank and did the same. Next thing, here he comes again, around to the steps and up into the plane. He sat down and turned the lights and motor on. You might say I was dumbfounded. I split while he was warming the motor up, for fear he'd ask me to go riding with him! Then McGarity, the pilot, came out and off they went.

Later, I sounded his eyeman, Duke, about Ray taking off with the door open next to him on the plane. He said he did that so he could check the sound of the engine. Sometimes he had told the pilot to sit her down at the nearest airport, because the engine didn't sound right to him, and they did it each time, and each time found something wrong.

Now, I've done quite a few gigs with Al Hibbler, too. We think we have our troubles, but both Al and Ray are blind, and they have really given me a lesson in gaiety.

Ray was the first leader I worked for who owned his own bus. B. B. King, the great blues man, owns his also. Life on Ray's bus was very different in one particular way. Horn blowing would happen anytime, day or night. I was stashed in front of Marcus Belgrave, and sometimes he would start rehearsing when I was trying to cop a nod. At first it was a drag, but after a while I would be looking for that big fat sound from him or Phil Guilbeau. They are very good trumpet men. Then maybe Fathead—David Newman—would get to blowing, and then I would almost be looking for Ray to swing out on organ any minute.

I used to dig some of those young cats doing the things we used to do with Basie. Phil and Marcus would pull up on a gig after riding all day, eat a box of popcorn or something, and blow like mad all night. Ed Lewis, who played with Basie when I did, used to be like that. He could eat a hamburger and blow for three days.

What was different about them was the musicians they talked about and admired. When I was on the road before, it used to be Louis and Roy, Hawk and Pres, Duke and Basie, and then Dizzy, Bird, and Jay Jay, but these youngsters were carrying on about Miles, Cannonball, Coltrane, Mulligan, Cleveland, Getz, Horace, Silver, and people like that, all the time. I didn't get into their arguments, but it used to amuse me to hear them getting warm and blowing their wigs the way we used to about very different people. It seemed to me then that the music had maybe changed more than the musicians. It has come a long way, and nobody knows about all of it. Some of the men they would discuss were just names to me, but I guess it would have been the same if I had started talking about Jimmy Harrison, Joe Smith, Big Green, Frank Newton, Bob Carroll, and cats like that.

One thing Ray and Basie had in common: You never knew you had a boss. The only way you knew either was around was if you saw them. But Ray really gets the best out of a rehearsal. He rehearses your tongues and everything else out. He's very quick to catch on and thinks everyone else should be likewise. He reminded me of Benny "King" Carter, and Benny will just about catch on before it happens.

I sure would have liked to have heard the big band play more of Ray's own things. We played some fine music by some top guys, and it was well played, but any good gang could have sounded as well as we did. The big difference was that he had the wonderful small combo within the big one.

That small combo really was in another bag. I've been a great admirer of head arrangements from the go, and it seemed as though they felt that way, too. During my three months with Ray, they played some new or different tunes every night, and what's more, they were all swinging. And what's more than that, they all had Ray Charles all through them! I used to see one or two manuscript books around, but no one seemed to use them until one night Ray called a tune that hadn't been played for about a year. "Just a minute," said one of the cats. So out came one of the books. Ray had been vamping on the organ in the meantime, and that seemed like a touch of Basie, too. Then they were ready, and all hell broke loose. Mr. Chambers, Leon Comegys, Keg Johnson, and I just sat there and looked and enjoyed the sounds as they took off. Hank Crawford, who played alto and acted as director, would also play the organ sometimes.

Of course, when the four Raelets hit the scene, there was nothing missing. Their singing was as close as our four bones, or the four trumpets, and they were so neat. But if there's one person who could do *without* a big band, it's Ray, because he's the most versatile in the business. He sings, he plays, and he arranges. Not that I don't wish we had more big bands. It's very hard to get the big band going again. It seems as though the public is always looking for new sounds and not caring about the rhythm underneath.

I am sorry I couldn't have done the band more good, but I was carrying bronchial pneumonia around for some time, and I didn't know it until just before the band went to Paris. I had made some arrangements for the band and hope I get to hear those blowing cats play them some day. They were "Mr. Charles, Lord," "South of the Border," and "Big Foot." It isn't the easiest band to write for, because after Hank Crawford and Ray get through, there isn't much to be said. Ray has a way of putting that rhythm section under his music that seems to be his alone. And the drummer is something else. He has a unique sort of rhythm that combines jungle, gospel, Latin, and modern swing.

When we played at Smalls' Paradise, which is now owned by Wilt the Stilt [Chamberlain], it carried me back quite a few days, because it was the largest band that had played the place since Elmer Snowden's was in there. As usual, Ray and the band turned them away.

Henderson Chambers and I "roomed" together on the bus. Behind us, with Marcus, was Rudy "Tooty" Powell. They very seldom slept, those two. As soon as Curly, the regular bus driver, slammed the door, they would open up the conservatory. Although Tooty wouldn't blow, Marcus would, for proof, and before you knew it you would be involved, too. Tooty is a tough man in any discussion, because he has a high voice. Mr. Chambers, Keg Johnson, Tooty, and I were about the oldest in the joint, but where Tooty got all his energy from I do not know. He would put darn near all the cats to sleep and then, just about ten minutes before we hit town, he would finally fall asleep himself.

The gang used to play 4-5-6, a game with three dice, until they were busted. One day, a brother who had been sleeping while they played, and who had some loot on him, started a tonk game with the cards up near the front of the bus. Jeff Brown was driving the bus at the time.

"Deal me in," Jeff says.

"Oh, Lord," I say to myself, "here's something new! This is the first time I've ridden behind a cat swinging down the highway with one hand and playing tonk with the other."

But he was so cool, I soon fell asleep.

Another time, we had a flat tire. We were all standing around beside the road when here comes Whitey, high as a kite.

"Hello, boys!"

"Say, man, how big do boys grow where you come from?"

"Don't go and get mad. I was brought up by some of you folks."

"Yeah? Well, you're gonna be brought down by some of us folks if you don't take off!"

The cat takes off. When he gets about a hundred feet away, he yells back:

"If I had you down South, I'd . . . "

That was it. Milk bottles, beer bottles, beer cans, whiskey bottles . . . the ofay does "The Skaters' Waltz," as Pres used to say when someone cut out.

Band rehearsals are never quite the same twice, but after the first twenty years you know pretty well what to expect. Putting together my experience with Ray and with other bands, I'll try to describe one that might be typical.

A three o'clock rehearsal as a rule starts at four. Some brother is always late. If there's a fine for being late, there'll still be one not on time, someone with a tale as long as from New York to Paris.

The band's strawboss is in charge till the leader gets there. Some straws are liked by the gang, and some are not. The one who can get his points over without dragging anyone is *it*. It's a trying job being in charge of five, ten, or even two people, especially if you're not the one that's paying them. You may be fortunate enough to have a gang of fine fellows who would like to see the band move forward as a whole. If that's to happen, there must be real cooperation from the first note of the rehearsal till the last note of the gig.

Some of the obstacles a straw may meet are jealousy, stubbornness, revenge, and too much ignorant oil. Then there's a feeling of superiority in some who know more music than straw and want the gang and the boss to know it, too. (They really showcase when there's an audience around.) The most common drag to straw and the entire gang is the cat who has mud in his eyes, the slow reader, but if he's a right guy everyone tries to help him. You can't always dig him at first, unless he has a solo or obbligato that is to be played as written, note for note, because, if he has big ears, he only needs to hear it once to play it as if he wrote it! He's called the Shadow, because he hides behind the cats with big eyes, the ones who can see around a corner.

Let's say the strawboss is in charge now.

"Okay, cats," he says, "let's make it I'm the big s--- til the bigger s--- comes. Take the first tune on the rack. Ready? Medium tempo. Let's put it right here—one, two, three, four . . . "

(Some straws say, "Take it all the way down from the left-hand corner, just for notes." That is, to see if the notes are correct. Another straw may ask for the introduction first, then the first chorus, second chorus, modulation, etc., until they've gone right through an arrangement a bit at a time to the coda.)

After we've worked on the number for a while, he says, "Left-hand corner. Let's make a record!" (He means, "Let's play it perfect!")

"Okay, now? Not too fast. Dig the foot, Mr. Drummer Man. Brass and saxes, listen for your first man. Ah-one, ah-two, ah-three, ah-four!"

So we run the number right through once.

"How did it sound, straw?"

"Okay to me, but the boss has to dig it. Anyway, let's take a break. Say fifteen minutes. He should be here then. He called and said he was at the office."

Soon the boss comes in.

"How'd it go, straw?"

"Sounds okay to me."

"Well, have no fear, the king is here," the boss says. "Was everyone on time?"

"Everyone but . . . I'd rather not say."

"Why do you think I'm paying you twice as much as everyone else? I know who it was. It was the second trumpet player."

"Yeah, that's right."

"Was he sober?"

"Nope."

"Well, that did it. Tell him to come by my room after rehearsal and get his two weeks. The only way we'll miss him is by his not lousing up the arrangements. We'll be home in a couple of days."

"Look, boss, it would be better to wait it out. If you let him go here you'll have to pay his fare home, and first class at that."

"Okay. Call the band and let me hear what you've done."

He goes to the piano and bangs out a few sounds. All bands have a little personal riff. It's also used to attract attention when you want to call someone far away in a crowd. Sometimes it's whistled, or blown on a horn, or beat out on a piano. About its most important use is to call the gang back after intermissions.

"Everybody here?" the boss calls.

"Yep," says the straw.

126

"Okay, I'll take it. Left–hand corner. One, two, three, four!"

He goes over to the straw after we've run the number down again.

"Say, what have you cats been playing? Cards or checkers? Because you sure as hell haven't been playing music! First thing, let's tune up. First trumpet, you are sharp."

"Thanks, man. My chick said the same thing."

"Fool, I mean your horn is sharp. So pull out." (He means a certain shank on the horn.)

"How do the saxes sound, Fess?" the lead alto asks.

"Sick. What does it say over that passage in Letter B?"

"Wait a minute. It says, 'As is.'"

"Oh! It sounds like 'Is as' to me! Isn't that supposed to be played in unison?"

"Sure is."

"Well, please try and do so. Second tenor, watch your part. I heard some clinkers."

"Man, that's one thing I can really do."

"What's that?"

"Read."

"Yeah, I know. The *New York News*, *Jet*, *Down Beat*, and all sorts of dirty books. Say, bass, keep your mind on your music. She will be there when you get home. Okay, gang? Let's wrap it up. Okay, we're off! One, two, three four . . . "

We ran it down again.

"Brass and rhythm are okay," the boss says. "Saxes, go over bar Number Ten in Letter C. I don't know who it is, but something is wrong, so let's dig who the Shadow is. Take it one at a time. In other words, let's go back to school days. First . . . Second . . . Third . . . Okay. Now the fourth sax take it. Oh, here he is!"

"I forgot to tell you, my horn has gotta go to the shop. My octave key isn't working."

"Okay, Fatso, tell me anything! Pay night my pocket won't be working if you mess that passage again."

"Okay, boss, I got it."

"I gotta go. Straw, take it down once and tell them the time for tonight."

"Right."

"Aw, I forgot. Where's the valet? Here, tell him to go get a taste

127

for the fellows. Tell them not to get high and start jamming, because we gotta be out of here in a half hour."

"We'll be out."

"So long, gang."

"So long."

"Man, that's a fine boss."

"Sure is."

One Tuesday morning, not long after the gig with Ray Charles, Jimmy Cleveland called me.

"Hey, Homes!" (He's also from Tennessee.) "I got something for you if you want it."

"Shoot."

"Want a week at the Apollo Theatre?"

"Do I? I want a week anywhere! Who's it with?"

"B. B. King."

"That's my man! I run for his guitar blowing and blues singing."

"Okay, you got it. I had to pay you back for the gig you threw me Christmas. Call B. B.'s manager."

"Thanks, Homes. And keep on wailing that fine bone. Thanks for calling."

"Okay. 'Bye now."

"Who was that?" my wife asked.

"That, my dear, was one of the baddest young cats that ever picked up a bone. I've got to call B. B. King's manager at once."

"Hello, is this Ted Curry?"

"Yeah."

"Dicky Wells calling to check as a stand-in for Jimmy Cleveland."

"I was expecting your call. Can you be in the Hole at 3 tomorrow to rehearse the show?" (This hole is a rehearsal hall down under the Apollo.)

We started at 3:15 with the first act. B. B. traveled with only two trumpets, two saxes, piano, bass, and drums, so he added five of us from Local 802, New York, to make for a bigger sound to play the acts. Most of the small bands do that. To our surprise, nearly all the acts had all the parts for twelve pieces, so everything went down okay until Honey Coles, the stage manager, told us to take fifteen. All the acts weren't there yet. In fact, some didn't show at all. We called them a lot of names, because we knew we would have to be up with the chickens next day, opening day, to rehearse with them.

A 9 o'clock rehearsal was called, and that meant we had to be there from 9 a.m. to 11:30 p.m. We finished rehearsing about half an hour before showtime, 12:20. The show went down okay, but it takes a day or so for a show to get relaxed, and, when it's put together for only a week, it's just begun to swing when it breaks up.

Now, I have most of B. B.'s albums home, and I have been on a show with him before, but I had never talked with him. He's some nice fellow. In fact, it seems as though he's too easygoing at times. (Leaders are going to convert me, yet! After Ray Charles, one of the nicest, then B. B. King next.) I went to his dressing room to carry a tune I had written for him. As we talked, I could see he was drug about something. Come to find out, a certain magazine had given the band and some of the acts a rough time. To add insult to injury, he was told not to have much to say over the mike, because it would lengthen the show too much. I couldn't dig telling the star of the show that, especially when at the same time some of the acts were milking the audience for an encore and talking like mad on the mike. One thing for sure, if you don't look after yourself, there are always people who will grab you and dart to hell with you.

A critic shouldn't really judge that kind of a show on the first day, but a bad write-up is always a warning that you need to improve or tighten up. I keep my worst write-ups, the same as the best and the in-betweens. It's good to try and analyze what the guys are saying before blowing your wig.

You can tell the men and women from the boys and girls from the way different acts squawk. If the boys and girls don't go over big, then the band's to blame. If you do go over big, the most they'll say is the band's okay. The men and women are no drag, whether or not they go over big. If their music wasn't well played, they say, "Okay, you'll have it right next time!" Believe me, we'll break our necks trying to please an appreciative act. That jug does wonders, too. I've heard some of the more experienced show people say, "Go get the band a jug, so those cats can open their eyes." It's not so much the juice as the spirit of the deal that counts.

B. B. King had some nice jive going at the mike the first couple of shows, and the public was with him, but when they cut him loose from the mike, it meant also cutting him loose from the audience.

Without a doubt, he's one of the best blues singers on earth. I can understand that not all people go for the blues, because different people like different music, but the blues sung right can be very moving. Dogs have been known to weep to death over the blues! If you have a nice spiel for the audience like B. B. had, and you get those smiles and hands between, before and after your solo, then you're doing okay. If your jive is right, they don't want you out of their sight.

A lot of the kids, who stay all day waiting for their humming, squealing, yelling, leaping and dancing groups, are down on the blues. They're too young to know they have the blues sometimes. But when they're disappointed to find a he or she leaving school or a party with someone new, they have the blues and don't know it.

More people love the blues than will admit it. Some will have you believe the blues are something to look down on. I dug a couple of babies about two years old in the aisle during one of the shows. They had their little dance working. That back beat had them, while at the same time the lyrics were moving their parents. There are good and bad blues, but, brother, there are very few people that the good old down-home blues won't move.

Carry on, B. B.!

In between shows the dressing-room conversation isn't much different from the kind on the bus. It often runs something like this:

"Say, where's Garbage Mouth?"

"Don't worry. He'll be here soon telling some of his sad-ass jokes."

"Speak of the devil . . . Here he comes."

"She's only the baker's daughter, but, oh, how I'd love to nibble on her cupcakes."

"See! What did I tell you?"

"Say, Garbage Mouth, a little hen is upstairs asking for you. Said she was going to sic something on you, and it ain't gonna be no dog."

"How she look?"

"Like a natural fox."

"Fellows, I almost forgot. That chick wants us to run her tune down before the next show."

"Nix, straw. I didn't peck yet. Anyway, she has no music."

"She said she would hum it to us."

"Local 802 says we don't have to play what we don't see."

"She said she would bring a jug."

"Oh, that's different."

"Garbage, I just come from upstairs, and the boss told me to tell you to play whatcha got and don't try to get hot."

"Where did you go after the last show? Looks as if you've been to the point of no return."

"I was eye-ballin' with a little dish in the front row. Man, I had the notion, but she didn't miss a motion."

"Okay, gang, that's three bells! All on!"

"Lock the door, last man. There's some weird-looking cats backstage."

Garbage starts to warm up, getting his chops ready for the show.

"Man, I have a cold and can't hear my horn."

"Well, dad, you ain't missing nothing."

"Shutup fool! Your ax sounds as if it has pneumonia."

"If you keep bugging me, I'll hang you before God gets the message."

"Say, straw, why the sad look?"

"I just came from your jive boss. Guess what?"

"Turn me on, man."

"He says the tax men are hanging him, and we'll have to take a cut when we go on the one-nighters."

"I got news for him. I'll die and go to hell before I take a cut."

"You could have left out those last eight words. We know where you're going, ol' man."

"Where do you get that 'ol' man' jive from?"

"From calling 'em like I see 'em!"

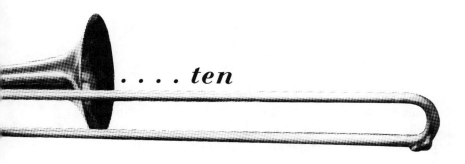

. . . . *ten*

Something Else

This chapter is a kind of summing-up in which Dicky Wells expresses great admiration for Tommy Dorsey, whom he regarded as "Mr. Trombone," and for Trummy Young, whose work with Louis Armstrong he considered something of a sacrifice. There are observations, not unrelated, about the effect of bebop and the fact that "the chorus lines went out." Philosophical about the changes in jazz, he encapsulates one of the problems facing musicians of his generation in a sentence: "The bands got smaller, but the ballrooms didn't."

S.D.

Erroll Garner really contributed something new to jazz. I don't think that since Earl Hines any pianist has brought anything in so valuable. Earl was the equivalent of Louis on piano. The grapevine says Teddy Brannon, who was with Jonah Jones, used to play in a similar style to Garner's present piano style. That may be, but you have to give Erroll credit for bringing it out. It's the same with Duke. He brings out the ideas of some of his guys in a way that they never could.

No one ever played like Pres before him. He had a different sound, a different delivery, and a way with a melody that was different to Hawk's. He definitely brought something. I heard Charlie Parker before he came to New York, and he was playing just the way he was before he passed, God bless him. When he came here with Jay McShann, he brought something most people hadn't heard before. You have to come to New York, to the *Apple*, to get yourself across. And then, when you make records, people hear you all over the country. Yet you don't always know where the ideas came from first. You can only say where you heard them first.

You have to give Tommy Dorsey credit, too, because for a trombone to sound like a trombone, there has to be a little Tommy there, somewhere. I've never heard enough praise for him. It's really been disgusting since he died. He gave out so much melody—the kind we need today from the trombone. After all, it's a voice-leading instrument.

He used to come to Harlem quite a bit, and he could swing,

135

too, but his tone was so fine people always wanted to hear him play pretty. His breathing was so good. His father taught him, and he always said his father was the greatest teacher in the world. Long ago, when we were still in Springfield, Ohio, and Claude Jones was with McKinney's Cotton Pickers, I can remember Claude telling us, "Say, you ought to hear this guy, Tommy Dorsey!"

We hadn't heard the records, then, but I think he impressed trombone players later the way Hawk did tenors. To play tenor, you had to sound a little like Hawk. Of course, when Lester Young came along he sounded like nobody but Lester Young and that's why he got so much credit, because he had a way with a melody that Hawk didn't have. There are many trombone players who have fine control of their horns, but no one with more than Tommy had, and none has better breathing than he had. The way he breathed in his horn, he was smooth as silk. He was Mr. Trombone. Out of a million good trombone players, you would tell him from the lot.

Tommy liked Lawrence Brown. Lawrence has real control, knows his instrument, and has a sophisticated style. It's a good thing everybody doesn't sound alike. There's nothing stiff about Tommy's style. It was very flexible, and there was that beautiful, flowing tone. Everything he did was just perfect. And he really had a tougher way to go than the guy who was just swinging along, because to play the horn right, and still have people love it—that was something else. He didn't use any special mute [it was a Shastock], but the reason he got a muted sound like no one else was because he had a sound like no one else to start with. I made him the only other mute like mine, and he used it the last time I saw him on stage, at the Capitol Theatre.

I went backstage and saw this guy sitting there with his head in his hands. It was Charlie Shavers, and someone said:

"Charles has a headache today. Tommy told him not to come on, but he came anyway."

I went over to him and said:

"Where's Tommy? I've got a mute for him."

"Oh, Uncle Tom! He's upstairs some place."

That's what he called him—"Uncle Tom." They had their little jive going, like all bands.

So I went to his dressing room, and Tommy played the mute

like he'd been playing it all the time. I wish I could sound as sweet with it as he did, but then he didn't have that little bluesy tone to go with it. I told him not to play too high, or he'd run into trouble. He could play high, too. He was laughing. He put it back in and played again. He said next time he recorded a blues he was going to use it, but he didn't live too long afterwards. He was a lovable guy, and Charlie told me he was great to work for. Of course, there were all those stories about fights with Jimmy. Brother bands don't seem to work out, but they got together before the end.

Those bands of Tommy's never sounded stiff to me, not like some I won't mention. Maybe that was because he was an easy-playing guy himself. And then he had so much variety in his book. If he hadn't died, I suppose he could have gone on success-fully for another twenty years, or more.

I remember Tommy was introduced to a kid once who every-body said was playing just like him.

"That's wonderful," Tommy said, "but why play like me? You've got ideas, haven't you? Go for yourself!"

There are a million ideas embedded in people, but they get turned back because their ear tells them to play like this guy or that guy who happens to sound good or to be having a success. So there are a million ideas that have never been exploited. From the technical side, it was right to listen to Tommy and to get something of his in your playing, but not to try to take his entire style and lose yours, or whatever you might have made. I sup-pose Miff Mole, for instance, could have played a melody like Tommy, but he had his own ideas.

Another wonderful trombone player was my good friend, Trummy Young. We lost something important to music when we let him get back to Honolulu. He had been heard about Washing-ton originally, and then with Earl Hines, but when he joined Jimmie Lunceford he became the talk of the profession. Sy Oliv-er spotlighted him in special arrangements, and Sy is like Duke in knowing what to do with a talented cat. Trummy was original, and he influenced a lot of guys. He had a good lip, brilliant tone, and was very good on glissandos. He really brought a modern turn to the instrument, and it was unusual then for a trombone player to be featured out front as much as he was. He sang, too, and besides his famous "Margie" he had his own catchy numbers, like "'Tain't What You Do," "Whatcha Know, Joe?" and "Easy Does It." He liked to listen to Pres and other saxophone players, and the use he made of their ideas gave him even more flexibility. A lot of people didn't understand what happened when he joined Louis Armstrong. Louis didn't want him to play high notes. In Dixieland, they don't want too many notes anyway, but they want punch. When you play low, the trombone tone is naturally broader. Over a long period, the effect of that is bad, physically and mentally. You need more pressure to play the high notes, and Trummy knew that as well as anyone else. Very few people could have done what he did for Louis so well, and I don't think he ever got enough credit for it, but he had made a big reputation in his career before that, so it was a kind of sacrifice.

An ideal trombone section in the early days would have been Jimmy Harrison, Tommy Dorsey, Miff Mole, and Tricky Sam. There would always have to be a place for Tricky. I'm glad to see his style being kept alive by guys like Al Grey and Booty Wood, not forgetting Quentin Jackson and Tyree Glenn. Tyree's is pretty, but I'd say Butter's is about the closest to Tricky's. The tearing sound, like you're tearing paper, is hard to master. Al Grey is going for the tough plunger sound, but Tricky had it so it sounded like *tissue* paper. Bubber Miley had it even thinner than Tricky, but that was because his mouthpiece was smaller. In order to learn how to do that, you have to go through the first stage, where it's a ruder sound. To me, that also sounds good, more "jungle." Tricky had control both ways—loud or smooth. I think it's a style that does things for jazz, and by adding more color and variety, Al and Butter [Quentin Jackson] helped the Basie bone section.

I'm sure they would rather have had Tricky than Dicky on that "Chatter Jazz" album I made for Victor with Rex Stewart, my friend from 'way back. We only made heads, but let me say here and now that Rex could say or do just about anything on his horn that he desired. He could come over and whisper in my ear, telling me what he wanted me to ask or answer him. We had a ball, although I was tongue-tied quite often.

When bop came into the picture, you might have thought that was the end of music like Tricky's but luckily there have always been some guys who loved it and were able to carry it on. And as long as Duke has a band, I guess there'll be someone playing that way.

Bop didn't strike me as really new at the time. Flatted fifths weren't new. Dig some of Don Redman's things. We thought of bebop as a drum style. As I understood it, Monk started the word as an explanation of how he wanted the drums to accent. Monk himself had a lot of simplicity and wasn't hard to appreciate. In the beginning, bop was too mixed up, and it wasn't swinging. Later on, they got it more interwoven, not so far out—more 'way in! Now J. J. [Johnson] is a wonderful musician, and he could hold it all together. The style brought out fine musicians, but at first it was pretty rough. I can remember the guys in Cab's band when Dizzy began his bopping.

"What is *that* back there?" they'd ask.

I don't know any who worked so hard as Diz, J. J., Monk, and, above all, Charlie [Parker], to get a foundation under the style, although maybe Charlie had to work less because he had it inside from the word "go." I believe guys like Louis, Hawk, Hodges, Tatum, Tommy Dorsey, Jimmy Harrison, Earl Hines, Erroll Garner, and Charlie all had it inside.

It wasn't so important to swing with bop. And then there was the difference in showcasing of musicians. When the bands played for dancing, not a lot of people paid them any mind unless something went wrong. So the musicians played more naturally and expressed themselves with more ease. And don't forget that with the big bands quite a lot of rhythm came from the different sections as well as from the rhythm men. Now you don't have that. Then, too, the chorus lines went out. They were more important than people realize. You might say we composed while they danced—a whole lot of swinging rhythm. That's when we invented new things and recorded them the next day.

There were a lot of reasons for the decline in popularity of the big bands, like agents, money, and transport. And then there was the tenor world. I think Illinois Jacquet really got the little band under way. He started that dancing while he was playing, and he added showmanship, so it wasn't so much a matter of what they were playing. A whole lot of show-off and acrobatics came into music then, and the tenor had the better sound for a group with only one horn. It was the cheap way out for proprietors, agents, and leaders.

The bands got smaller, but the ballrooms didn't. You took those little groups into places built for five or six thousand people and something was missing. Very often, too, small bands went South that had been big bands under the same leader *on records*. The people would turn out and not be satisfied. Then when a big band came to town, the people stayed away because they figured they would be cheated again in the same way.

During the war, the young progressive guys moved in while many of the older musicians were in the army, and some of their music was pretty far out. Some of the big bands made a mistake, too. They got too heavy, and their arrangements were too complicated. That was why the Savoy Sultans remained more popular at the Savoy than bands that were bigger and more famous. The had very good rhythm. Two of the most popular bands at the Savoy in the forties were Cootie Williams's and Lucky Millinder's for the same reason.

I guess in the end jazz will have to strike a balance. A lot depends on where you are playing and for what kind of people. I remember the manager at Smalls' telling me one time, "When the music makes the customers pat their feet, they keep on buying drinks, so that's the kind we like."

People are enjoying jazz in different ways now. Some are dancing to it, some are drinking to it, and some are thinking to it, but I don't know whether it is *living* with so many as it once did.

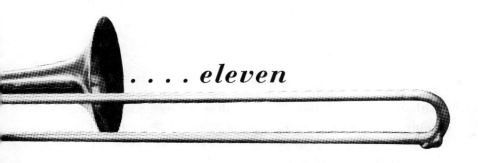

. . . . eleven

Coda: Cats, Bears, and Bulls

The coda is melancholy. Although he continued to play on weekends and record dates, in September 1967 Dicky Wells finally joined the day people and took a job on Wall Street, where many other jazz players of his generation had found a haven. He took the work seriously and always maintained a good appearance. And he did not complain.

He was mugged twice after collecting rents from a property he owned in Brooklyn, and twice in New York. The last and most vicious attack put him in the hospital. Brain damage was feared, but he made a good recovery and played his horn again. He died of cancer on 12 November, 1985.

S.D.

I got my first day gig in September 1967. I had heard that many of my musician friends were working in the Wall Street district, so I asked one of my godbrothers, Les Carr, to look out for me. He laid the word on my man, Herbie Cowans, the drummer, who had had an offer from A.E. Ames, Inc., of 2 Wall Street. He couldn't take it up because of a U.S.O. tour. I had no references, so I carried down a couple of albums I had made. One, produced by Stanley Dance, was *Bones for a King* on Felsted, and there couldn't have been a better title for a better man—Tommy Dorsey. The other, *Dicky Wells in Paris* on Prestige, was produced by Hugues Panassié, and it had done very well in Europe. The bad cats on it were Bill Coleman and Django Reinhardt, plus some members of the band of one of the sweetest leaders I ever worked for, Teddy Hill.

The big man at the office was Mr. Ken Murton, a Canadian, and I had no idea he was a jazz fan until he asked to borrow the albums. He called the boss out of the purchase and sale room, and I soon found I had a job. When I asked if I could take a month or so off a year for tours, they told me it would be all right if I got a good replacement.

Never for one moment have I regretted taking that day gig. The gang there is really great, and I still get to blow, mostly weekends. I have also had some good record dates with Jimmy Rushing. My reason for taking the gig had to do with the fact I never had the best tummy, and I was not so happy about the food when traveling. I used to dig Cat Eye and Moon.

Those cats could eat nails. And I don't forget the Holy Main, Basie. He used to eat steak and then ask the waiter to bring him half a chicken. Bean [Coleman Hawkins] and Benny Carter, as I said before, used to carry on like that when I was with Smack. Jimmy Harrison didn't have the best stomach either, but that man could blow more bone on a hotdog than the law allows.

Then there was the falling apart of big bands, the closing out of locations, and the cutting down on the beautiful bone sections. Demand for my horn had begun to cool off, which wasn't helping my pocket any! What I would have loved to have found was a place in a small group like Stuff Smith's or John Kirby's in a location like the Savoy or Smalls' Paradise. But such gigs no longer exist, and Moon [Buddy Tate] has had the only swinging dance band around for some time.

There was another reason why I wanted to be on Wall Street. It's the onliest place in the world where there are so many musicians—both ex and active—working by day. There are black and white, too, so this Wall Street band is real integrated. I have met quite a few ofay cats who were in concert, dance, or symphony. The bread isn't the best, but it isn't the worst, so I thank God and the others in the Wall Street band for such a place to gig. There must be at least a hundred cats down there, cats who are on and off the scene. Tommy Benford, Julian Dash, Bobby Johnson, Herbie Cowans, Les Carr, Bobby Williams, John Williams, Edgar Dowell, Joe Britton, Alphonse Steele, and George Stevenson are some I see often.

Another advantage of being home, besides the food, is that I can attend to my duties as a landlord. Not having any family help apart from the Enemy (my wife, Cherry, that is) it was tough for me. To collect rents in Brooklyn, you ought to be a ghost, and an Oxford ghost at that, so they can't see you at night. I had some sweet tenants at first, but my pad must have been the first stop after the cornfields for those that came later. There was fighting and cursing, and the only time I was "Mr." Wells was when there was a shortage. Most of the time I was "Mr. M. F.," and the last straw was upside my head. Then I had to split.

Brooklyn is one up on New York, because I was only mugged once in New York, when they left the Ole Rag on the sidewalk at

130th Street and Lenox. It happened twice in Brooklyn, but I came out breathing. They were all soul brothers in action, no greys, so I am still for the cat who treats me as I treat him—black, green, white, or blue.

Dicky Wells and Stanley Dance in 1971. Courtesy Duncan Butler.

Afterword

I met Dicky Wells for the first time at the Savoy Ballroom in 1937. I had arranged to meet a friend there who had traveled from England with me. Although this friend was then conducting a heavy affair with the hatcheck girl at the Black Cat in the Village, he was not much interested in jazz. So I was surprised to find him engaged in conversation with Russell Procope at a table. Apparently he had mistaken Procope's uniform for a waiter's and had ordered a sherry as the musician wended his way across the room at intermission. It was fairly typical of Procope that he returned with *two* sherries and sat himself down to explain the local scene to the stranger. After I had joined them, Procope introduced me to Dicky Wells when he passed by.

I saw both of them later in the year when the Teddy Hill band played at the London Palladium. They were busy gambling backstage at the time, but they were very hospitable.

The magnificent records Dicky Wells made soon afterwards in Paris for Hugues Panassié prompted me to record him when I had opportunities in 1958 and 1959 for Felsted, a label that had been specially created to harbor a series of "mainstream" jazz albums. At a party in Felsted, a village near where I lived, I had run into Sir Edward Lewis, the head of British Decca. It was a lively evening, but we were soon talking shop. I complained that most of the jazz on his various labels was either Dixieland or bebop and that what I considered the heart of the matter was being neglected. He called from London the next morning, said he agreed with my views, and asked if I knew of anyone who might be able to record in the U. S. the kind of music his company lacked. I was available, and I volunteered.

I had been on a good many record sessions before, but never in the role of what is nowadays falsely called "the producer." (The musicians, in my opinion, are the producers.) However, beginner's luck held, and under the leadership of Dicky Wells, Buster Bailey, Rex Stewart, Earl Hines, Budd Johnson, Buddy Tate, Billy Strayhorn, and

Cozy Cole, some eighteen sessions were completed with a reasonable degree of success. The one complication was the advent of stereo, which more or less coincided with the making of these records. RCA's engineers proved sympathetic and apart from a confrontation between one of them and Jo Jones, who objected to being boxed in by partitions, most problems were overcome.

Although I was able to record Dicky Wells several times after the Felsted dates, he always seemed particularly proud of the *Trombone Four-in-Hand* album, on which his solos, arrangements, and com-positions were recorded to his satisfaction.

Finally, I should say that before this book was written he had been in the habit of spelling his nickname "Dickie." During one conversation I rather innocently asked why so many American males favored the feminine diminutive. "I guess because it looks prettier," he answered. But almost from that day he spelled it differently and became "Dicky," a fact that seems to disturb some discographers and record collectors quite unnecessarily.

S.D.

.... *appendix A*

The Romantic Imagination
of Dickie Wells

André Hodeir

Hugues Panassié gave Dicky Wells considerable praise in his pioneering work, *Le Jazz Hot*, in 1934, and three years later he devoted an entire article to him in the magazine *Jazz Hot* (No. 20). This focused French attention on the trombonist very valuably.

"I first heard of Dickie Wells some seven years ago," he wrote, "when I asked the Negro pianist Freddie Johnson if there was a coloured trombone player who could be compared with Jimmy Harrison. After thinking for a moment, Freddie replied that there was only one who could challenge Jimmy Harrison, and he was called Dickie Wells. Immediately, on Freddie's advice, I bought *Springfield Stomp* and *In a Corner* by Cecil Scott, which contained marvelous trombone solos. All the same, I had to wait till 1933, with Spike Hughes's numerous discs, before I really knew Dickie Wells."

By 1937, Panassié had taken advantage of Wells's presence in Paris with the Teddy Hill orchestra to record him at two sessions for the newly formed Swing label. The remarkable musicianship that had so impressed him on the Hughes records was more than confirmed:

"The first thing that strikes you when you come in contact with Dickie Wells's playing is his extraordinary power of expression, his irresistible fire. From this point of view, Dickie and Higginbotham were clearly the two trombonists who produce the most brutal physical shock. They also have in common a sombre, majestic tone—more sombre with Higginbotham, more majestic in Dickie.

"Dickie Wells's tone is incidentally of such a quality that it is worthwhile pausing a little on it. It is very rare to hear a trombonist with a tone so full, so ample, and at the same time as pleasant in the low as in the upper registers. Dickie's very pronounced vibrato—produced by his lips—perhaps the most pronounced of all hot vibratos which I have heard on trombone, adds still more to the beauty of this tone.

"Dickie's melodic style is so simple, so direct, that it is difficult to characterize it. Often, instead of developing the melodic line of the theme, he concentrates it. Some exuberant phrases, often pleasantly fantastic, which appear here and there, are only an accidental contrast— their effect is admirable. The simplicity of his melodic lines allied to his power of performance allow Dickie to get an incomparable swing." [*Jazz Hot* was printed in French *and* English, but the magazine's translators did not always do justice to Panassié's elegant and lucid French.]

Many years later, André Hodeir's famous appreciation appeared in the same magazine and was reprinted in his book *Hommes et problèmes du jazz* in 1954. That Hodeir wrote off Wells's career somewhat prematurely was an unfortunate result of a tour of France during which the musician's work was ravaged, as he explained, by cold and cognac. By kind permission of the publishers, Da Capo Press, Inc., of New York, Hodeir's enlightening essay follows in the English translation from his book, whose American edition was retitled *Jazz: Its Evolution and Essence.*

S.D.

Does life begin at forty? That's what the title of a prewar comedy asserted. The jazzman does not bear out this optimistic philosophy, for it seems that his life—his musical life, of course—usually comes to an end around that age. Some striking exceptions, such as Sidney Bechet, do not invalidate what I believe could be stated as a general rule. All you have to do is go over the principal musicians now in their forties. Is it not perfectly clear that, although some of them may have a great deal of talent left, their current work is only a pale reflection of their former splendor? They are the survivors of the men they were rather than the same men living on; or, if they are the same, they are carried along only by an ever-diminishing momentum.

The European composer, at least under favorable circumstances, moves toward purity without losing his essential driving force and grows greater with meditation. By comparison, the jazzman may well be thought to be at a disadvantage. His fate is too precariously tied up with his youth for him not to feel bitter regrets as he grows old, if he sees clearly what is happening. Is the cause of this almost inevitable decline physical or psychological? Does it come from a stiffening of the muscles or a loss of breath power that diminishes the ability to swing? Or does it come from the impossibility of continually finding something new, which results in the boredom of repetition and a loss of the necessary joy in playing? It is probably a combination of both. Such as it is, there is something pathetic in a destiny that corresponds to the development of the human body rather than to that of the mind and spirit.

Dickie Wells entered his forties quite a few years ago. He was born in Centerville, Tennessee, on June 10, 1907, and began his musical career at the age of fifteen in the obscure Booker Washington band. Around 1925 he went to New York, where he worked with Charlie Johnson and later with the Scott brothers. After playing with Luis Russell in 1931, he stayed for a few months with Elmer Snowden and Bennie Carter before joining Fletcher Henderson's orchestra in 1933. After that famous group disbanded, he joined Teddy Hill's band and came to Europe with it. It was in Paris, in 1937, that he made records under his own name for the first time. Upon his return to the United States, he was signed by Count Basie, with whom he remained until after the war, when he joined Sy Oliver's orchestra. After some further peregrinations, including another stay in Europe (1952), he was to be seen not too long ago at the Savoy in Boston—leading, of all things, a Dixieland band!

The Early Days of Dickie Wells

As far back in his past as records permit us to look, Dickie Wells has always been an innovator with a powerful personality. The earliest recordings of his that we have—"Happy Hour" and "Symphonic Screach," made with Lloyd Scott in 1927—show him surrounded by depressing musicians: a clarinetist (Cecil Scott, no doubt) to whom even Johnny Dodds could have shown a thing or two about getting the notes in the right place rhythmically, a trumpeter striving in vain to imitate Red Nichols, and a rhythm section that would disgrace an amateur hour. Caught in this Gehenna, the nineteen-year-old trombonist improvises on the first side a break which suggests that he might really be able to swing, and on the second he turns out a first-rate solo that reveals unusual temperament.

Try to imagine the time when these recordings were made— January 1927. Jack Teagarden and Jimmy Harrison had scarcely rescued the trombone from the oompah of tailgate style. Stimulating each other to greater efforts but with different ability, they were trying to enlarge their instrument's field of action and to make it a vehicle for expressive melodic thought. Whatever may be thought of their respective work, it must be admitted that they created a kind of classicism from which Dickie Wells, a born romantic, profited greatly. Yes, the Dickie Wells of "Symphonic Screach" owes a lot to his elders Jimmy Harrison, Teagarden, and also Charlie "Big" Green. Even without them, he would undoubtedly have made the trombone expressive; but undoubtedly it would have taken him longer to do so. In spite of this, his solo in "Symphonic Screach" is already marked by a personal style. The tone is denser, the accent more somber and grandiose, and the phrasing more supple than Harrison's.

Nearly three years later, we find Dickie Wells again with Cecil Scott, who had by then succeeded his brother as a leader of the band. The group had improved noticeably, thanks largely to the presence of two young trumpeters named Bill Coleman and Frankie Newton. Although the rhythm section does not set him off to advantage, Dickie Wells shows in the course of a twenty-four-bar exposition that he had made real progress rhythmically; he does not always get the notes perfectly in place (cf. the end of the first sixteen-bar group), but he does not use corny syncopation in the principal phrase and he swings well. The whole of this solo, starting with the initial glissando toward the upper register, is resolutely ahead of its time. In "Springfield Stomp," Dickie Wells improvises a series of breaks of which at least one reveals his individual tendencies by its mobility and vehemence; but it is with "Bright Boy Blues" that the constricting framework of the traditional trombone chorus is broken for the first time, at least on records. Very likely following the path blazed by Armstrong (though it was undoubtedly his own path as well), the twenty-two-year-old Wells here creates a chorus that places him in the front rank of jazz musicians, right up there with Hodges, Hawkins, and Hines. The personality asserted here is an authentic one, and the style no longer retains any elements borrowed from predecessors. There is much more than a suggestion of his idea of using contrasts (changes in register and, to a lesser extent in this particular record, rhythmic diversity), and it is this idea, along with his beautiful, deep tone and the fact that no other trombonist has so much melodic inventiveness, which has made

154

it necessary even for those who hate all superlatives to call him the most remarkable musician on his instrument.

The Elements of His Style

Dickie Wells's tone, which is full of well-controlled emotion of high quality, would be enough by itself; I mean that, like Armstrong and Hodges, he is one of those jazzmen for whom melodic inventiveness is a supplementary and almost superfluous gift, since they manage to express themselves completely by their tone. All they have to do is blow into their instruments to achieve something personal and move the listener. Dickie Wells gets this expressive quintessence out of the most thankless instrument of all. When played without majesty, the trombone easily becomes wishy-washy and unbearable. Dickie Wells is majesty personified, in style and particularly in tone. Of course, he does not neglect his instrument's special possibilities. He rather often uses the slide, which is its principal element; his famous chorus in "Sweet Sue," with Spike Hughes, is only one example among many. But he uses it like a born nobleman, with perfect taste and an aristocratic nonchalance that is as far removed from the deliquescence of Lawrence Brown as from the triviality of Kid Ory.

Dickie Wells has an admirable knowledge of how to bring out the full value of his tone by inflection and vibrato. This is where his discreet use of the slide is especially marvelous. A record like Spike Hughes's "Arabesque" is particularly instructive in this respect, and I'm sorry not to be a trombonist so that I could make a profitable instrumental analysis of it. Wells frequently uses what might be called terminal vibrato. The note (usually isolated or at the end of a phrase) is level at first, but after an instant it begins to vibrate more and more intensely up to its brutal end. Graphically, this might by expressed as in Ex. 1.

Example 1: Terminal vibrato

This method is certainly not new, and there are others who sometimes use it equally well (I will mention only Louis Armstrong, who uses it even more as a vocalist than on the trumpet); but it is so perfectly integral a part of Dickie Wells's playing that it seems hard not to recognize it as an important element. We will note later how it plays a role in the very construction of many of his choruses. For the moment, let me simply cite the two records that I believe to be the best examples of his use of terminal vibrato: "Music at Sunrise" with Spike Hughes, and "Panassié Stomp," with Count Basie. The latter also brings out another distinguishing trait of Dickie Wells's style, the ornamented note. It is fairly close to what is called a mordent in classical music (that is, the quick alternation of a principal tone with an auxiliary one). What it involves is a small group of neighboring notes played legato, and the note being ornamented is usually high ("How Come You Do Me," with Spike Hughes) or at least higher than the note that follows (Ex. 2). Ornamented notes occur rather frequently in Dickie Wells's choruses, even in rapid tempos.

Example 2: Ornamented note

Like all great jazz musicians, Wells is a skillful instrumentalist as well. He never shows off his virtuosity (a childish thing to do, anyway, since the trombone does not have the trumpet's brilliance, which excuses some trumpeters' abuses of their instrument's virtuoso possibilities); but whenever the occasion demands it, he shows a mastery that is not at all usual for his time. In Teddy Hill's "Marie," his chorus is very amusing and easily handled in spite of a very lively tempo. I know of only one recording in which his technique is faulty—the Spike Hughes version of "Sweet Sue," where he plays some notes off pitch. This is unimportant in view of the high level maintained in the rest of his solos.

Dickie Wells is not only an expressive and moving soloist with a good instrumental technique. He is also one of those who swing the most. His ease and rhythmic precision are all the more extraordinary because one rarely hears his equal even on instruments that are less heavy and less difficult to handle than the

156

trombone. Perhaps not enough attention has been paid to the fact that the shape of some instruments makes them less adaptable to swing than others; for every ten trumpeters who swing, it is hard to find one trombonist. It is certain that in records like Spike Hughes's "Firebird," "Air in D Flat," "Bugle Call Rag," and "How Come You Do Me," Teddy Hill's "Here Comes Cookie," Basie's "Texas Shuffle," and his own "Between the Devil and the Deep Blue Sea," Dickie Wells plays with more intense swing than any but a few trumpeters have attained. Sometimes, in the manner of Lester Young, he even sacrifices everything else to swing, concentrating all his rhythmic powers on one or two notes repeated at greater or lesser length. Examples of this procedure may be found in Basie's "Texas Shuffle" and even in a record that goes back as far as 1933, Spike Hughes's "Bugle Call Rag."

Symmetry and Contrast

We have just reviewed briefly the principal elements in Dickie Wells's playing. Now let us consider how he uses them to serve his musical thought, and how this thought is organized. This involves one of the most delicate subjects in the study of jazz— that is the construction of choruses. The question has scarcely been touched, and we cannot deal with it in detail here. Let us merely note that, because of its clarity and simplicity, the work of Dickie Wells lends itself pretty well to the succinct analyses we are going to devote to it.

It seems incontestable that Wells is one of the most perfect constructors of choruses in the history of jazz. He has not only a sense of contrast, as we have already observed, but also—and perhaps to an even greater extent—a sense of balance. I mentioned near the beginning of this chapter that he is a born romantic. I believe this is true in a certain sense, for few musicians have his vivid imagination, his sweeping ardor, his impetuous effervescence, and his profoundly dramatic accent; but these expressive qualities, which make him one of the most sensitive soloists, are supported by a firm foundation in his sense of balance, and this is what distinguishes him from equally admirable but less well organized musicians (Roy Eldridge, for instance).

The art of Dickie Wells seems to be governed by two essential ideas, symmetry and contrast. (By symmetry, I mean the rhythmic or melodic repetition of a given motif; by contrast, the violent opposition of upper and lower registers, of *forte* and *piano*, of motion and repose.) They may appear contradictory; but all you have to do to be convinced of the necessity of both is to imagine what a musician's playing would be like if either one were missing. A style based on contrast alone would be incoherent, and one that is too symmetrical would be monotonous. In varying degrees, these two qualities are found linked together in the work of all great musicians; but no one unites them better than Dickie Wells.

He often shows this desire for symmetry right at the start of a solo. His choruses frequently begin with a kind of doublet—that is, a short phrase that is repeated, either identically or transposed, after a brief pause. This procedure, which the great trombonist seems to be particularly fond of, has the excellent effect of airing out the first bars of a chorus, permitting a subsequent gradation of contrasts that would risk decreasing the tension if presented in the opposite order. This initial doublet is found in some of his best solos: Spike Hughes's "Sweet Sorrow Blues" (in which the phrase includes a very expressive inflection) and Basie's "London Bridge Is Falling Down," "Taxi War Dance," and "Miss Thing," among others.

Another favorite procedure of Dickie Wells is what might be called the entry note. It is an isolated note that does not appear to be attached to the chorus; on the contrary, it seems quite independent of what follows. It shows up at the beginning of some solos, serving no apparent melodic purpose, as if the musician had just wanted to check the pitch or tone of his instrument. However, its musical meaning cannot be denied. To my way of understanding, it serves as a link; by means of this simple note, Wells skillfully manages to form a connection between his chorus and the preceding one. Such a connection is too often neglected by most improvisers, who don't care what relation their variation has to the one before. Moreover, this entry note is nearly always expressive. Wells makes up for its apparent melodic insignificance by using a warm and moving vibrato (generally of the "terminal" type mentioned earlier). Interesting examples of the entry note may be found in Teddy Hill's "When the

Robin Sing His Song Again" and particularly in "Hot Club Blues," where it is immediately followed by a doublet (a rather infrequent but very effective combination). Naturally, none of this is systematic; and Dickie Wells does not refrain from using other kinds of entries. One of the most original is surely his glissando break in Teddy Hill's "A Study in Brown."

His taste for symmetry is again reflected in the way he breaks up his choruses, but it is animated by an inventive imagination that prevents him from making his divisions too uniform. Examples of choruses cut up in four-bar divisions are fairly rare (Spike Hughes's "Air in D Flat" is one, so is Basie's "Down for Double"). Actually, Wells's sense of symmetry is manifested in more subtle ways, because they are closely connected with the ways in which he shows his sense of contrast. In the chorus of "Sweet Sorrow Blues," for example, after the initial doublet the phrase develops and comes to a drop into the lower register, then drops again (symmetry) but this time in the middle register (contrast). Similarly, in the chorus of Spike Hughes's "How Come You Do Me" the repetition of certain motifs (symmetry) is set off by their rhythmic disjunction (contrast).

It definitely seems that Wells's taste for contrast exceeds his taste for symmetry and is the dominant element in his style. (This does not invalidate my earlier statement that balance is Wells's principal quality.) There is scarcely a single solo in which it is not manifested, in one way or another. Let us take his chorus in Spike Hughes's "Pastoral" as an example. Wells takes sixteen bars in a moderate tempo. The first eight are rather static; they open with a repeated note, and the ensuing melodic development is very calm. On the other hand, the following eight bars are much more animated; Wells uses a staccato phrasing that forms a sharp break with what went before. In Hughes's "Bugle Call Rag," Wells starts by swinging on a repeated note, then suddenly takes off into the upper register and accentuates the tension of the phrase by inflection before going into a very mobile final drop. The first eight bars of his solo in Fletcher Henderson's "King Porter Stomp" (Vocalion version) are constructed in very angular fashion, with very dry notes that are "shot out"; the other eight bars begin with an upper-register held note that is taut in sonority but still forms a perfect rhythmic contrast with what went before. On the other hand, Dickie

Wells knows how to use a calm vibrato to create a feeling of relaxation at the end of a violent episode (as in Basie's "Texas Shuffle"). A tranquil, intimate chorus with little contrast, such as the one in "Dicky's Dream" (also made with Basie), must be considered an exception. Actually, his taste for contrast is so great that he will even oppose his chorus to the preceding one. We have a striking example of this in Hughes's "Someone Stole Gabriel's Horn," where Wells follows the sax's very regularly divided solo with its exact rhythmic and plastic antithesis, full of glissandos and irregularly broken up.

Let us now examine the style of Dickie Wells from a strictly rhythmic point of view. His choruses may often be divided into regular sections, but within these sections he exercises a rare amount of rhythmic imagination. He uses notes of greatly varying length and combines them very freely. In Spike Hughes's "Firebird," for example, he plays on the beat, in the manner of the New Orleans trombonists (though naturally he is incomparably better about getting the notes in the right place and about swinging). In Basie's "London Bridge" he plays a long series of quarter notes on the beat, ending with two syncopated notes (one of Louis Armstrong's favorite procedures). On the other hand, in Hughes's "Music at Midnight" he uses much less regular rhythms, such as a triplet of syncopated quarter notes. His chorus in Basie's "Taxi War Dance" contains an unusual number of short notes (eighths), whereas welcome contrasts between long and short notes give his "Panassié Stomp" solo rare rhythmic suppleness. Another rhythmically interesting chorus is the one in Teddy Hill's "Marie." Although the tempo is very fast, Dickie Wells comes on with a series of eighths; then he slows up somewhat with a mixture of eighths and quarter notes, and even some half-note triplets that form a curious contrast to the work of the rhythm section (three against four); and he ends very humorously with a break made up of eighth notes again. In Spike Hughes's "Air in D Flat," the diversity of rhythmic values counterbalances the symmetry of four-bar division; each of these four phrases stands in rhythmic contrast to the others.

To see the freedom and rhythmic diversity of Wells's phrasing, it is sufficient to study a simple eight-bar phrase taken from "I Found a New Baby," which he recorded in France in 1937. Notice (Ex. 3) the long, vibrated note—it might be compared to

160

Example 3: Eight-bar phrase from "I Found a New Baby"

an entry note—in the first measure; the syncopated phrase that follows; the descending phrase, straddling the bar line between the fourth and fifth measures, which is also syncopated but with longer, dislocated notes (dotted quarters), and which comes to rest on the second beat of the fifth measure (note here that the glissandos further amplify the feeling of rhythmic uncertainty caused by the dislocation of the syncopated notes); and finally the very classical descending phrase of measures 6–8, which might almost have been taken from an Armstrong chorus. Here again, it would be a mistake to believe that the phrase is any the less cohesive for showing imaginative variety. Moreover, Dickie Wells is perfectly capable of developing a chorus according to the strictest rhythmic progression. Even in the tight quarters of an eight-bar bridge, he can begin statically, step things up, and finish by playing eight to the bar. His short solos in Teddy Hill's "Here Comes Cookie" and "When the Robin Sings His Song Again" are almost twinlike examples of this. It will be observed, especially in the second, that Wells has a tendency to "swallow" the sixteenth notes of his dotted-eighth-and-sixteenth groups; this fits in very nicely with this particularly supple and nonchalant way of swinging.

Melodically, there is the same alternation between imagination and conformity. Although Wells has a predilection for changes in register (those of "A Study in Brown" are typical), he has nothing against staying in the upper register (as in Spike Hughes's "Fanfare") or in the middle range. He rarely tries to make an effect with a high note, although examples that might be noted are the high F in Basie's "Down for Double" and the somewhat unfortunate glissando in the Kansas City Six's "I Got Rhythm". Much more interesting is his liking for wide intervals (something few trombonists have, I believe), which is demonstrated on this same side, notably during his first bridge (Ex. 4). (Note also, in this excerpt, the great rhythmic originality expressed by the triplet of half notes in measure 19 and the triplet of syncopated quarter notes in measure 22.)

Example 4: Wide intervals from "I Got Rhythm"

A great deal more remains to be said about such an astonishing musician, but that would take us beyond the limits of a study like this. Before concluding, however, I should like to go over what I consider his most interesting records. In roughly chronological order, they are as follows: Lloyd Scott's "Symphonic Screach" and Cecil Scott's "Bright Boy Blues," which I discussed near the beginning of this chapter. Luis Russell's "Goin' to Town," which is a kind of recorded synthesis of all Wells's principal characteristics: attack, glissando, vibrato, "bite," and freedom of rhythmic construction. Nearly all the Spike Hughes series, and particularly "How Come You Do Me," which swings extremely well in a moderate tempo and shows off other aspects of Wells's playing, such as the ornamented high note, dislocation and rhythmic contrast, and harmonious construction; "Fanfare" (vehemence); "Sweet Sorrow Blues" (simplicity); "Arabesque" (ease); "Air in D Flat" (balance in spite of contrasts); and "Bugle Call Rag" (modernism of style). Teddy Hill's "Here Comes Cookie," "Marie," and "A Study in Brown." Count Basie's "Texas Shuffle," "Panassié Stomp," "Love Jumped Out," "Jimmy's Blues," "Nobody Knows," and particularly "Harvard Blues" (Okeh version), the orchestra's masterpiece in a slow tempo. Finally, under his own name, "Between the Devil and the Deep Blue Sea," which has a bridge that is a little gem, and the admirable "Dicky Wells Blues," which would be one of the truly great jazz records if the rhythm section were up to the level of the soloist—it is, alas, very far from it!—and if even Wells himself had not weakened somewhat in the last two choruses.

There is perhaps no way to conclude except by returning to our starting point, which was not exactly optimistic. It is unpleasant to observe the decline of a musician one likes. Many people refuse to do so. Nevertheless, the sincere critic must face the facts. How can the fact be avoided that Wells's solos, even with Basie, became increasingly rare towards the end of the war and kept diminishing in quality? I am thinking of "Tush" (with Earle Warren, April 1944) and "Four O'Clock Drag" (with the Kansas

City Six at about the same time), both of which are among his weakest choruses; the second, a slow blues, gives the painful impression that Wells has lost the feeling and has to force himself to play.

A few years ago, it was still possible to think that these were simply lapses. But Dickie Wells came to Europe in 1952. We hoped to hear the brilliant soloist again; instead, all we heard time after time was a worn-out, diminished, unrecognizable Wells. The fate that condemns nine jazzmen out of ten to end up caricatures of their past greatness has caught up with the great trombonist. Under these circumstances, it is best to forget the Wells of today in order to remember the marvelous soloist he was before the war.

. . . . *appendix B*

A Dicky Wells Discographical Listing
Compiled by Chris Sheridan

ABBREVIATIONS

Instruments

a-h	alto horn	narr	narration
as	alto saxophone		
		org	organ
b	string bass		
bj	banjo	p	piano
bs	baritone saxophone		
btb	bass trombone	ss	soprano saxophone
cel	celesta	tb	trombone
cl	clarinet	tp	trumpet
ct	cornet	ts	tenor saxophone
		tu	tuba
d	drums		
		u/k	unknown
E♭-h	E♭ horn		
elb	electric bass	vb	vibraphone/vibraharp
		v or vo	vocal
f	flute		
flh	fluegelhorn	xyl	xylophone
g	guitar		

Vocalists

Performances involving a singer are indicated by a "v" after the title, followed by the initials of the performer. Thus, vFN indicates a vocal by Frankie Newton. Full names are included in the lists of personnel preceding each session.

Record Labels

All originate in the United States unless indicated below or in text. Album numbers in italics are vinyl or CD issues; those in Roman are 78 rpm.

ABC-Par	ABC-Paramount	JazzA	Jazz Archives
Atl	Atlantic	JP	Jazz Panorama (Swe)
		JS	Jazz Selection (F)
Band	Bandstand	JSoc	Jazz Society (Swe)
BB	Bluebird	JzU	Jazz Unlimited (D)
BlH	Blue Heaven		
Bruns	Brunswick	Key	Keynote
Bway	Bluesway		
		Mer	Mercury
Cam	Camden	Met	Metronome (Swe)
Car	Caracol (F)	MJR	Master Jazz Recordings
CassO	Cassettes Only		
Col	Columbia	Par	Parlophone (E)
ColC	Collectors Classics (D)	Ph	Philips
Com	Commodore	Pr	Prestige
EmA	EmArcy	Rhap	Rhapsody (E)
Ev	Everybodys	Riv	Riverside
ExR	Extreme Rarities		
		SH	Swing House (E)
Fel	Felsted (E)	Sig	Signature
Fest	Festival	SoS	Sounds of Swing
FH	First Heard (E)	Spl Edn	Special Edition
Flute	Flutegrove (E)	Spot	Spotlite (E)
FTOR	First Time on Records	Steep	SteepleChase (D)
		Stv	Storyville (D)
GE	Golden Era	SwT	Swing Treasury
GOJ	Giants of Jazz		
		UA	United Artists
Hind	Hindsight		
HMV	His Master's Voice	Van	Vanguard
HRS	Hot Record Society	Vg	Vogue (F)
		Vic	Victor
Imp	Impulse	VJM	Vintage Jazz Mart (E)
		Voc	Vocalion
J&J	Jazz & Jazz (I)		

Countries of origin

Aus	Australia	I	Italy
D	Denmark	Swe	Sweden
E	United Kingdom	Swi	Switzerland
F	France		

ACKNOWLEDGMENTS

The information forming the basis of this discographical listing has been accumulated over a number of years, and from a great many sources, many of which must remain unsung. I am especially grateful, however, for the help given this project by Stanley Dance, Frank Liniger, Tony Middleton, Bill Rankin, and Bob Weir. Any shortcomings remain mine. —C.S.

BIBLIOGRAPHY

Allen, Walter C. *Hendersonia (The Music of Fletcher Henderson and His Musicians)*. *Jazz Monographs* No. 4, Highland Park, N.J.: Walter C. Allen, 1974.

Evensmo, Jan. *Jazz Solography Series* No. 14. (Includes "The Trombone of Dickie Wells.") Oslo: Jan Evensmo, 1983.

Jepsen, Jorgen Grunnet. *Jazz Records 1942–1962* (various vols.). Copenhagen: Knudsen, 1962, 1990.

Panassié, Hugues. *Discographie critique des meilleurs disques de jazz*. Paris: R. Laffont, 1958.

Rust, Brian. *Jazz Records 1897–1942*. Westport, Conn.: Arlington House, 1978.

Sheridan, Chris. *Count Basie: A Bio-Discography*. Westport, Conn.: Greenwood Press, 1986.

Weir, Bob. *Buck Clayton Discography*. Chigwell, Essex: Storyville Publications, 1989.

LLOYD SCOTT & HIS ORCHESTRA

Gus McClung, Kenneth Roane (tp); Wells (tb); Fletcher Allen, John Williams (cl/as); Cecil Scott (cl/ts/bs); Don Frye (p); Hubert Mann (bj); Chester Campbell (tu); Lloyd Scott (d).
NYC, January 10, 1927:

37529-1	Harlem Shuffle	
37529-2	Harlem Shuffle	Vic 21491
37530-2	Symphonic Scrontch	Vic 20495
37531-1	Happy Hour Blues	
37531-2	Happy Hour Blues	Vic 20495

NB: All five takes on *RCA(F) 741 066*.

CECIL SCOTT & HIS BRIGHT BOYS

Bill Coleman (tp); Frankie Newton (tp/vo); Wells (tb); Harold McFerran, John Williams (as); Cecil Scott (cl/ts/bs); Don Frye (p); Rudolph Williams (bj); Mack Walker (tu); Lloyd Scott (d).
NYC, November 19, 1929:

57709-1	Lawd, Lawd (vFN/band members)	Vic V-38098
57710-1	In a Corner	Vic V-38098
57711-2	Bright Boy Blues	Vic V-38117
57712-1	Springfield Stomp	Vic V-38117

NB: All four takes on *RCA (F) 741 066*.

LUIS RUSSELL & HIS ORCHESTRA

Henry 'Red' Allen (tp/vo); Gus Aiken, Robert Cheek (tp); Wells (tb); Albert Nicholas (cl/as); Henry Jones (as); Greely Walton (ts); Luis Russell (p); Will Johnson (bj/g); Pops Foster (b); Paul Barbarin (d/vb); Chick Bullock (vo).
NYC, August 28, 1931:

70195-1	You Rascal, You (vHRA)	Vic 22793
70196-1	Goin' to Town (vCB)	Vic 22789
70197-1	Say the Word (vCB)	Vic 22789
70198-1	Freakish Blues	Vic 22815

NB: All four takes also on *VJM(E) VLP.57*.

BENNY CARTER & HIS ORCHESTRA
Louis Bacon, Frankie Newton, u/k (tp); Wells (tb); Wayman Carver (f/as); Benny Carter (cl/as); Chew Berry (ts); Teddy Wilson (p); u/k (g); Dick Fulbright (b); Sidney Catlett (d); u/k female (vo).
NYC, June 23, 1932:
1765-1   Tell All Your Daydreams to Me (v)   Crown 3321

Add u/k (ts); omit vocalist.
NYC, October 5, 1932:
73772-1   Hot Toddy   Vic rejected
73772-2   Hot Toddy   Vic rejected
73773-1   Jazz Cocktail   Vic rejected
73773-2   Jazz Cocktail   Vic rejected
73774-1   Black Jazz   Vic rejected
73774-2   Black Jazz   Vic rejected

SMALLS' PARADISE ENTERTAINERS (ELMER SNOWDEN & HIS ORCHESTRA)
Leonard Davis, Roy Eldridge (tp); George Washington, Wells (tb); Otto Hardwicke (as); Wayman Carver (f/as); Al Sears (ts/bs); Don Kirkpatrick (p); Elmer Snowden (bj); Dick Fulbright (b/tu); Sidney Catlett (d); u/k female (vo).
Vitaphone movie short *Smash Your Baggage*, NYC, 1933:
              Bugle Call Rag   *IAJRC 12*
              Tiger Rag   *IAJRC 12*
              Tiger Rag #2   *IAJRC 12*
              Stop the Sun, Stop the Moon   *IAJRC 12*
              My Man's Gone (v)   *IAJRC 12*
              Concentratin' on You   *IAJRC 12*
              Don't Let Your Love Go Wrong   *IAJRC 12*

HENRY ALLEN, COLEMAN HAWKINS, & THEIR ORCHESTRA
Henry 'Red' Allen (tp/vo); Wells (tb); Russell Procope (cl/as); Coleman Hawkins (ts); Don Kirkpatrick (p); Lawrence Lucie (g); John Kirby (b/tu); Walter Johnson (d).
NYC, March 27, 1933: (Brunswick)
13183-A   Someday Sweetheart (vHRA)   *Pirate (Swe)*
                                               MPC-513
13184-A   I Wish I Could Shimmy Like   *Pirate (Swe)*
            My Sister Kate (vHRA)   *MPC-513*

SPIKE HUGHES & HIS NEGRO ORCHESTRA
Shad Collins, Leonard Davis, Bill Dillard (tp); Wilbur DeParis, George Washington, Wells (tb); Wayman Carver (f/as); Benny Carter (cl/as/vo); Howard Johnson (cl/as); Coleman Hawkins (cl/ts); Rod Rodriguez (p); Lawrence Lucie (g); Ernest Hill (b); Kaiser Marshall or Sidney Catlett* (d).
NYC, April 18, 1933:
B-13257-A   Nocturne   Decca F-3563
B-13258-A   Someone Stole Gabriel's Horn (vBC)   Decca F-3563
B-13259-A   Pastorale*   Decca F-3606
B-13260-A   Bugle Call Rag*   Decca F-3606

170

Henry 'Red' Allen, Leonard Davis, Bill Dillard (tp); Wilbur DeParis, George Washington, Wells (tb); Wayman Carver (f/cl/as); Benny Carter, Howard Johnson (cl/as); Coleman Hawkins (cl/ts); Chew Berry (ts); Luis Russell (p); Lawrence Lucie (g); Ernest Hill (b); Sidney Catlett (d).
NYC, May 18, 1933:

B-13352-A	Arabesque	Decca F-3639
B-13353-A	Fanfare	Decca F-3639
B-13354-A	Sweet Sorrow Blues	Decca F-5101
B-13355-A	Music at Midnight	Decca F-3836
B-13356-A	Sweet Sue, Just You (1)	Decca F-3972

Howard Scott (tp) & Rod Rodriguez (p) replace Davis or Dillard & Russell; Carter (cl/ss/as).
NYC, May 19, 1933:

B-13359-A	Air in B-Flat	Decca F-5101
B-13360-A	Donegal Cradle Song	Decca F-3717
B-13361-A	Firebird	Decca F-3717
B-13362-A	Music at Sunrise	Decca F-3836
B-13363-A	How Come You Do Me Like You Do? (1) (vHRA)	Decca F-3972

NB: (1) by Allen (tp); Wells (tb); Carver (f); Carter (as); Hawkins, Berry (ts); Rodriguez (p); Lucie (g); Spike Hughes (b); Catlett (d).

HENRY ALLEN, COLEMAN HAWKINS, & THEIR ORCHESTRA
Henry 'Red' Allen (tp/vo); Wells (tb); Hilton Jefferson (as); Coleman Hawkins (ts); Horace Henderson (p); Bernard Addison (g/bj); John Kirby (b/tu); Walter Johnson (d).
NYC, July 21, 1933:

13616-1	The River's Takin' Care of Me (vHRA)	Banner 32840
13617-1	Ain'tcha Got Music? (vHRA)	Banner 32840
13618-1	Stringin' Along on a Shoe String (vHRA)	Banner 32829
13619-1	Shadows on the Swanee (vHRA)	Banner 32829

FLETCHER HENDERSON & HIS ORCHESTRA
Henry 'Red' Allen, Russell Smith, Bobby Stark (tp); Wells, Sandy Williams* (tb); Hilton Jefferson, Russell Procope (cl/as); Coleman Hawkins (cl/ts); Fletcher Henderson (p); Bernard Addison (g); John Kirby (b); Walter Johnson (d).
NYC, August 18, 1933:

13827-1	Yeah! Man	Voc 2527
13827-2	Yeah! Man	Bruns(F) A-9771
13828-1	King Porter's Stomp	Voc 2527
13828-2	King Porter's Stomp	Bruns(F) A-9771
13829-1	Queer Notions*	Voc 2583
13830-1	Can You Take It?*	Voc 2583
13830-1	Can You Take It?*	Col 35671

Claude Jones (tb) & Horace Henderson (p) replace Sandy Williams & Fletcher Henderson.
NYC, September 22, 1933:

W265135-1	Queer Notions	Col (E) CB 678
W265135-2	Queer Notions	Col (F) DF.1400

171

W265136-1	Talk of the Town	Col 2825-D
W265136-2	Talk of the Town	rejected
W265136-3	Talk of the Town	Col (Au) DO-1064
W265137-2	Night Life	Col (E) CB 727
W265138-2	Nagasaki	Col 2825-D

HORACE HENDERSON & HIS ORCHESTRA

Henry 'Red' Allen (tp/vo); Russell Smith, Bobby Stark (tp); Claude Jones, Wells (tb); Hilton Jefferson, Russell Procope (cl/as); Coleman Hawkins (cl/ts); Horace Henderson (p); Bernard Addison (g); John Kirby (b/tu); Walter Johnson (d).
NYC, October 3, 1933:

W265150-2	Happy Feet	Par R 1792
W265151-1	Rhythm Crazy	Par R 1743
W265152-1	Ol' Man River (vHRA)	Par R 1766
W265153-2	Minnie the Moocher's Wedding Day	Par R 2031
W265154-1	Ain'tcha Glad?	Par R 1717
W265155-1	I've Got To Sing a Torch Song	Col (E) CB 701

HENRY ALLEN & HIS ORCHESTRA

Henry 'Red' Allen (tp/vo); Wells (tb); Buster Bailey (cl/as); Hilton Jefferson (as); Horace Henderson (p); Lawrence Lucie (g); John Kirby (b/tu); Walter Johnson (d).
NYC, May 1, 1934:

15146-1	I Wish I Were Twins (vHRA)	Banner 33081
15147-1	I Never Slept a Wink Last Night (vHRA)	Banner 33081
15148-2	Why Don't You Practice What You Preach? (vHRA)	Banner 33054
15149-1	Don't Let Your Love Go Wrong (vHRA)	Banner 33054

WINGY MANONE & HIS ORCHESTRA

Wingy Manone (tp); Wells (tb); Artie Shaw (cl); Bud Freeman (ts); Teddy Wilson or Jelly Roll Morton* (p); Frank Victor (g); John Kirby (b); Kaiser Marshall (d).
NYC, August 15, 1934:

15629-A	Easy Like	*Merritt 6*
15629-B	Easy Like	*Merritt 6*
15630-A	In the Slot	*Merritt 6*
15630-B	In the Slot	*Merritt 6*
15631-A	Never Had No Lovin'*	*Merritt 6*
15631-B	Never Had No Lovin'*	Spl Edn 5011-S
15632-A	I'm Alone without You*	Spl Edn 5011-S
15632-B	I'm Alone without You*	*Rhap RHA 6030*

TEDDY HILL & HIS ORCHESTRA

Bill Dillard (tp/vo); Bill Coleman, Roy Eldridge (tp); Wells (tb); Russell Procope (cl/as); Howard Johnson (as); Chew Berry, Teddy Hill (ts); Sam Allen (p); John Smith (g); Dick Fulbright (b); Bill Beason (d).
NYC, February 26, 1935:

16923-1	Lookie, Lookie, Here Comes Cookie	Banner 33384
16924-1	Got Me Doin' Things (vBD)	Banner 33384

| 16925-1 | When the Robin Sings His Song Again | Banner 33397 |
| 16926-1 | When Love Knocks at Your Heart (vBD) | Banner 33397 |

HENRY ALLEN & HIS ORCHESTRA
Henry 'Red' Allen (tp/vo); Wells (tb); Cecil Scott (cl); Chew Berry (ts); Horace Henderson (p); Bernard Addison (g); John Kirby (b); George Stafford (d).
NYC, April 29, 1935:

17395-1	Rosetta (vHRA)	Voc 2965
17396-1	Body & Soul (vHRA)	Voc 2965
17397-1	I'll Never Say 'Never Again' Again (vHRA)	Voc 2956
17398-1	Get Rhythm in Your Feet (vHRA)	Voc 2956

TEDDY HILL & HIS ORCHESTRA
Shad Collins, Bill Dillard, Frankie Newton (tp); Wells (tb); Russell Procope (cl/as); Howard Johnson (as); Teddy Hill (ts); Cecil Scott (cl/ts/bs); Sam Allen (p); John Smith (g); Dick Fulbright (b); Bill Beason (d).
NYC, April 1, 1936:

18911-1	Uptown Rhapsody	Voc 3294
18912-1	Christopher Columbus	rejected
18912-2	Christopher Columbus	rejected

NYC, May 4, 1936:

19175-1	At the Rug Cutters' Ball	Voc 3247
19176-1	Blue Rhythm Fantasy	Voc 3247
19177-1	Passionette	Voc 3294

Add Beatrice Douglas (vo).
NYC, March 26, 1937:

06462-1	The Love Bug Will Bite You (vBand)	BB B-6897
06463-1	Would You Like To Buy a Dream? (vBD)	BB B-6897
06464-1	Big Boy Blue (vBD/TH)	BB B-6908
06465-1	Where Is the Sun? (vBD)	BB B-6898
06466-1	The Harlem Twister	BB B-6908
06467-1	My Marie	BB B-6898

Same.
NYC, April 23, 1937:

07925-1	I Know Now (vBD)	BB B-6954
07926-1	The Lady Who Couldn't Be Kissed (vBD)	BB B-6954
07927-1	The You and Me That Used To Be (vBD)	BB B-6941
07928-1	A Study in Brown	BB B-6943
07929-1	Twilight in Turkey	BB B-6943
07930-1	China Boy	BB B-6941

Dizzy Gillespie (tp) & Robert Carroll (ts) replace Frankie Newton & Cecil Scott.
NYC, May 17, 1937:

| 010206-1 | San Anton' (vBD) | BB B-6988 |

010207-1	I'm Happy, Darling, Dancing With You	BB B-6989
010208-1	Yours & Mine (vBD)	BB B-7013
010209-1	I'm Feeling Like a Million (vBD)	BB B-7013
010210-1	King Porter's Stomp	BB B-6988
010211-1	Blue Rhythm Fantasy	BB B-6989

DICKY WELLS & HIS ORCHESTRA
Bill Coleman (tp/vo); Shad Collins*, Bill Dillard* (tp); Wells (tb); Django
Reinhardt (g); Dick Fulbright (b); Bill Beason (d).
Paris, July 7, 1937:

OLA-1884-1	Bugle Call Rag*	Swing(F) 6
OLA-1885-1	Between the Devil & the Deep Blue Sea*	Swing(F) 6
OLA-1886-1	I Got Rhythm*	Swing(F) 27
OLA-1887-1	Sweet Sue	Swing(F) 16
OLA-1888-1	Hangin' Around Boudon (vBC)	Swing(F) 16
OLA-1889-1	Japanese Sandman	Swing(F) 27

Shad Collins*, Bill Dillard+ (tp); Wells (tb); Howard Johnson (as); Sam Allen
(p); Roger Chaput (b); Bill Beason (d).
Paris, July 12, 1937:

OLA-1894-1	I've Found a New Baby*+	Swing(F) 3
OLA-1895-1	Dinah*+	Swing(F) 39
OLA-1896-1	Nobody's Blues But My Own	Swing(F) 39
OLA-1897-1	Hot Club Blues+	Swing(F) 3

Omit Collins, Dillard & Johnson.
Same date:

| OLA-1898-1 | Lady Be Good | Swing(F) 10 |
| OLA-1899-1 | Dicky Wells Blues | Swing(F) 10 |

COUNT BASIE & HIS ORCHESTRA
Buck Clayton, Harry Edison, Ed Lewis (tp); Dan Minor, Benny Morton,
Wells (tb); Earle Warren (as); Herschel Evans, Lester Young (ts); Jack Wash-
ington (as/bs); Count Basie (p); Freddie Green (g); Walter Page (b); Jo Jones
(d); Helen Humes, Jimmy Rushing (vo).
CBS 'America Dances' broadcast, NYC, July 9, 1938:

	One O'Clock Jump (theme)	ColC CC-9
	Every Tub	ColC CC-9
	Song of the Wanderer (vHH)	ColC CC-9
	Flat Foot Floogie (vJR)	ColC CC-9
	Lady Be Good	ColC CC-9
	Boogie Woogie (vJR)	ColC CC-9
	One O'Clock Jump	ColC CC-9
	I Let a Song Go Out of My Heart (vJR)	Palm 30-06

Add Harry James (tp*).
CBS broadcast, Famous Door, NYC, July 23, 1938:

	Time Out	unissued
	One Hour (vHH)	unissued
	Jumpin' at the Woodside	unissued
	I Hadn't Anyone till You (vJR)	unissued
	King Porter's Stomp*	IAJRC 14

174

| Lady Be Good | *JP LP 2* |
| Everybody Loves My Baby (nc) | unissued |

Omit James.
CBS broadcast, Famous Door, NYC, August 9, 1938:

One O'Clock Jump (theme)	*JP LP 23*
King Porter's Stomp	*JP LP 23*
I've Got a Date With a Dream (vJR)	unissued
Lady Be Good (nc)	unissued

CBS broadcast, Famous Door, NYC, August 12, 1938:

| I Haven't Changed a Thing (vHH) | *JazzA JA-41* |

NYC, August 22, 1938:

64471-A	Stop Beatin' Round the Mulberry Bush (vJR)	Decca 2004
64471-B	Stop Beatin' Round the Mulberry Bush (vJR)	Decca 2004
64472-A	London Bridge is Falling Down (vJR)	Decca 2004
64473-A	Texas Shuffle	Decca 2030
64474-A	Jumpin' at the Woodside	Decca 2212

CBS broadcast, Famous Door, NYC, August 23, 1938:

Yeah! Man	*JP LP 23*
John's Idea	*JP LP 23*
Melody in F	*JP LP 23*
Must We Just Be Friends? (vHH)	unissued

CBS broadcast, Famous Door, NYC, August 24, 1938:

Nagasaki	*JP LP 23*
Doggin' Around	*JP LP 23*
One O'Clock Jump (theme)	*JP LP 23*

PEE WEE RUSSELL'S RHYTHMAKERS

Max Kaminsky (tp); Wells (tb); Pee Wee Russell (cl); Al Gold (ts); James P. Johnson (p); Freddie Green (g); Wellman Braud (b); Zutty Singleton (d/vo).
NYC, August 31, 1938:

23391-1	Baby, Won't You Please Come Home?	HRS 10000
23391-2	Baby, Won't You Please Come Home?	HRS 17
23392-1	There'll Be Some Changes Made	HRS 1001
23392-2	There'll Be Some Changes Made	*Merritt 9*
23393-1	Horn of Plenty Blues (vZS)	HRS 1001
29994-1	Dinah	HRS 1000

NB: Wells not present on two other titles from this session.

COUNT BASIE & HIS ORCHESTRA

Personnel as before.
CBS broadcast, Famous Door, NYC, September 6, 1938:

| Indiana | *JazzA JA-41* |
| Out the Window (nc) | *JazzA JA-41* |

CBS broadcast, Famous Door, NYC, September 13, 1938:

	Wo-Ta-Ta	*JazzA JA-41*
	Indiana (nc)	*JazzA JA-41*
	Love of My Life (vHH)	*JazzA JA-41*
	John's Idea	*JazzA JA-41*

BILLIE HOLIDAY & HER ORCHESTRA
Buck Clayton (tp); Wells (tb); Lester Young (cl/ts); Margaret 'Queenie' Johnson (p); Freddie Green (g); Walter Page (b); Jo Jones (d); Billie Holiday (vo). NYC, September 15, 1938:

23467-1	The Very Thought of You (vBH)	Voc 4457
23468-1	I Can't Get Started (vBH)	Voc 4457
23468-2	I Can't Get Started (vBH)	
23469-1	I've Got a Date with a Dream (vBH)	
23469-2	I've Got a Date with a Dream (vBH)	Voc 4396
23470-1	You Can't Be Mine (vBH)	Voc 4396

NB: All takes on *Columbia C-34837*.

COUNT BASIE & HIS ORCHESTRA
Personnel as before.
CBS broadcast, Famous Door, NYC, October 9, 1938:

	Nagasaki	*JP LP 23*
	Doggin' Around	*JP LP 23*
	One O'Clock Jump (theme)	*JP LP 23*

NYC, November 16, 1938:

64746-A	Dark Rapture (vHH)	Decca 2212
64747-A	Shorty George	Decca 2325
64748-A	The Blues I Like To Hear (vJR)	Decca 2284
64749-A	Do You Wanna Jump, Children? (vJR)	Decca 2224
64750-A	Panassié Stomp	Decca 2224

Add Shad Collins, Hot Lips Page* (tp).
Spirituals To Swing concert, Carnegie Hall, NYC, December 23, 1938:

	One O'Clock Jump	*Van VRS 8523*
	Blues with Lips*	*Van VRS 8523*
	Rhythm Man	*Van VRS 8523*

IDA COX & HER BAND
Shad Collins (tp); Wells (tb); Buddy Tate (ts); James P. Johnson (p); Freddie Green (g); Walter Page (b); Jo Jones (d); Ida Cox (vo).
Same concert:

	Four Day Creep	*Van VRS 8524*

COUNT BASIE & HIS ORCHESTRA
Buck Clayton, Shad Collins, Harry Edison, Ed Lewis (tp); Dan Minor, Benny Morton, Wells (tb); Earle Warren (as); Herschel Evans, Lester Young (ts); Jack Washington (as/bs); Count Basie (p); Freddie Green (g); Walter Page (b); Jo Jones (d); Helen Humes (vo).
NYC, January 5, 1939:

64851-A	My Heart Belongs to Daddy (vHH)	Decca 2249
64852-A	Sing for Your Supper (vHH)	Decca 2249

176

Chew Berry (ts) replaces Evans.
NYC, February 3, 1939:

64979-A	Cherokee, Part 1	Decca 2406
64980-A	Cherokee, Part 2	Decca 2406
64981-A	Blame It on My Last Affair (vHH)	Decca 2284
64981-B	Blame It on My Last Affair (vHH)	Decca 2284

Add Jimmy Rushing (vo).
NYC, February 4, 1939:

64982-A	Jive at Five (1)	Decca 2922
64983-A	Thursday (vHH)	Decca 2325
64984-A	Evil Blues (vJR)	Decca 2922
64985-A	Lady Be Good	Decca 2631

NB: (1) by Clayton, Collins, Edison, Wells, Young, Washington, & rhythm only.

BASIE'S BAD BOYS
Buck Clayton, Shad Collins (tp); Wells (tb); Lester Young (cl/ts); Count Basie (p/org); Freddie Green (g); Walter Page (b); Jo Jones (d); Jimmy Rushing (vo).
Chicago, February 13, 1939:

24510-1	I Ain't Got Nobody	*Col G-31224*
24511-1	Goin' to Chicago (vJR)	*Col G-31224*
24512-1	Live & Love Tonight	*Col G-31224*
24513-1	Love Me or Leave Me	*Col G-31224*

NB: All titles also on *CBS(F) 66101*.

COUNT BASIE & HIS ORCHESTRA
As before, except Buddy Tate (ts) replaces Chew Berry.
NYC, March 19, 1939:

W24238-1	What Goes Up Must Come Down (vJR)	Voc 4734
W24238-2	What Goes Up Must Come Down (vJR)	
W24239-1	Rock-a-Bye Basie	Voc 4747
W24240-1	Baby, Don't Tell on Me (vJR)	Voc 4747
W24240-2	Baby, Don't Tell on Me (vJR)	
W24241-1	One Hour (vHH)	Voc 4748
W24241-2	One Hour (vHH)	
W24242-1	Taxi War Dance	Voc 4748
W24242-2	Taxi War Dance	

NB: All takes also on *CBS(F) 66101*.

NYC, March 20, 1939:

W24243-1	Don't Worry 'bout Me (vHH)	Voc 4734
W24243-2	Don't Worry 'bout Me (vHH)	
W24244-1	Jump for Me	Voc 4886

NB: All takes also on *CBS(F) 66101*.

NYC, April 5, 1939:

W24337-A	And the Angels Sing (vHH)	Voc 4784
W24338-A	If I Didn't Care (vHH)	Voc 4784
W24339-A	Twelfth Street Rag	Voc 4886
W24340-A	Miss Thing, Part 1	Voc 4860
W24341-A	Miss Thing, Part 2	Voc 4860

NB: All takes also on *CBS(F) 66101*.

Chicago, May 19, 1939:
WC2594-C	Lonesome Miss Pretty	*Col CL 6079*
WC2595-B	Bolero at the Savoy (vHH)	unissued
WC2595-C	Bolero at the Savoy (vHH)	*Col G-31224*
WC2596-C	Nobody Knows (vJR)	Voc 5169
WC2697-C	Pound Cake	Voc 5085

NB: All except WC2595-B on *CBS(F) 66101*.

NBC broadcast, Hotel Sherman, Chicago, June 4, 1939:
Southland Shuffle	*JazzA JA-41*
One O'Clock Jump (nc)	unissued

NBC broadcast, Hotel Sherman, Chicago, June 5, 1939:
Moten's Swing	*JazzA JA-41*
Darktown Strutters' Ball	*JazzA JA-41*
One O'Clock Jump (theme)	*JazzA JA-41*

NBC broadcast, Hotel Sherman, Chicago, June 10, 1939:
I've Found a New Baby	*JP LP 23*
Thinking of You (nc)	unissued

Chicago, June 24, 1939:
WC2632-A	You Can Count on Me (vHH)	Voc 4967
WC2632-B	You Can Count on Me (vHH)	
WC2633-A	You & Your Love (vHH)	Voc 4967
WC2634-A	How Long Blues (vJR)	Voc 5010
WC2634-B	How Long Blues (vJR)	
WC2635-A	Sub-Deb Blues (vHH)	Voc 5010

NB: All takes on *CBS(F) 66101*.

CBS 'America Dances' broadcast, Famous Door, NYC, July 15, 1939:
One O'Clock Jump (theme)	unissued
Swingin' the Blues	*JazzA JA-42*
Rock-a-Bye Basie	*JazzA JA-41*
Don't Worry 'bout Me (vHH)	*JazzA JA-42*
Time Out	*JazzA JA-42*
Boogie Woogie Blues (vJR)	unissued
Roseland Shuffle	*JazzA JA-42*
White Sails (vHH)	unissued
Clap Hands, Here Comes Charlie	*JazzA JA-42*
One O'Clock Jump	unissued

NYC, August 4, 1939:
W24978-A	Moonlight Serenade (vHH)	Voc 5036
W24979-A	Song of the Islands	Voc 5169
W24980-A	I Can't Believe That You're in Love with Me (vJR)	Voc 5036
W24981-A	Clap Hands, Here Comes Charlie	Voc 5085

NB: All takes also on *CBS(F) 66101*.

FRANKIE NEWTON & HIS CAFE SOCIETY ORCHESTRA
Frankie Newton (tp); Wells (tb); Stanley Payne, Tab Smith (as); Kenneth Hollon (ts); Kenny Kersey (p); Ulysses Livingston (g); Johnny Williams (b); Eddie Dougherty (d).
NYC, August 15, 1939:

W25203-1	Vamp	Voc 5410
W25204-1	Parallel Fifths	Voc 5410

COUNT BASIE KANSAS CITY SEVEN
Buck Clayton (tp); Wells (tb); Lester Young (ts); Count Basie (p); Freddie Green (g); Walter Page (b); Jo Jones (d).
NYC, September 5, 1939:

W25296-1	Dickie's Dream	*CBS(F) 65384*
W25296-2	Dickie's Dream	*CBS(F) 65384*
W25296-3	Dickie's Dream (breakdown)	unissued
W25296-4	Dickie's Dream	Voc 5118
W25297-1	Lester Leaps In	*CBS(F) 65384*
W25297-2	Lester Leaps In	Voc 5118

NB: Above in actual take order; all except W25296-3 also on *CBS(F) 66101*.

COUNT BASIE & HIS ORCHESTRA
Personnel as before.
LA, November 6, 1939:

WCO26276-A	The Apple Jump	OKeh 5862
WCO26277-A	I Left My Baby (vJR)	Col 35231
WCO26278-A	Riff Interlude	Col 35231
WCO26279-A	Volcano	OKeh 6010

NB: All takes also on *CBS(F) 66101*.

LA, November 7, 1939:

WCO26280-A	Between the Devil & the Deep Blue Sea (vHH)	Col 35357
WCO26281-A	Ham 'n' Eggs	Col 35357
WCO26282-A	Hollywood Jump	Col 35338
WCO26283-A	Someday Sweetheart (vHH)	Col 35338

NB: All takes also on *CBS(F) 66101*.

JAM SESSION
Harry Edison, poss. Buck Clayton, u/k (tp); Benny Morton, Wells (tb); Lester Young, poss. Buddy Tate (ts); Albert Ammons, Count Basie, Fletcher Henderson, Pete Johnson, Meade Lux Lewis (p); Charlie Christian (g); Artie Bernstein, Walter Page (b); Nick Fatool, Jo Jones (d).
Spirituals To Swing Concert, Carnegie Hall, NYC, December 24, 1939:

Lady Be Good	*Van VRS 8524*

COUNT BASIE & HIS ORCHESTRA
Al Killian (tp) & Vic Dickenson (tb) replace Shad Collins & Benny Morton.
WBZ broadcast, Southland Theatre Restaurant, Boston, February 20, 1940:

One O'Clock Jump	*ColC CC-11*
Ebony Rhapsody	*ColC CC-11*
Riff Interlude	*ColC CC-11*
Darn That Dream (vHH)	*ColC CC-11*

Take It, Pres	*ColC CC-11*
Baby, Don't Tell on Me (vJR)	*ColC CC-11*
One Hour (vHH)	*JP LP 23*
I Got Rhythm	JSoc AA-602

NB: All titles also on *JSoc(Swe) AA-512*.

WBZ broadcast, Southland Theatre Restaurant, Boston, March 1, 1940:

Indiana	*Ev EV-3006*
Time Out	unissued
Twelfth Street Rag	*Ev EV-3006*

WBZ broadcast, Southland Theatre Restaurant, Boston, March 7, 1940:

Louisiana	*JazzA JA-42*
Green Bay	*JazzA JA-42*

WBZ broadcast, Southland Theatre Restaurant, Boston, March 9, 1940:

Basin Street Blues	*Ev EV-3006*
St. Louis Blues (nc)	unissued
Topsy	*Ev EV-3006*
One O'Clock Jump (theme)	unissued

WBZ broadcast, Southland Theatre Restaurant, Boston, March 12, 1940:

Doggin' Around	unissued
Tickle-Toe	unissued
I Left My Baby (vJR)	*Ev EV-3006*

WBZ broadcast, Southland Theatre Restaurant, Boston, March 13, 1940:

Rockin' in Rhythm	*Ev EV-3006*

NYC, March 19, 1940:

WCO26655-1	I Never Knew	Col 35521
WCO26656-1	Tickle-Toe	Col 35521
WCO26657-A	Let's Make Hay While The Moon Shines	Col 35500
WCO26657-B	Let's Make Hay While The Moon Shines	*Col G-31224*
WCO26657-?	Let's Make Hay While The Moon Shines	unissued
WCO26658-A	Louisiana	Col 35448
WCO26658-B	Louisiana	*Epic EG 7151*

NB: All except WCO26657-? also on *CBS(F)66101*.

NYC, March 20, 1940:

CO26659-A	Easy Does It	Col 35448
CO26660-A	Let Me See	OKeh 6330
CO26660-B	Let Me See	

NB: All takes also on *CBS(F) 66101*. Wells absent from two other titles recorded at this session.

Add Tab Smith (as).
NYC, May 31, 1940:

W26870-A	Blow Top	*Epic EG 7151*
W26870-B	Blow Top	OKeh 5629
W26871-A	Gone with 'What' Wind	*Epic LN 1117*
W26871-B	Gone with 'What' Wind	OKeh 5629

180

W26872-A	Superchief	OKeh 5673
W26873-A	You Can't Run Around (vJR)	OKeh 5673

NB: All takes also on *CBS(F) 66101*.

Omit Tab Smith.
Chicago, August 8, 1940:

WC3254-A	Evenin' (vJR)	OKeh 5732
WC3255-A	The World Is Mad, Part 1	OKeh 5816
WC3256-A	The World Is Mad, Part 2	OKeh 5816
WC3257-A	Moten's Swing	OKeh 5732
WC3258-A	It's Torture (vHH)	OKeh 5773
WC3259-A	I Want a Little Girl (vJR)	OKeh 5773

NB: All takes also on *CBS(F) 66101*.

NYC, October 30, 1940:

CO29006-1	All or Nothing At All (vHH)	OKeh 5884
CO29006-2	All or Nothing At All (vHH)	*Tax(Swe) m-8027*
CO29007-1	The Moon Fell in the River (vHH)	OKeh 5884
CO29007-2	The Moon Fell in the River (vHH)	
CO29008-1	What's Your Number?	OKeh 5897
CO29008-2	What's Your Number?	
CO29008-3	What's Your Number?	
CO29009-1	Draftin' Blues (vJR)	OKeh 5897
CO29009-2	Draftin' Blues (vJR)	
CO29009-3	Draftin' Blues (breakdown) (vJR)	
CO29009-4	Draftin' Blues (breakdown) (vJR)	

NB: All takes also on *CBS(F) 66101*.

NYC, November 19, 1940:

CO29087-1	Five O'Clock Whistle	
CO29087-2	Five O'Clock Whistle	
CO29087-3	Five O'Clock Whistle	OKeh 5922
CO29088-1	Love Jumped Out	*Col G-31224*
CO29088-2	Love Jumped Out	
CO29088-3	Love Jumped Out	OKeh 5963
CO29089-1	My Wanderin' Man (vHH)	OKeh 5922
CO29089-2	My Wanderin' Man (vHH)	
CO29089-3	My Wanderin' Man (vHH)	
CO29090-1	Broadway	OKeh 6095
CO29090-2	Broadway	

NB: All takes also on *CBS(F) 66101*.

Add Tab Smith (as); Paul Bascomb (ts) replaces Lester Young.
NYC, December 13, 1940:

CO29246-1	It's the Same Old South (vJR)	OKeh 5963
CO29246-2	It's the Same Old South (vJR)	
CO29246-3	It's the Same Old South (vJR)	*Col G-31224*
CO29247-1	Stampede in G Minor	OKeh 5987
CO29247-2	Stampede in G Minor	
CO29247-3	Stampede in G Minor	
CO29248-1	Who Am I? (vHH)	OKeh 5987

CO29249-1	Rockin' the Blues	OKeh 6010
CO29249-2	Rockin' the Blues!	

NB: All takes also on *CBS(F) 66101*.

Ed Cuffee (tb) replaces Vic Dickenson & Don Byas (ts) replaces Paul Bascomb.
NYC, January 20, 1941:

CO29521-1	It's Square but It Rocks (vHH)	OKeh 6047
CO29521-2	It's Square but It Rocks (vHH)	
CO29521-3	It's Square but It Rocks (vHH)	
CO29521-4	It's Square but It Rocks (vHH)	
CO29522-1	I'll Forget (vHH)	OKeh 6122

NB: All takes also on *CBS(F) 66101*.

NYC, January 22, 1941:

CO29533-1	You Lied to Me (vHH)	OKeh 6267
CO29534-1	Wiggle Woogie	OKeh 6157
CO29534-2	Wiggle Woogie	
CO29535-1	Beau Brummel	OKeh 6122
CO29535-2	Beau Brummel	
CO29535-3	Beau Brummel	
CO29535-4	Beau Brummel	

NB: All takes also on *CBS(F) 66101*.

NYC, January 28, 1941:

CO29580-1	Music Makers	OKeh 6047
CO29580-2	Music Makers	
CO29581-1	Jump the Blues Away	OKeh 6157
CO29581-2	Jump the Blues Away	
CO29582-1	Deep in the Blues (vHH)	
CO29582-2	Deep in the Blues (vHH)	unissued
CO29583-1	The Jitters	OKeh 6095
CO29583-2	The Jitters	*Tax(Swe) m-8027*
CO29583-r	The Jitters	
CO28584-1	Tuesday at Ten	OKeh 6071
CO28585-1	Undecided Blues (vJR)	OKeh 6071

NB: All takes except CO29582-2 also on *CBS(F) 66101*. CO29583-r is a rehearsal take.

Add Coleman Hawkins (ts*).
Chicago, April 10, 1941:

C3677-1	I Do Mean You	OKeh 6180
C3678-1	9:20 Special*	OKeh 6244
C3678-2	9:20 Special*	
C3679-1	H & J	OKeh 6365
C3679-2	H & J	
C3680-1	Feedin' The Bean*	OKeh 6180
C3680-2	Feedin' The Bean*	
C3681-1	Goin' to Chicago Blues (vJR)	OKeh 6244

NB: All takes also on *CBS(F) 66101*, except C3680-2, which is on *CBS(F) 66102*.

Kenny Clarke (d*) replaces Jo Jones. Earle Warren also (vo).
NYC, May 21, 1941

CO30520-1	You Betcha My Life* (vEW)	
CO30520-2	You Betcha My Life* (vEW)	OKeh 6221
CO30520-3	You Betcha My Life* (breakdown) (vEW)	
CO30521-1	Down, Down, Down*	OKeh 6221
CO30521-2	Down, Down, Down*	OKeh 6221
CO30521-3	Down, Down, Down*	
CO30522-1	Tune Town Shuffle	OKeh 6267
CO30522-2	Tune Town Shuffle	
CO30522-3	Tune Town Shuffle	
CO30523-1	I'm Tired of Waiting for You (vJR)	
CO30523-2	I'm Tired of Waiting for You (vJR)	unissued

NB: All takes except CO30523-2 also on *CBS(F) 66101*.

Eli Robinson & Robert Scott (tb); Maxine Johnson (vo) replace Ed Cuffee, Dan Minor, & Helen Humes.
RCM film soundies, NYC, July/August, 1941:

Airmail Special	*ExR LP 1004*
Take Me Back, Baby (vJR)	*Stv SLP 6000*

CBS broadcast, Cafe Society Uptown, NYC, September 19, 1941:

There'll Be Some Changes Made (vJR)	*JzU JU-4*
9:20 Special	unissued
You Betcha My Life	unissued
Tuesday at Ten	*JzU JU-4*
One O'Clock Jump (theme)	unissued

CBS broadcast, Cafe Society Uptown, NYC, September 20, 1941:

Yes Indeed (vJR)	*JzU JU-4*
Tom Thumb	*JzU JU-4*
9:20 Special	*JzU JU-4*
I Guess I'll Have To Dream the Rest (vEW)	*JzU JU-4*
Basie Boogie	unissued
There'll Be Some Changes Made (vJR)	*JzU JU-5*
Gone with 'What' Wind	unissued
One O'Clock Jump (theme)	unissued

CBS broadcast, Cafe Society Uptown, NYC, September 23, 1941:

Diggin' for Dex	*JzU JU-5*
Be Fair (vEW)	unissued
Love Jumped Out	*JzU JU-5*
Tune Town Shuffle	*JzU JU-5*
My Melancholy Baby (vJR)	*JzU JU-5*
Every Tub	*JzU JU-5*

Add Lynne Sherman (vo).
NYC, September 24, 1941:

CO31353-1	My Old Flame (vLS)	OKeh 6527

CO31353-2	My Old Flame (vLS)	
CO31354-1	Fiesta in Blue	OKeh 6440
CO31354-2	Fiesta in Blue	
CO31354-3	Fiesta in Blue	
CO31354-4	Fiesta in Blue	
CO31354-5	Fiesta in Blue	
CO31355-1	Tom Thumb	OKeh 6527
CO31356-1	Take Me Back, Baby (vJR)	OKeh 6440

NB: All takes also on *CBS(F) 66102* except CO31353-1/2, which are on *CBS(F) 66101*.

Paul Robeson (vo) replaces Lynne Sherman.
NYC, October 1, 1941:

CO31373-1	King Joe, Part 1 (vPR)	OKeh 6475
CO31373-2	King Joe, Part 1 (vPR)	
CO31374-1	King Joe, Part 2 (vPR)	OKeh 6475
CO31374-2	King Joe, Part 2 (vPR)	
CO31375-1	Moon Nocturne (vEW)	OKeh 6449
CO31376-1	Something New	OKeh 6449
CO31376-2	Something New	*PH P 07873 R*

NB: All takes also on *CBS(F) 66102*.

CBS broadcast, Cafe Society Uptown, NYC, October 2, 1941:

Out the Window (nc)	unissued
I Want a Little Girl (vJR)	*JzU JU-5*
Rockin' the Blues	*JzU JU-5*
What Word Is Sweeter than Sweetheart? (vEW)	unissued
Something New	*JzU JU-5*
Topsy	*JzU JU-5*
Airmail Special (nc)	unissued

CBS broadcast, Cafe Society Uptown, NYC, October 6, 1941:

Wiggle Woogie (nc)	unissued
Flamingo	unissued
Tom Thumb	*JzU JU-5*
One-Two-Three-O'Lairy (vJR)	unissued
I Do Mean You	*JzU JU-5*
Tuesday at Ten	unissued
Moten's Swing (theme)	unissued

CBS broadcast, Cafe Society Uptown, NYC, October 7, 1941:

[Untitled Original]	*JzU JU-5*
Down, Down, Down	*JzU JU-5*
Take Me Back, Baby (vJR)	*JzU JU-4*
Blue Lou	unissued
I Found You in the Rain (vEW)	unissued
Broadway	*JzU JU-4*
Sweet Georgia Brown (nc)	*JzU JU-4*

184

CBS broadcast, Cafe Society Uptown, NYC, October 21, 1941:
        H & J   *JzU JU-4*
        Diggin' for Dex   *JzU JU-4*
        Goin' to Chicago (vJR)   *JzU JU-4*

CBS broadcast, Cafe Society Uptown, NYC, October 25, 1941:
        Baby, Don't Tell on Me (vJR)   *JzU JU-4*
        Swinging the Blues   *JzU JU-4*
        One O'Clock Jump (theme)   *JzU JU-4*

Add Lynne Sherman (vo).
NYC, November 3, 1941:

CO31642-1	I Struck a Match in the Dark (vEW)	OKeh 6508
CO31642-2	I Struck a Match in the Dark (vEW)	unissued
CO31642-3	I Struck a Match in the Dark (vEW)	unissued
CO31642-4	I Struck a Match in the Dark (vEW)	unissued
CO31643-1	Platterbrains	
CO31643-2	Platterbrains	OKeh 6508
CO31643-3	Platterbrains	
CO31644-1	All of Me (vLS)	Col 36675
CO31644-2	All of Me (vLS)	
CO31644-3	All of Me (extract) (vLS)	

NB: All issued takes also on *CBS(F) 66102*.

NYC, November 17, 1941:

CO31765-1	Feather Merchant	Col 36845
CO31765-2	Feather Merchant	
CO31765-3	Feather Merchant	
CO31766-1	Down for Double	OKeh 6584
CO31766-2	Down for Double	*Epic LN 3169*
CO31767-1	More than You Know (vLS)	OKeh 6584
CO31767-2	More than You Know (vLS)	
CO31768-1	Harvard Blues (vJR)	OKeh 6564
CO31768-2	Harvard Blues (vJR)	*Tax(Swe) m-8027*
CO31769-1	Coming Out Party	*Tax(Swe) m-8027*
CO31769-2	Coming Out Party	OKeh 6564

NB: All takes also on *CBS(F) 66102*.

Add Harry Nemo (vo).
NYC, January 21, 1942:

CO32274-1	One O'Clock Jump	OKeh 6634
CO32274-2	One O'Clock Jump	
CO32275-1	Blue Shadows & White Gardenias (vEW)	OKeh 6626
CO32276-1	'Ay Now (vHN)	OKeh 6626
CO32276-2	'Ay Now (vJR/band)	
CO32276-3	'Ay Now (vHN/band)	
CO32277-1	For the Good of Your Country (vJR)	
CO32277-2	For the Good of Your Country (vJR)	

NB: All takes also on *CBS(F) 66102*.

Jerry Blake (as) replaces Tab Smith.
Chicago, April 3, 1942:

C4225-1	Basie Blues	Col 36601
C4225-2	Basie Blues	
C4226-1	Outskirts of Town (vJR)	Col 36601
C4227-1	Time on My Hands (vEW)	

NB: All takes also on *CBS(F) 66102*.

Caughey Roberts (as) replaces Jerry Blake.
LA, July 27, 1942:

HCO888-1	Rusty Dusty Blues (vJR)	Col 36675
HCO889-1	Ride On (vEW/band)	Col 36647
HCO890-1	Lose the Blackout Blues (vJR)	*Tax(Swe) m-8025*
HCO891-1	Time on My Hands (vEW)	Col 36685
HCO892-1	It's Sand, Man!	Col 36647
HCO893-1	Ain't It the Truth?	Col 36845
HCO893-2	Ain't It the Truth?	
HCO893-3	Ain't It the Truth?	
HCO894-1	For the Good of Your Country (vJR)	Col 36685

NB: All takes also on *CBS(F) 66102*.

Add Louis Taylor (tb); Jimmy Powell (as) replaces Caughey Roberts.
Soundtrack for UA film *Stage Door Canteen*, Astoria, R.I., February 8–10, 1943:

Quicksand	*ExR LP 1002*

Snooky Young (tp) replaces Al Killian. Thelma Carpenter (vo).
AFRS Jubilee 28 transcription, LA, June 7, 1943:

Basie Boogie	*SwT LP-101*
Don't Get Around Much Anymore (vTC)	unissued
Dance of the Gremlins	*SwT LP-101*
Baby, Won't You Please Come Home? (vJR)	unissued
Green	*SwT LP-101*
Them There Eyes (vTC)	unissued
One O'Clock Jump	unissued

AFRS Command Performance 70 transcription, Hollywood, mid-June 1943:

Dance of the Gremlins	V-Disc 34
G. I. Stomp (Red Bank Boogie)	V-Disc 34

AFRS Down Beat 60 transcriptions, Hollywood, June or July 1943:

One O'Clock Jump (theme)	*SH-SWH-23*
Rhythm Man	V-Disc 175
You'll Never Know (vEW)	*SH SWH-23*
Blue Lou	*JP LP 18*
The Chicks I Pick Are Slender Tender & Tall (vJR)	*Queen (I) Q-025*
As Time Goes By (vTC)	unissued
It's Sand, Man!	*Palm Club(F) 31*
Boogie Woogie (vJR)	*JP LP 18*

186

Yeah! Man	V-Disc 175
Jazz Me Blues	JSoc AA-552
One O'Clock Jump (theme)	unissued

Ida James (vo) replaces Thelma Carpenter.
AFRS Jubilee 32 transcriptions, Hollywood, July 5, 1943:

Airmail Special	*SH SWH-41*
After You've Gone (vIJ)	*SH SWH-41*
St. Louis Blues (vJR)	*SH SWH-41*
Cabin in the Sky (vEW)	*SH SWH-41*
Exactly Like You (vJR)	unissued
I Won't Say I Will (vIJ)	*SH SWH-41*
Swing Shift (nc)	*SH SWH-41*
One O'Clock Jump (theme)	unissued

Bobby Brooks Quartet (vo) replaces Ida James.
Soundtrack for Universal film, *Top Man*, Universal City, California, August 1–6, 1943:

Basie Boogie	unissued
Basie Boogie	*Ri-Disc(Swi) RD-9*
Wrap Your Troubles in Dreams (vBBQ)	unissued

Harry Edison, Ed Lewis, Joe Newman, Snooky Young (tp); Eli Robinson, Robert Scott, Louis Taylor, Wells (tb); Jimmy Powell (as); Earle Warren (as/vo); Buddy Tate, Lester Young (ts); Rudy Rutherford (cl/bs); Count Basie (p); Freddie Green (g); Rodney Richardson (b); Jo Jones (d); Thelma Carpenter, Jimmy Rushing (vo).
AFRS GI Jive Transcription, NYC, November/December 1943:

Jumpin' at the Woodside	*JSoc 64711*

AFRS Jubilee transcriptions, NYC, prob. December 6, 1943:

One O'Clock Jump (theme)	unissued
Jumpin' at the Woodside	*FH FH-55*
Baby Won't You Please Come Home? (vJR)	unissued
Do Nothin' till You Hear from Me (vTC)	*SH SWH-41*
Don't Believe Everything You Dream (vEW)	*SH-SWH-23*
I've Found a New Baby	*SwT LP-101*
One O'Clock Jump (theme)	unissued
I've Found a New Baby (alt)	*HEP(E) CD-38*
Andy's Blues	*HEP(E) CD-38*
Outskirts of Town (vJR)	*HEP(E) CD-38*
Jumpin' at the Woodside (alt)	*HEP(E) CD-38*
My Ideal (vTC)	*HEP(E) CD-38*
Do Nothin' till You Hear from Me (alt) (vTC)	*HEP(E) CD-38*
Lady Be Good	unissued

NB: Items 1–7 comprised AFRS Jubilee 55.

DICKY WELLS & HIS ORCHESTRA
Bill Coleman (tp); Wells (tb); Lester Young (ts); Ellis Larkins (p); Freddie
Green (g); Al Hall (b); Jo Jones (d).
NYC, December 21, 1943:

T19003-1	I Got Rhythm	Sig 90002
T19004-1	I'm Fer It, Too	Sig 90002
T19004-2	I'm Fer It, Too	*JS ELP 7001*
T1919-1	Hello Babe	*JS ELP 7001*
T1919-2	Hello Babe	Sig 28115
T1920-1	Linger Awhile	Sig 28115

NB: All takes also on *RCA(F) FXM3-7324*.

COUNT BASIE & HIS ORCHESTRA
As before, except Al Killian (tp) & Ted Donnelly (tb) replace Snooky Young
& Robert Scott. Omit Freddie Green.
Lang-Worth transcriptions, NYC, January 10, 1944:

Do Nothin' till You Hear from Me (vTC)	*Palm(E) 30-12*
Don't Believe Everything You Dream (vEW)	*Palm(E) 30-12*
Don't Cry Baby (vJR)	*Palm(E) 30-12*
I've Had This Feeling Before (vEW)	*Palm(E) 30-12*
Sent for You Yesterday (vJR)	*Palm(E) 30-12*
Wiggle Woogie	*Palm Club(F) 31*
I Couldn't Sleep a Wink Last Night (vEW)	*BlH BH6-605*
Basie Boogie	*Palm(E) 30-12*
9:20 Special	*Palm Club(F) 31*
Down for Double	*Palm Club(F) 31*
I've Found a New Baby	*BlH BH6-605*
Rock-a-Bye Basie	*Palm(E) 30-12*
Swing Shift	*JP LP 18*
Red Bank Boogie	*Palm(E) 30-12*
Rockin' the Blues	*Palm(E) 30-12*
One O'Clock Jump (short)	*FTOR FTR 2501*
One O'Clock Jump (long)	*BlH BH1-109*
Shoo Shoo Baby (vTC)	unissued

KANSAS CITY SEVEN
Buck Clayton (tp); Wells (tb); Lester Young (ts); Count Basie (p); Freddie
Green (g); Rodney Richardson (b); Jo Jones (d).
NYC, March 22, 1944:

HL21-1	After Theater Jump	
HL21-2	After Theater Jump	Key K-1302
HL22-1	Six Cats & a Prince	
HL22-2	Six Cats & a Prince	Met B517
HL22-3	Six Cats & a Prince	Key K-1303
HL24-1	Destination K.C.	*EmA MG 26010*
HL24-2	Destination K.C.	Key K-1303

NB: Wells not on HL23-1; all takes also on *Phonogram/Keynote (J) 18JP-1054*.

KANSAS CITY SIX
Bill Coleman (tp); Wells (tb); Lester Young (ts); Joe Bushkin (p); John Simmons (b); Jo Jones (d).
NYC, March 28, 1944:

A-4746-1	Three Little Words	*Com XFL 15352*
A-4746-2	Three Little Words	*Com XFL 15352*
A-4746-3	Three Little Words	Com C 573
A-4746	Three Little Words	*Com XFL 15352*
A-4747-1	Jo-Jo	Com C 555
A-4747-2	Jo-Jo	*Com XFL 15352*
A-4747-3	Jo-Jo (breakdown)	
A-4747-4	Jo-Jo	*Com XFL 15352*
A-4747-1/3	Jo-Jo (composite)	*Com XFL 15352*
A-4748-1	I Got Rhythm	Com C 555
A-4748-2	I Got Rhythm	*Com XFL 15352*
A-4748	I Got Rhythm	*Com XFL 15352*
A-4749-1	Four O'Clock Drag	*Com XFL 15352*
A-4749-2	Four O'Clock Drag	Com C 573
A-4749-2/1	Four O'Clock Drag (composite)	*Com XFL 15352*

NB: All takes also on *Mosaic MR23-128*.

COUNT BASIE & HIS ORCHESTRA
As before; add Freddie Green (g).
Carnegie Hall, NYC, April 2, 1944:

Ain't Misbehavin'	*Ev EV-3002*
I'm Gonna Sit Right Down & Write	unissued
Myself a Letter (vJR)	

AFRS One Night Stand 198, Blue Room, Hotel Lincoln, NYC, April 7, 1944:

One O'Clock Jump (theme)	unissued
Diggin' for Dex	*Car LP-431*
My Ideal (vTC)	*J&J JJ 604*
Blue Lou	*J&J JJ 604*
Ain't It the Truth?	*Car LP-431*
Take Me Back, Baby (vJR)	*SwT LP 101*
And So Little Time	*J&J JJ 604*
Journey to a Star (vEW)	*J&J JJ 604*
Jumpin' at the Woodside	*JP LP 2*
One O'Clock Jump (theme)	unissued

WOR-Mutual broadcast, Blue Room, Hotel Lincoln, NYC, April 10, 1944:

One O'Clock Jump (theme)	unissued
My! What a Fry!	*Ev EV-3002*
Absent-Minded (nc)	unissued
One O'Clock Jump (theme)	*Ev EV-3002*

WOR-Mutual & CBS broadcasts, Blue Room, Hotel Lincoln, NYC, April 14, 1944:

Bangs	*Ev EV-3004*
Ain't But the One (vBand)	*Ev EV-3004*
Don't Cry, Baby (nc)	unissued

| | I've Found a New Baby | Ev EV-3002 |
| | King Porter's Stomp | Ev EV-3004 |

AFRS One Night Stand transcriptions, Blue Room, Hotel Lincoln, NYC, April 17, 1944:

	One O'Clock Jump (theme)	unissued
	Avenue C	Queen(I) Q-025
	Tess' Torch Song (vTC)	Queen(I) Q-025
	I'm Gonna Sit Right Down & Write Myself a Letter (vJR)	Queen (I) Q-025
	Rock-a-Bye Basie	Queen(I) Q-025
	And So Little Time (vEW)	unissued
	Dance of the Gremlins	Queen(I) Q-025
	When They Ask about You (vTC)	Queen(I) Q-025
	One O'Clock Jump (theme)	unissued

EARLE WARREN & HIS ORCHESTRA
Same as last except Clyde Hart (p) replaces Count Basie.
NYC, April 18, 1944:

S5440-1	Empty Hearted (vEW)	Savoy 507
S5441-1	Circus in Rhythm	Savoy 508
S5441-2	Circus in Rhythm	Savoy MG 12071
S5441-3	Circus in Rhythm	
S5442-1	Poor Little Plaything (vEW)	Savoy 508
S5442-2	Poor Little Plaything (vEW)	
S5443-1	Tush	
S5443-2	Tush	Savoy 507

NB: All takes except S5440-1 also on Savoy SJL-2202.

COUNT BASIE & HIS ORCHESTRA
As before.
CBS broadcast, Blue Room, Hotel Lincoln, NYC, April 21, 1944:

| | Kansas City Stride | Ev EV-3002 |
| | One O'Clock Jump (theme) | unissued |

AFRS ONS 228 transcriptions, Blue Room, Hotel Lincoln, NYC, April 24, 1944:

	Hey! Rube	unissued
	I Dream of You (vTC)	unissued
	Basie Blues	unissued
	Irresistable You (vEW)	unissued
	Ain't Misbehavin'	SwT LP 101
	I'm in Love with Someone (vTC)	unissued
	Jumpin' at the Woodside	SwT LP 101
	9:20 Special	unissued

WOR-Mutual broadcast, same venue & date:

	One O'Clock Jump (theme)	unissued
	I've Found a New Baby	unissued
	Tess' Torch Song (vTC)	unissued
	Jazz Me Blues	Ev EV-3002
	I Couldn't Sleep a Wink Last Night (nc) (vEW)	unissued

190

Blue Lou	*Ev EV-3004*
My Melancholy Baby (nc) (vJR)	unissued
Avenue C	unissued
One O'Clock Jump (theme)	unissued

WOR-Mutual broadcasts, Blue Room, Hotel Lincoln, April–May 1944:

One O'Clock Jump (theme)	unissued
Dinah	*Ev EV-3002*
And So Little Time	unissued
Blue Room Jump (Andy's Blues)	*Ev EV-3002*
One O'Clock Jump (theme)	unissued
Tush	*Ev EV-3002*
This I Love Above All (vEW)	unissued

AFRS Down Beat transcriptions, NYC, May 5, 1944:

One O'Clock Jump (theme)	*Queen (I) Q-025*
I've Found a New Baby	JSoc AA-604
Avenue C	JSoc AA-604
Do Nothing till You Hear from Me (vTC)	*Queen (I) Q-025*
Basie Boogie	*JP LP 18*
Harvard Blues (vJR)	*Queen(I) Q-025*
My Ideal (vTC)	*Joyce LP 1062*
Exactly Like You (vJR)	*J&J JJ 604*
Beaver Junction	*J&J JJ 604*
One O'Clock Jump (theme)	*Queen (I) Q-025*

WOR-Mutual broadcast, Blue Room, Hotel Lincoln, NYC, May 13, 1944:

One O'Clock Jump (theme)	unissued
Hey! Rube	unissued
Tush	*Car LP 431*
This Is a Lovely Way To Spend an Evening (vTC)	unissued
Rock-a-Bye Basie	unissued
Harvard Blues (nc)	unissued
Jazz Me Blues	*Car LP 431*
I Couldn't Sleep a Wink Last Night (vEW)	unissued
I Never Knew (vJR)	unissued
One O'Clock Jump (theme)	unissued

WOR-Mutual broadcast, Blue Room, Hotel Lincoln, NYC, May 17, 1944:

Every Tub	*IAJRC 17*

Add Freddie Bryant (vo).
WOR-Mutual broadcast, Blue Room, Hotel Lincoln, NYC, same date:

I Never Knew	unissued
This I Love Above All (vFB)	unissued
Let's Mop It (vTC)	unissued
I Want a Little Girl (vJR)	unissued
Dance of the Gremlins	*Car LP 431*
How Blue the Night (vTC)	unissued

191

Too Much in Love (vEW)	unissued
Blue Room Jump (Andy's Blues)	*Car LP 431*
One O'Clock Jump (theme)	unissued

Omit Bryant.
CBS broadcast, Blue Room, Hotel Lincoln, NYC, May 20, 1944:

Call Me Darling (vTC)	*Ev EV-3002*
Ain't It the Truth?	*Ev EV-3002*

CBS broadcast, Blue Room, Hotel Lincoln, NYC, May 22, 1944:

It's Sand, Man!	*SwT LP 101*
I Dream of You (vTC)	unissued
Circus in Rhythm	*SwT LP 101*
Time Alone Will Tell (vEW)	unissued
I'm in Love with Someone (vTC)	unissued
Swing Shift	*SwT LP 101*
Gee, Baby, Ain't I Good to You? (vJR)	*SwT LP 101*
Jumpin' at the Woodside	*Ev EV-3002*
One O'Clock Jump (theme)	unissued
Gee, Baby, Ain't I Good to You? (vJR)	unissued
One O'Clock Jump (theme)	unissued

NB: Items 1–8 used for AFRS ONS 269.

Add Freddie Bryant (vo).
Lang-Worth transcriptions, NYC, May 25, 1944:

Tush	*BlH BH3-308*
This I Love above All (vFB)	*BlH BH1-109*
Circus in Rhythm	*BlH BH6-605*
I Dream of You (vTC)	*BlH BH3-308*
Ain't It the Truth?	*BlH BH6-605*
Time Alone Will Tell (vFB)	*Palm(E) 30-12*
I'm Gonna Sit Right Down & Write Myself a Letter (vJR)	*JP LP 18*
Let's Jump	*Palm(E) 30-12*

Omit Bryant.
Liederkranz Hall, NYC, May 27, 1944:

VP711-XP33591	Kansas City Stride	V-Disc 258
VP712-XP33592	Beaver Junction	V-Disc 258
VP731-XP33597	Circus in Rhythm	V-Disc 289
VP732-XP33598	Aunt Hagar's Country Home (vEW)	*JSoc AA-506*
VP733-XP33599	Gee, Baby, Ain't I Good to You? (vJR)	V-Disc 552
J509-ND7TC-1412	Basie Strides Again (Along Avenue C)	V-Disc 813
	Call Me Darling (vTC)	unissued

WOR-Mutual broadcast, Blue Room, Hotel Lincoln, NYC, May 29, 1944:

One O'Clock Jump (theme)	unissued
Blue Lou	unissued
Call Me Darling (vTC)	*Car LP 431*
Jazz Me Blues	unissued
Harvard Blues (nc) (vJR)	unissued
My! What a Fry!	*Car LP 431*
Time on My Hands (vEW)	unissued
Avalon	*Car LP 431*
One O'Clock Jump (theme)	unissued

CBS broadcast, Blue Room, Hotel Lincoln, NYC, May 30, 1944:

The Jumpin' Jive	unissued
I'm in Love with Someone (vTC)	unissued
Kansas City Stride	unissued
Tess' Torch Song (vTC)	unissued
There'll Be Some Changes Made (vJR)	*Car LP 431*
Let's Jump	unissued
Time Alone Will Tell (vEW)	unissued
Jumpin' at the Woodside	unissued
One O'Clock Jump (theme)	unissued

AFRS transcriptions, NYC, poss May, 1944:

One O'Clock Jump (theme)	*JP LP 18*
Let's Jump	JSoc AA-555
Andy's Blues	*JSoc 67411*
Jumpin' at the Woodside	*JP LP 18*

JAMMIN' THE BLUES
Harry Edison (tp); Wells (tb); Illinois Jacquet, Lester Young (ts); Marlowe Morris (p); Barney Kessel (g); Red Callender (b); Sidney Catlett (d); Marie Bryant (vo).
Film soundtrack, LA, early August 1944:

Blues for Marvin	*JazzA JA-18*
One Hour (vMB)	*JazzA JA-18*

NB: Wells not on other performances from this film.

COUNT BASIE & HIS ORCHESTRA
Harry Edison, Al Killian, Ed Lewis (tp); Ted Donnelly, Eli Robinson, Louis Taylor, Wells (tb); Jimmy Powell (as); Earle Warren (as/vo); Buddy Tate, Lester Young (ts); Rudy Rutherford (cl/bs); Basie (p); Freddie Green (g); Rodney Richardson (b); Jo Jones (d); Thelma Carpenter, Jimmy Rushing (vo).
AFRS Jubilee transcriptions, LA, September 11, 1944:

One O'Clock Jump (theme)*	unissued
Avenue C*	unissued
Avenue C (alt)	*Hep CD-38*
More than You Know* (vTC)	unissued
More than You Know (alt) (vTC)	*Hep CD-38*
Basie Boogie*	*Car LP 432*
Basie's Bag (Basie Boogie: alt)	*Hep CD-38*
Harvard Blues* (vJR)	unissued

Harvard Blues (alt) (vJR)	*Hep CD-38*
I'll Be Seeing You* (vEW)	unissued
I'll Be Seeing You (alt) (vEW)	unissued
Jumpin' at the Woodside*	*JP LP 2*
Jumpin' at the Woodside (alt)	*HEP CD-38*
Let's Jump	*HEP CD-38*
One O'Clock Jump (theme)*	unissued

NB: *transcribed for AFRS Jubilee 96.

Add the King Sisters (vo), Illinois Jacquet (ts+).
AFRS Jubilee transcriptions, LA, September 18, 1944:

One O'Clock Jump (theme)*	unissued
Let's Jump*	unissued
Swing Shift	*Hind HSR-224*
Gee, Baby, Ain't I Good to You?* (vJR)	unissued
Gee, Baby, Ain't I Good to You? (alt) (vJR)	*Hind HSR-224*
Snoqualmie Jo-Jo* (vKS)	unissued
Do Nothin' till You Hear from Me* (vTC)	unissued
Beaver Junction	*Hep CD-38*
+My! What a Fry!*	unissued
+My! What a Fry! (alt)	*Hep CD-38*
One O'Clock Jump (theme)*	unissued

NB: *transcribed for AFRS Jubilee 97.

Jimmy Keith (ts) & Buddy Rich (d) replace Lester Young & Jo Jones. Add Artie Shaw (cl).
AFRS Jubilee transcriptions, Hollywood, September 25, 1944:

One O'Clock Jump (theme)*	*SH SWH-23*
Rhythm Man*	*Car LP 432*
I'm Gonna Sit Right Down & Write Myself a Letter* (vJR)	unissued
Lady Be Good*	*SoS LP 125*
Lady Be Good (alt)	*Hind HSR-224*
Blues*	*SoS LP 125*
Bird Calls (Blues: alt)	*Hind HSR-224*
Embraceable You* (vTC)	unissued
Kansas City Stride*	*SH SWH-23*
One O'Clock Jump (theme)*	unissued

NB: *transcribed for AFRS Jubilee 98.

Illinois Jacquet (ts) replaces Jimmy Keith. Add Joe Newman (tp).
AFRS Jubilee transcriptions, Hollywood, October 2, 1944:

One O'Clock Jump (theme)*	unissued
Dinah*	*Car LP 432*
Dinah (alt)	*Hep CD-38*
Baby, Won't You Please Come Home?* (vJR)	*Car LP 432*
Baby, Won't You Please Come Home? (alt) (vJR)	*Hep CD-38*
Rock-a-Bye Basie*	*Car LP 432*

	Rock-a-Bye Basie (alt)	*Hind HSR-224*
	Call Me Darling* (vTC)	*GE LP 55001*
	Call Me Darling (alt) (vTC)	*Hind HSR-224*
	One O'Clock Jump*	*Car LP 432*
	One O'Clock Jump (alt)	*Hep CD-38*
	One O'Clock Jump (short)	*Car LP 432*

NB: *transcribed for AFRS Jubilee 99.

Poss. Jesse Price (d) replaces Buddy Rich.
NBC For the Record broadcast, NYC, October 30, 1944:

My! What a Fry!	*GE LP 55001*
Harvard Blues (vJR)	V-Disc 369
One O'Clock Jump (theme)	unissued

WMCA broadcast, Apollo Theatre, NYC, November 1, 1944:

One O'Clock Jump	*Ev EV-3003*

Al Stearns (tp), Lucky Thompson (ts) & Shadow Wilson (d) replace Ed Lewis, Illinois Jacquet & Jesse Price.
NYC, December 6, 1944:

CO33953-1	Taps Miller	Col 36831
CO33954-1	Jimmy's Blues (vJR)	Col 36831
CO33954-2	Jimmy's Blues (vJR)	
CO33955-1	I Didn't Know about You (vTC)	Col 36766
CO33956-1	Red Bank Boogie	Col 36766
CO33956-2	Red Bank Boogie	

NB: All takes on *CBS(F) 66102*.

Ed Lewis (tp) replaces Al Stearns.
WOR-Mutual broadcast, Blue Room, Hotel Lincoln, NYC, December 1944:

One O'Clock Jump (theme)	unissued
Swing Shift	*Ev EV-3004*
Beaver Junction	*Ev EV-3004*

CBS broadcast, Blue Room, Hotel Lincoln, NYC, December 23, 1944:

One O'Clock Jump (theme)	unissued
It's Sand, Man!	*Ev EV-3004*
Blue Room Jump (Andy's Blues)	*Ev EV-3004*
Kansas City Stride	*Ev EV-3004*
One O'Clock Jump (theme)	unissued

WOR-Mutual broadcast, Blue Room, Hotel Lincoln, NYC, December 27, 1944:

Red Bank Boogie	unissued
Taps Miller (nc)	*Ev EV-3004*
Jumpin' at the Woodside	unissued

WOR-Mutual broadcast, Blue Room, Hotel Lincoln, NYC, January 1, 1945:

Love Jumped Out	*Ev EV-3004*
After a While (nc) (vEW)	unissued
One O'Clock Jump (theme)	unissued

Joe Marshall (d) replaces Shadow Wilson.
CBS Playhouse No. 2, NYC, January 11, 1945:

VP1115	Taps Miller	V-Disc 419
VP1116	Jimmy's Blues (vJR)	V-Disc 460
VP1116	Take Me Back, Baby (vJR)	V-Disc 460
VP1120	Playhouse No. 2 Stomp	V-Disc 493
VP1176	Just an Old Manuscript	V-Disc 575
VP1280	On the Upbeat	V-Disc 468
	All of Me	unissued
	Call Me Darling (vTC)	unissued

NB: All issued takes on *JSoc AA-505*.

Shadow Wilson (d) & Maxine Johnson (vo) replace Joe Marshall & Thelma Carpenter.
AFRS One Night Stand 551 transcriptions, Blue Room, Hotel Lincoln, NYC, January 25, 1945:

One O'Clock Jump (theme)	*CassO 0514*
Red Bank Boogie	*CassO 0514*
This Heart of Mine (vMJ)	*CassO 0514*
I'm Gonna See My Baby (vJR)	*CassO 0514*
Paging Mr. Green	*CassO 0514*
Sleigh Ride in July	*CassO 0514*

CBS broadcast, Blue Room, Hotel Lincoln, NYC, January 31, 1945:

[Unidentified title] (nc)	unissued
I Didn't Know about You (vMJ)	unissued
One O'Clock Jump (theme)	unissued
I'm Fer It, Too	*Ev EV-3004*
Taps Miller	unissued
Avenue C	*Ev EV-3004*
One O'Clock Jump (theme)	unissued

AFRS One Night Stand 551 transcriptions, Blue Room, Hotel Lincoln, NYC, February 2, 1945:

Swing Shift	*Flute FL-7*
Solo Flight	
Wish You Were Waiting for Me (vMJ)	
Together (vJR)	
Hey! Rube (nc)	

NB: All titles also on *Cassette Only 0514*.

NBC Fitch Bandwagon program, Blue Room, Hotel Lincoln, NYC, February 4, 1945:

One O'Clock Jump (theme)	*GOJ LP 1004*
Aces & Faces	*GOJ LP 1004*
Don't Cry, Baby (vJR)	*GOJ LP 1004*
Just an Old Manuscript	*GOJ LP 1004*
One O'Clock Jump (theme)	*GOJ LP 1004*

AFRS One Night Stand 592 transcriptions, Blue Room, Hotel Lincoln, NYC, February 1945:

One O'Clock Jump (theme)	unissued
I'm Confessin' (vJR)	unissued
I Walked In (vEW)	unissued
Blue Room Jump (Andy's Blues)	*Flute FL-7*
Back Door Romp (Andy's Blues)	*Flute FL-7*
I Didn't Know about You (vMJ)	unissued
'Tain't Me (vJR)	*Flute FL-7*

Lang-Worth Transcriptions, NYC, February 13, 1945:

Sugar Hill Shuffle	*JP LP 18*
I Should Care (vEW)	unissued
Just an Old Manuscript	*JP LP 18*
Wish You Were Waiting for Me (vMJ)	*BlH BH3-308*
Harvard Blues (vJR)	*Palm(E) 30-12*
Please Don't Say No (vEW)	*BlH BH1-109*
I Didn't Know about You (vMJ)	*BlH BH1-109*
I'm Fer It, Too	*JP LP 18*

Coca Cola Spotlight Bands 607, USAAF Base, Dover, NJ, February 24, 1945:

Avenue C	unissued
Wish You Were Waiting for Me (vMJ)	unissued
Harvard Blues (vCB)	*Ev EV-3004*
Evelina (vEW)	unissued

NYC, February 26, 1945:

CO34352-1	Avenue C	Col DF3468
CO34352-2	Avenue C	
CO34352-3	Avenue C	
CO34352-4	Avenue C	
CO34353-1	*This Heart of Mine (vLS)	Col 36795
CO34354-1	*That Old Feeling (vLS)	Col 36795
CO34354-2	*That Old Feeling (vLS)	

NB: *add Lynne Sherman (vo) & unidentified strings. All takes also on *CBS(F) 66102*.

FREDDIE GREEN & HIS KANSAS CITY SEVEN
Buck Clayton (tp); Wells (tb); Lucky Thompson (ts); Sammy Benskin (p); Green (p); Al Hall (b); Shadow Wilson (d); Sylvia Sims (vo).
NYC, May 7, 1945:

DU4907	I'm in the Mood for Love (vSS)	Duke 113
DU4909	Sugar Hips	Duke 113
	Get Lucky	Duke 114
	I'll Never Be the Same	Duke 114

COUNT BASIE & HIS ORCHESTRA
Buck Clayton, Harry Edison, Karl George, Al Killian, Ed Lewis (tp); Ted Donnelly, J. J. Johnson, Eli Robinson, Wells (tb); Jimmy Powell (as); Earle Warren (as/vo); Buddy Tate, Lucky Thompson (ts); Rudy Rutherford (cl/bs);

Count Basie (p); Freddie Green (g); Rodney Richardson (b); Shadow Wilson (d); Taps Miller, Jimmy Rushing (vo).
NYC, May 14, 1945:

VP1356	High Tide (vTM)	V-Disc 483
VP1357	Sent for You Yesterday (vJR)	V-Disc 534
VP1357	Jimmy's Boogie Woogie (vJR)	V-Disc 534
VP1686	Tippin' on the Q.T.	V-Disc 627
JBB296	San Jose	V-Disc 744
JBB296	B-Flat Blues	V-Disc 744
JBB297	Sweet Lorraine (vEW)	V-Disc 802

Omit Buck Clayton; add Preston Love (as), Pearl Bailey & Maxine Johnson (vo).
WNEW Tribute to Glenn Miller broadcast, Paramount Theatre, NYC, June 5, 1945:

One O'Clock Jump (theme)	*Met MNR 1213*
B-Flat Blues	*Met MNR 1213*
I'm Gonna See My Baby (vMJ)	*Met MNR 1213*
Duration Blues (vPB)	*Met MNR 1213*
Red Bank Boogie	unissued

Snooky Young (tp), George Dorsey (as) & Ann Moore (vo) replace Al Killian, Earle Warren, Jimmy Powell, Pearl Bailey & Maxine Johnson.
AFRS Jubilee 141 transcriptions, Hollywood, July 9, 1945:

One O'Clock Jump (theme)	unissued
Basie Boogie	*Joyce LP 5002*
What Can I Say Dear? (vAM)	*Joyce LP 5002*
Gotta Be This or That	*Joyce LP 5002*
Andy's Blues	*Joyce LP 5002*

COUNT BASIE ALL STARS
Harry Edison, Snooky Young (tp); Ted Donnelly, Wells (tb); Lucky Thompson (ts); Rudy Rutherford (bs); Count Basie (p); Freddie Green (g); Rodney Richardson (b); Shadow Wilson (d); Jimmy Rushing (vo).
Lamplighter broadcast, Streets of Paris club, LA, July 15, 1945:

Royal Garden Blues	*Origin OJL 8101*
Body & Soul	*Origin OJL 8101*
Evenin' (vJR)	*Origin OJL 8101*
I Got Rhythm	*Origin OJL 8101*

COUNT BASIE & HIS ORCHESTRA
As before. Martha Lewis, Jimmy Rushing (vo).
AFRS Jubilee 142 transcriptions, Hollywood, July 16, 1945:

One O'Clock Jump (theme)	unissued
Avenue C	*Flute FL-7*
I Never Knew (vJR)	*FH FH-22*
Hey! Rube	*Palm POM-1*

June Richmond, Delta Rhythm Boys (vo).
AFRS Jubilee 143 transcriptions, Hollywood, July 23, 1945:

One O'Clock Jump (theme)	unissued
Queer Street	*Joyce LP 5001*

Are You Living, Old Man? (vJRi)	*Joyce LP 5001*
Old Man River (vJRi)	*Joyce LP 5001*
I'm Beginning To See the Light (vDRB)	*Joyce LP 5001*
Hey! John (vDRB)	*Joyce LP 5002*
High Tide (vBand)	*Joyce LP 5002*

Jimmy Rushing (vo) replaces June Richmond. Add Lena Horne, Bing Crosby (vo).
AFRS Jubilee Christmas Show, Hollywood, August 8, 1945:

Jingle Bells (nc) (vDRB)	unissued
One O'Clock Jump (theme)	unissued
Jumping at Ten	*Car CAR-427*
Just A-Settin' & A-Rockin' (vDRB)	*SH SWH-29*
My Silent Love (vLH)	*SH SWH-29*
Jingle Bells (nc)	unissued
Gotta Be This or That (vBC)	*SH SWH-29*
Jumpin' at the Woodside	*FH FH-22*
Silent Night (vLH)	unissued

Ann Moore (vo) replaces Lena Horne & Bing Crosby.
AFRS Jubilee 147 transcriptions, Hollywood, September 10, 1945:

One O'Clock Jump (theme)	unissued
Rambo	*Joyce LP 5001*
Mean to Me (vAM)	*Joyce LP 5001*
Boogie Woogie (vJR)	*Joyce LP 5001*
Astructed (Andy's Blues)	*Joyce LP 5001*

AFRS Jubilee 148 transcriptions, Hollywood, September 17, 1945:

One O'Clock Jump (theme)	unissued
I've Found a New Baby	*Flute FL-7*
Blue Skies (vJR)	*Flute FL-7*
Jivin' Joe Jackson (vAM)	*Flute FL-7*
Taps Miller	*Flute FL-7*
One O'Clock Jump (theme)	unissued

AFRS Jubilee 149 transcriptions, Hollywood, September 24, 1945:

One O'Clock Jump (theme)	unissued
Rhythm Man	unissued
Gotta Be This or That (vDRB)	unissued
Jazz Me Blues	unissued
Please Don't Talk about Me When I'm Gone (vJR)	*Flute FL-7*
It's Sand, Man!	*Band BS 7128*

Lena Horne (vo).
AFRS Jubilee 150 transcriptions, Hollywood, October 1, 1945:

One O'Clock Jump (theme)	unissued
San Jose	*Flute FL-7*
One for My Baby (vLH)	unissued
Good for Nothin' Joe (vLH)	unissued
Tush	*Flute FL-7*

Emmett Berry (tp) & Illinois Jacquet (ts) replace Karl George & Lucky Thompson. Ann Moore & Jimmy Rushing (vo).
Hollywood, October 9, 1945:

HCO1563-1	Blue Skies (vJR)	Col 37070
HCO1564-1	Jivin' Joe Jackson (vAM)	Col 36889
HCO1565-1	High Tide	Col 36990
HCO1565-2	High Tide	
HCO1565-3	High Tide	
HCO1566-1	Queer Street	Col 36889
HCO1566-2	Queer Street	
HCO1566-3	Queer Street	

NB: All takes also on *CBS(F) 66102*.

Department of State transcriptions, probably Hollywood, October 1945:

Wild Bill's Boogie	unissued
Baby, Don't You Cry (vJR)	*Palm Club(F) 03*
Sent for You Yesterday (vJR)	*Palm Club(F) 03*
That's All She Wrote	*Palm Club(F) 03*
Queer Street	*Palm Club(F) 04*

BENNY CARTER & HIS ORCHESTRA
Emmett Berry, Neal Hefti, Joe Newman, Shorty Rogers (tp); Alton Moore, Wells, Sandy Williams, Trummy Young (tb); Tony Scott (cl); Benny Carter (as/tp); Russell Procope (as); Don Byas, Flip Phillips (ts); Willard Brown (bs/as); Sonny White (p); Al Casey (g); John Simmons (b); J. C. Heard (d).
NYC, January 7, 1946:

168	Diga Diga Doo	DeLuxe 1028
169	Who's Sorry Now?	DeLuxe 1009
170	Some of These Days	DeLuxe 1012

NB: All takes also on *Swingtime (D) ST 1013*.

DICKY WELLS BIG SEVEN
George Treadwell (tp); Wells (tb); Budd Johnson (ts); Cecil Scott (bs); Jimmy Jones (p); Al McKibbon (b); Jimmy Crawford (d); Sarah Vaughan (vo).
NYC, March 21, 1946:

1033	We're Through (vSV)	HRS 1019
1034	Bed Rock	HRS 1019
1035	Opera in Blue	HRS 1018
1036	Drag Nasty (The Walk)	HRS 1018

BUCK CLAYTON'S BIG EIGHT
Buck Clayton (tp); Wells, Trummy Young (tb); George Johnson (as); Billy Taylor (p/cel*); Brick Fleagle (g); Al McKibbon (b); Jimmy Crawford (d).
NYC, July 24, 1946:

1047	Saratoga Special	HRS 1027
1048	Sentimental Summer*	HRS 1027
1049	Harlem Cradle Song	HRS 1028
1050	My Good Man, Sam	HRS 1028
1051	I Want a Little Girl	HRS 1029

SY OLIVER & HIS ORCHESTRA
Bill Coleman, Skeets Reid, Lyman Vunk, Lamar Wright (tp); Gus Chappell,

Bill Granzow (tb); Dicky Wells, Henry Wells (tb/vo); Eddie Barefield, George Dorsey (as); Gale Curtis, Fred Williams (ts); Willard Brown (bs); Billy Kyle (p); Aaron Smith (g); George Duvivier (b); Wally Bishop (d); Sy Oliver (vo). NYC, January 9, 1947:

	A Slow Burn	MGM 10004
	Hey! Daddy-O (vSO/DW)	MGM 10004
	For Dancers Only	unissued
	If You Believe in Me (vHW)	MGM 10255

DUSTY FLETCHER
Dusty Fletcher (monologue) acc. Hot Lips Page (tp); Wells (tb); Budd Johnson (ts); Billy Kyle (p); Aaron Smith (g); George Duvivier (b); Jack 'The Bear' Parker (d). NYC, January 30, 1947:

NSC224	I'm Going Back There, Part 1	National 4014
NSC225	I'm Going Back There, Part 2	National 4014
NSC226	Dusty Fletcher's Mad Hour, Part 1	National 4013
NSC227	Dusty Fletcher's Mad Hour, Part 2	National 4013

ILLINOIS JACQUET & HIS ORCHESTRA
Miles Davis, Marion Hazel, Fats Navarro, Joe Newman (tp); Gus Chappell, Ted Kelly, Eli Robinson, Wells (tb); Ray Perry, Jimmy Powell (as); Illinois Jacquet, George 'Big Nick' Nicholas (ts); Leo Parker (bs); Bill Doggett or Leonard Feather* (p); Al Lucas (b); Shadow Wilson (d).

94-4	For Europeans Only	Aladdin 180
95-3	Big Dog*	Aladdin 180
96-4	You Left Me Alone	Aladdin 179
97-2	Jivin' with Jack the Bellboy	Aladdin 179

SY OLIVER & HIS ORCHESTRA
Bill Coleman, Frank Galbraith, Wallace Wilson, Lamar Wright (tp); Gus Chappell, Fred Robinson, Dicky Wells (tb); Henry Wells (tb/vo); George Dorsey (as); Eddie Barefield (as/ts); Ernie Powell (ts); Willard Brown (bs); Buddy Weed (p); Aaron Smith (g); George Duvivier (b); Jimmy Crawford (d); Sy Oliver (vo). NYC, April 1, 1947:

	I Want To Be Loved (vSO/HW)	MGM 10030
	Lamar's Boogie	MGM 10133
	25 Words or Less (vSO)	unissued
	Walking the Dog (vSO/Band)	MGM 11092

COUSIN JOE WITH DICKY WELLS' BLUE SEVEN
Shad Collins (tp); Wells (tb); Pete Brown (as); Billy Kyle (p); Danny Barker (g); Lloyd Trotman (b); Woodie Nichols (d); Cousin Joe (vo). NYC, mid-1947:

SRC439	Come Down Baby (vCJ)	Signature 1013
SRC440	Bachelor's Blues (vCJ)	Signature 1012
SRC441	Don't Pay Me No Mind (vCJ)	Signature 1013
SRC442	Stoop to Conquer (vCJ)	Signature 1012
SRC443	Blues, Part 1	unissued
SRC444	Blues, Part 2	unissued

COUNT BASIE & HIS ORCHESTRA
Emmett Berry, Harry Edison, Ed Lewis, Snooky Young (tp); Ted Donnelly,
Bill Johnson, George Matthews, Wells (tb); Preston Love, Charles Price (as);
Paul Gonsalves, Buddy Tate (ts); Jack Washington (bs); Count Basie (p);
Freddie Green (g); Walter Page (b); Jo Jones (d); Bob Bailey, Jimmy Rushing
(vo).
Chicago, October 19, 1947:

D7VB1090-1	Don't You Want a Man Like Me? (vJR)	Vic 20-2602
D7VB1091-1	Blue & Sentimental (vBB)	Vic 20-2602
D7VB1092-1	Seventh Avenue Express	Vic 20-3003
D7VB1093-1	Mr. Roberts' Roost	Vic 20-3255

LA, December 8, 1947:

D7VB2167-1	Sophisticated Swing	Vic 20-3255
D7VB2168-1	Guest in a Nest	Vic 20-2771
D7VB2168-2	Guest in a Nest	unissued
D7VB2169-1	Your Red Wagon (vJR)	Vic 20-2677
D7VB2170-1	Money is Honey (vJR)	Vic 20-2771

Jeanne Taylor (vo) replaces Bob Bailey.
LA, December 9, 1947:

D7VB2171-1	Just a Minute	Vic 20-3051
D7VB2171-2	Just A Minute	unissued
D7VB2172-1	Baby, Don't Be Mad at Me (vJT)	Vic 20-2948
D7VB2173-1	I've Only Myself to Blame (vJT)	Vic 20-2850
D7VB2173-2	I've Only Myself to Blame (vJT)	unissued

Emmett Berry, Harry Edison, Jimmy Nottingham, Clark Terry (tp); Ted
Donnelly, Bill Johnson, George Matthews, Wells (tb); Bernie Peacock (as);
Earle Warren (as/vo); Paul Gonsalves, Wardell Gray (ts); Jack Washington
(bs); Count Basie (p); Freddie Green (g); Singleton Palmer (b); Shadow Wilson (d); Jimmy Rushing, Dinah Washington (vo).
WMGM broadcast, Royal Roost, NYC, September 11, 1948:

X-1	*Session 106*
Futile Frustration	*Session 106*
Am I Asking Too Much? (vDW)	*Session 106*
Evil Gal Blues (vDW)	*Session 106*
Good Bait	*Session 106*
Moon Nocturne (nc) (vEW)	*Session 106*
Paradise Squat	*Session 106*
I Want To Cry (vDW)	*Session 106*
Blue Skies (vJR)	*Session 106*
The King	*Session 106*

WMGM broadcast, Royal Roost, NYC, September 14, 1948:

Spasmodic	*Ozone 6*
Robbins' Nest	unissued
Blue Skies (vJR)	unissued
X-1	*Spot SPJ-134*
Moon Nocturne (vEW)	unissued
Far Cry	*Ozone 6*

I Want to Cry* (vDW)		unissued
The King		*Spot SPJ-134*

NB: *Beryl Booker (p) replaces Count Basie.

WMGM broadcast, Royal Roost, NYC, September 18, 1948:

The Peacock		*Alto 702*
Swedish Pastry		*Alto 702*
Maybe You'll Be There		unissued
X-1		unissued
Jimmy's Blues (vJR)		unissued
San Jose		unissued
The King		unissued
One O'Clock Jump (theme)		unissued

Anita O'Day (vo) replaces Dinah Washington.
WMGM broadcasts, Royal Roost, NYC, September 25, 1948:

Spasmodic		*Alto 702*
Robbins' Nest		*Alto 702*
High Tide		*Alto 702*
San Jose		*Alto 702*
Boot Whip* (vAoD)		*Alto 702*
That's That (vAoD)		*Alto 702*
The King		*Alto 702*

NB: *Lou Stein (p) replaces Count Basie.

Butch Ballard (d) replaces Shadow Wilson. Omit Anita O'Day.
AFRS Jubilee 310 transcriptions, NYC, November, 1948:

One O'Clock Jump (theme)		unissued
It Serves Me Right		*Spot SPJ-134*
Little Dog		*Spot SPJ-134*
Sent for You Yesterday (vJR)		unissued
Hey! Pretty Baby		unissued
One O'Clock Jump (theme)		unissued

Emmett Berry, Harry Edison, Jimmy Nottingham, Clark Terry, Gerald Wilson (tp); Ted Donnelly, Melba Liston, George Matthews, Wells (tb); Charles Price (as); Earle Warren (as/vo); Paul Gonsalves, Bill Parker (ts); Jack Washington (bs); Count Basie (p); Freddie Green (g); Singleton Palmer (b); Butch Ballard (d); Bobby Troup (vo).
LA, April 11, 1949:

D9VB600-1	Brand New Doll (vBT)	Vic 20-3449
D9VB600-2	Brand New Doll (vBT)	unissued
D9VB601-1	Cheek to Cheek	Vic 20-3449
D9VB601-2	Cheek to Cheek	unissued
D9VB602-1	Just an Old Manuscript	*RCA(F) 75.428*
D9VB602-2	Just an Old Manuscript	unissued
D9VB603-1	Katy	*HMV 7EG-8221*
D9VB603-2	Katy	unissued

Omit Melba Liston; Taps Miller & Jimmy Rushing (vo) replace Bobby Troup.
NYC, June 29, 1949:

D9VB1766-1	She's a Wine-O (vJR)	Vic 20-3542

| D9VB1767-1 | Did You Ever See Jackie Robinson Hit the Ball? (vJR) | RCA(F) 741.042 |
| D9VB1768-1 | Shoutin' Blues | Vic 20-3514 |

NYC, July 13, 1949:

D7VB906-2	After You've Gone (vJR)	Vic 20-3558
D9VB1767-2	Did You Ever See Jackie Robinson Hit the Ball? (vTM/band)	Vic 20-3514
D9VB1821-1	St. Louis Baby (vTM/?)	Vic 20-3601
D9VB1822-1	Convertible Cadillac (vEW)	unissued

NB: Wells absent from one other unissued title.

NYC, July 22, 1949:

D9VB1897-1	Wonderful Thing	HMV(E) 7EG-8147
D9VB1898-1	The Slider	rejected
D9VB1899-1	Mine Too	Vic 20-3699
D9VB1900-1	Walking Slow Behind You (vJR)	Vic 20-3572

Add Billy Valentine (vo) & poss. Jimmy Tyler (ts).
NYC, August 5, 1949:

D9VB1898-1	The Slider	Vic 20-3542
D9VB2138-1	Normania (Blee Blop Blues)	Vic 20-3601
D9VB2139-1	Rocky Mountain Blues (vBV)	Vic 20-3572

BILLIE HOLIDAY WITH BUSTER HARDING & HIS ORCHESTRA

Emmett Berry, Buck Clayton, Jimmy Nottingham (tp); George Matthews, Wells (tb); George Dorsey, Rudy Powell (as); Joe Thomas, Lester Young (ts); Sol Moore (bs); Horace Henderson (p); Mundell Lowe (g); George Duvivier (b); Shadow Wilson (d); Billie Holliday (vo).
NYC, August 17, 1949:

| W75147-A | 'Tain't Nobody's Business If I Do (vBH) | Decca 24726 |
| W75148-A | Baby Get Lost (vBH) | Decca 24726 |

COUNT BASIE OCTET

Harry Edison (tp); Wells (tb); George Auld (ts); Gene Ammons (ts/bs); Count Basie (p); Freddie Green (g); Al McKibbon (b); Gus Johnson (d); Deep River Boys, 'Google Eyes' (vo).
NYC, February 6, 1950:

E0VB3187-1	If You See My Baby (vGE)	HMV(E) 7EG-8221
E0VB3187-2	If You See My Baby	unissued
E0VB3188-1	Solid As a Rock (vDRB)	Vic 20-3699
E0VB3189-1	Rat Race	Vic LPM-1112
E0VB3190-1	Sweets	RCA(F) 75.428

JOEY THOMAS ORCHESTRA

Frank Galbraith (tp); Wells (tb); Walter Thomas (as); Harry Johnson (ts); Andy Brown (bs); Bill Doggett (p); Abie Baker (b); Jimmy Crawford (d); Freddie Jackson, Charles Singleton, Joey Thomas (vo).
NYC, March 28, 1951:

	Investigation Blues	Decca 48210
	There Ain't Room Enough	Decca 48210
	Bad Luck Child	Decca 48215
	Sarah Kelly from Plumbnelly	Decca 48215

JIMMY RUSHING (vo) acc. Dick Vance (tp); Wells (tb); Rudy Powell (as); Harold Clark (ts); Al Williams (p); Walter Page (b); Ralph Jones (d). NYC, October 5, 1951:

K8084	I'm So Lonely (vJR)	King 4502
K8085	Go Get Some More, You Fool (vJR)	King 4564
K8086	Hi-Ho Sylvester (vJR)	King 4502
K8087	That's The Way I Feel (vJR)	King 4564

PAUL QUINICHETTE & HIS ORCHESTRA
Buck Clayton (tp); Wells (tb); Paul Quinichette (ts); Count Basie (p/org); Freddie Green (g); Walter Page (b); Gus Johnson (d). NYC, January 30, 1952:

YB4815-1	Shad Roe	Mer 8287
YB4816-1	Paul's Bunion	Mer 70020
YB4817	Crew Cut	*EmA EP1-6035*
YB4818-1	The Hook	Mer 8287

NB: Wells absent from rest of session. All titles also on *EmA(J) 175J-5/6*.

JIMMY RUSHING (vo) acc. Frank Galbraith (tp); Wells (tb); Pete Clark (as); Buddy Tate (ts); Fletcher Smith (p); Jimmy Shirley (g); Walter Page (b); Bobby Donaldson (d). NYC, September 23, 1952:

K8287	In the Moonlight (vJR)	King 4588
K8288	She's Mine, She's Yours (vJR)	King 4606
K8289	Where Were You? (vJR)	King 4588
K8290	Somebody's Been Spoiling These Women (vJR)	King 4606

BILL COLEMAN & HIS SWING STARS
Bill Coleman (tp/vo); Wells (tb); Guy Lafitte (cl/ts); Randy Downes (p); Buddy Banks (b); Zutty Singleton (d). Paris, October 18, 1952:

	One O'Clock Jump	*Ph(F) N 76006 R*
	Black & Blue	Ph(F) 72128
	Ghost of a Chance	*Ph(F) N 76006 R*
	St. James Infirmary Blues (vBC)	*Ph(F) N 76006 R*
	Out of Nowhere (vBC)	*Ph(F) N 76006 R*
	The Sheik of Araby	*Ph(F) N 76006 R*
	Royal Garden Blues	*Ph(F) N 76006 R*
	Knuckle Head	Ph(F) 72129
	Baby, Won't You Please Come Home? (vBC)	*Ph(F) N 76008 R*
	Solitude	*Ph(F) N 76008 R*
	Red Top	*Ph(F) N 76008 R*
ACP 2344	Drum Face	Ph(F) 72130
	Perdido (vBC)	*Ph(F) N 76008 R*
	The Saints (vBC)	Ph(F) 72129

205

ACP 2346	Muskrat Ramble	Ph(F) N 70900 H
ACP 2340	St. Louis Blues, Part 1 (vBC)	Ph(F) 72131
ACP 2341	St. Louis Blues, Part 2	Ph(F) 72131

EARL HINES & HIS NEW SOUND ORCHESTRA

Gene Redd (tp); Wells (tb); Leroy Harris (cl/as/bs); Jerome Richardson (f/ts/vo); Earl Hines (p/cel/vo); Paul Binnings (b); Hank Milo (d); The Hines Varieties (Redd/Wells/Harris/Richardson) (vo).
LA, July/August 1954:

Crazy Rhythm (vTHV)	*Nocturne EP-7*
Hollywood Hop	*Nocturne EP-7*
A Jumpin' Something	*Nocturne EP-7*
The Web	Nocturne 103
Almost Like Being in Love	Nocturne 105
I Don't Hear Sweet Music	Nocturne 105
Gone with the Wind	*Tops L 1599*

JIMMY RUSHING & ADA MOORE WITH BUCK CLAYTON & HIS ORCHESTRA

Emmett Berry, Buck Clayton (tp); Wells (tb); Eddie Barefield (as); Budd Johnson (ts); Willard Brown (bs/as); Sir Charles Thompson (p); Steve Jordan (g); Aaron Bell (b); Jo Jones (d); Ada Moore, Jimmy Rushing (vo/narr).
NYC, August 18, 1955:

Any Place I Hang My Hat Is Home (vAM)	*Col CL 778*
Pretty Little Baby (vJR)	*Col CL 778*
I've Got a Feeling I'm Falling (vAM)	*Col CL 778*
One Hour (vJR/AM)	*Col CL 778*
Ain't She Sweet?	*Col CL 778*

NYC August 19, 1955:

You're My Thrill (vAM)	*Col CL 778*
Between the Devil & the Deep	*Col CL 778*
Blue Sea (vAM)	
Gee, Baby, Ain't I Good to You (vJR)	*Col CL 778*

Ken Kersey (p), Milt Hinton (b) & Osie Johnson (d) replace Sir Charles Thompson, Aaron Bell & Jo Jones. Eddie Barefield (cl/as).
NYC, August 23, 1955:

Any Place I Hang My Hat Is Home (vAM)	*Col CL 778*
Cool Breeze Women (vJR)	*Col CL 778*
I Can't Give You Anything but Love	*Col CL 778*
The Blues	*Col CL 778*
Any Place I Hang My Hat Is Home (vAM)	*Col CL 778*
After You've Gone (vJR)	*Col CL 778*
Closing Theme	*Col CL 778*

FRANKIE LAINE WITH BUCK CLAYTON & HIS ORCHESTRA

Buck Clayton (tp); Urbie Green, Wells (tb); Hilton Jefferson (as); Budd Johnson, Al Sears (ts); Dave McRae (bs); Sir Charles Thompson (p); Skeeter Best (g); Milt Hinton (b); Bobby Donaldson (d); Frankie Laine (vo).
ZEP 37342   Until the Real Thing Comes Along (vFL) *Col CL 808*

ZEP 37343	If You Were Mine (vFL)	*Col CL 808*
ZEP 37344	My Old Flame	*Col CL 808*

RED PRYSOCK & HIS ORCHESTRA
Frank Galbraith (tp); Wells (tb); Red Prysock (ts); Clarence Wright (bs); Roland Johnson (vb); Oliver Blair (p); Herbert Gordy (b); Jerome Potter (d). NYC, February 23–28, 1956:

W489	Rock & Roll Party	Mer 70918
W490	Rock & Roll Mambo	Mer 70918
W496	Fruit Boots	Wing 90070
W497	Plaid Laces	Wing 90070
	Let's Get It	*Mer MG 20211*
	Red's Blues	*Mer MG 20211*
	Red Rock	*Mer MG 20211*
	What Next?	*Mer MG 20211*
	Shakers	*Mer MG 20211*
	Rolling & Rocking	*Mer MG 20211*
	Fox	*Mer MG 20211*
	Lulu	*Mer MG 20211*

JIMMY RUSHING WITH BUCK CLAYTON & HIS ORCHESTRA
Billy Butterfield, Buck Clayton, Ed Lewis (tp); Urbie Green, Wells (tb); Hilton Jefferson, Rudy Powell (as); Budd Johnson (ts); Dave McRae (bs); Hank Jones (p); Steve Jordan (g); Milt Hinton (b); Jo Jones (d); Jimmy Rushing (vo). NYC, November 8, 1956:

CO56723	Old-Fashioned Love (vJR)	*Col CL 963*
CO56724	Lullaby of Broadway (vJR)	*Col CL 963*
CO56725	Some of These Days (vJR)	*Col CL 963*

REX STEWART & THE HENDERSON ALL-STARS
Rex Stewart (ct); Emmett Berry; Taft Jordan, Joe Thomas (tp); J.C. Higginbotham, Benny Morton, Wells (tb); Buster Bailey (cl); Garvin Bushell, Hilton Jefferson (as); Coleman Hawkins, Ben Webster (ts); Haywood Henry (bs); Red Richards (p); Al Casey (g); Bill Pemberton (b); Jimmy Crawford (d). NYC, late November 1957:

	Sugarfoot Stomp	*Jazztone J1285*
	King Porter Stomp	*Jazztone J1285*
	King Porter Stomp (spliced alt)	*Urania US 2012*

Dick Vance (tp) & Norman Thornton (bs) replace Emmett Berry & Haywood Henry. NYC, November 29, 1957:

	Honeysuckle Rose	*Jazztone J1285*
	Wrappin' It Up	*Jazztone J1285*
	The Way She Walks (Rex's Tune)*	*Jazztone J1285*

NB: *Omit Ben Webster.

Rex Stewart (ct); J.C. Higginbotham, Benny Morton, Wells (tb); Hilton Jefferson (as); Coleman Hawkins (ts); Red Richards (p); Al Casey (g); Bill Pemberton (b); Jimmy Crawford (d). NYC, December 2, 1957:

Casey Stew	*Jazztone J1285*
A Hundred Years from Today	*Jazztone J1285*
Three Thieves	*Jazztone J1285*
'Round About Midnight	*Jazztone J1285*

COUNT BASIE ALL-STARS

Emmett Berry, Doc Cheatham, Roy Eldridge, Joe Newman (tp); Vic Dicken-
son, Frank Rehak, Wells (tb); Earle Warren (as); Coleman Hawkins, Lester
Young (ts); Harry Carney (bs); Count Basie (p); Freddie Green (g); Eddie
Jones (b); Jo Jones (d); Jimmy Rushing (vo).
CBS-TV 'The Sound of Jazz' rehearsal, NYC, December 5, 1957:

| I Left My Baby (vJR) | *Col CL 1098* |
| Dicky's Dream | *Col CL 1098* |

Emmett Berry, Doc Cheatham, Joe Newman, Joe Wilder (tp); Roy Eldridge
(tp/flh); Vic Dickenson, Benny Morton, Wells (tb); Earle Warren (as); Coleman Hawkins, Ben Webster (ts); Gerry Mulligan (bs); Count Basie (p); Freddie Green (g); Eddie Jones (b); Jo Jones (d); Jimmy Rushing (vo).
WCBS-TV 'The Sound of Jazz' broadcast, NYC, December 8, 1957:

Open All Night (Fast & Happy Blues)	*Pumpkin 116*
Blues (nc)	*Pumpkin 116*
I Left My Baby (vJR)	*Pumpkin 116*
Dicky's Dream	*ExR LP 1002*

DICKY WELLS & HIS ORCHESTRA

Vic Dickenson, George Matthews, Benny Morton, Wells (tb); Skip Hall (p);
Major Holley (b); Jo Jones (d).
NYC, February 3, 1958:

Bones for the King	*Fel FAJ 7006*
Sweet Daddy Spo-De-O	*Fel FAJ 7006*
You Took My Heart	*Fel FAJ 7006*

Buck Clayton (tp); Wells (tb); Buddy Tate (ts/bs); Rudy Rutherford (cl/bs);
Skip Hall (p); Everett Barksdale (g); Major Holley (b); Jo Jones (d).
NYC, February 4, 1958:

Come & Get It (-1)	unissued
Come & Get It (-3)	*Fel FAJ 7006*
Stan Dance (-2)	unissued
Stan Dance (-3)	*Fel FAJ 7006*
Stan Dance (insert for -3)	*Fel FAJ 7006*
Hello Smack (-2)	unissued
Hello Smack (-3)	*Fel FAJ 7006*

BUDDY TATE ALL-STARS

Buck Clayton (tp); Wells (tb); Earle Warren (as/bs); Buddy Tate (ts); Skip
Hall (p); Lord Westbrook (g); Aaron Bell (b); Jo Jones (d).
NYC, February 12, 1958:

Moon Eyes (-1)	unissued
Moon Eyes (-2)	unissued
Moon Eyes (-3)	*Fel FAJ 7004*
Rockin' Steve (-1)	unissued
Rockin' Steve (-2)	unissued

Rockin' Steve (-3)		*Fel FAJ 7004*
Rompin' With Buck (-2)		unissued
Rompin' With Buck (-4)		unissued
Rompin' With Buck (-5)		unissued
Rompin' With Buck (-S*)		*Fel FAJ 7004*

NB: *Combines material from previous takes.

JIMMY RUSHING & HIS ORCHESTRA

Emmett Berry, Buck Clayton, Mel Davis, Bernie Glow (tp); Vic Dickenson, Urbie Green, Wells (tb); Earle Warren, Rudy Powell (as); Coleman Hawkins, Buddy Tate (ts); Danny Bank (bs); Nat Pierce (p); Danny Barker (g); Milt Hinton (b); Jo Jones (d); Jimmy Rushing (vo).

CO60472	I'm Coming Virginia (vJR)	*Col CL 1152*
CO60473	Mister Five by Five (vJR)	*Col CL 1152*
CO60474	June Night (vJR)	*Col CL 1152*
CO60475	Rosalie (vJR)	*Col CL 1152*

Doc Cheatham (tp), Frank Rehak (tp) & Osie Johnson (d) replace Bernie Glow, Vic Dickenson & Jo Jones.
NYC, February 26, 1958:

CO60476	Knock Me a Kiss (vJR)	*Col CL 1152*
CO60477	Jimmy's Blues (vJR)	*Col CL 1152*
CO60478	Someday Sweetheart+ (vJR)	*Col CL 1152*
CO60479	Harvard Blues (vJR)	*Col CL 1152*

NB: *Nat Pierce (cel). +Rudy Powell (cl).

NYC, February 27, 1958:

CO60480	It's a Sin To Tell a Lie (vJR)	*Col CL 1152*
CO60481	Trav'lin Light (vJR)	*Col CL 1152*
CO60482	When You're Smiling (vJR)	*Col CL 1152*
CO60483	Somebody Stole My Gal (vJR)	*Col CL 1152*

THE BIG EIGHTEEN

Billy Butterfield, Buck Clayton, Charlie Shavers, Rex Stewart (tp); Lawrence Brown, Vic Dickenson, Lou McGarity, Wells (tb); Walt Levinsky (cl/as); Hymie Schertzer (as); Sam Donahue, Boomie Richman (ts); Ernie Caceres (bs); Johnny Guarnieri (p); Barry Galbraith (g); Milt Hinton (b); Jimmy Crawford (d).
NYC, June 10, 1958:

J2JB4446	Swingtime in the Rockies	*Vic LPM-1983*
J2JB4447	Easy Does It	*Vic LPM-1921*
J2JB4448	Five O'Clock Drag	*Vic LPM-1921*

Peanuts Hucko (cl/ts) replaces Walt Levinsky.
NYC, June 17, 1958:

J2JB4585	Feet Draggin' Blues	*Vic LPM-1983*
J2JB4586	Summit Ridge Drive	*Vic LPM-1983*
J2JB4587	Tuxedo Junction	*Vic LPM-1921*
J2JB4588	Blues on Parade	*Vic LPM-1921*

NYC, June 24, 1958:

J2JB4987	Okay for Baby	*Vic LPM-1983*
J2JB4988	March of the Toys	*Vic LPM-1921*
J2JB4989	Skyliner	*Vic LPM-1983*
J2JB4990	Parade of the Milk Bottle Caps	*Vic LPM-1983*

Yank Lawson (tp) & Walt Levinsky (cl/as) replace Billy Butterfield & Peanuts Hucko.

NYC, July 8, 1958:

J2JB5329	Celery Stalks at Midnight	*Vic LPM-1983*
J2JB5330	I'm Praying Humble	*Vic LPM-1921*
J2JB5331	Hors D'Oeuvre	*Vic LPM-1921*
J2JB5332-1	Liza	rejected

Rex Stewart (ct); Buck Clayton, Yank Lawson, Charlie Shavers (tp); Bob Ascher, Sy Berger, Lou McGarity, Wells (tb); Walt Levinsky (cl/as); Hymie Schertzer (as); Sam Donahue, Boomie Richman (ts); Ernie Caceres (bs); Johnny Guarnieri (p); Barry Galbraith (g); Russ Saunders (b); Don Lamond (d).

NYC, July 15, 1958:

J2JB5332-2	Liza	*Vic LPM-1921*
J2JB5488	The Campbells Are Swinging	*Vic LPM-1921*
J2JB5489	Organ Grinder's Swing	*Vic LPM-1983*
J2JB5490	Ton O'Rock Jump	*Vic LPM-1983*
J2JB5491	Quaker City Jazz	*Vic LPM-1983*

REX STEWART & THE HENDERSON ALL-STARS

Rex Stewart (ct); Taft Jordan, Allan Smith, Joe Thomas, Paul Webster (tp); Leon Comegys, Benny Morton, Wells (tb); Garvin Bushell, Hilton Jefferson (cl/as); Buddy Tate, Bob Wilber (cl/ts); Haywood Henry (bs); Dick Cary (Eb-h); Red Richards (p); Chauncey Westbrook (g); Bill Pemberton (b); Mousie Alexander (d); Clarence 'Big' Miller (vo).

Great South Bay Jazz Festival, Great River, Long Island, August 1–2, 1958:

	Wrappin' It Up	*UA UAL 4009*
	D-Natural Blues	*UA UAL 4009*
	Medley: These Foolish Things/Willow Weep for Me/Over the Rainbow	*UA UAL 4009*
	Hello, Little Girl (vCBM)	*UA UAL 4009*
	Georgia Sketches, Parts 1–3	*UA UAL 4009*
	Down South Camp Meeting	unissued
	What'cha Call 'Em Blues	unissued
	Blues	unissued

JOE THOMAS & HIS ALL-STAR GROUP

Johnny Letman, Joe Thomas (tp); Wells (tb); Buster Bailey (cl); Buddy Tate (ts); Herbie Nichols (p); Everett Barksdale (g); Bill Pemberton (b); Jimmy Crawford (d).

NYC, October 27, 1958:

| 3174 | Sweethearts on Parade | *Atl 1303* |
| 3175 | Blues for Baby | *Atl 1303* |

3176	I Can't Believe That You're in Love with Me	*Atl 1303*
3177	Crazy Rhythm	*Atl 1303*

BUCK CLAYTON & HIS ALL-STARS
Emmett Berry, Buck Clayton (tp); Wells (tb); Earle Warren (cl/as); Buddy Tate (ts); Al Williams (p); Gene Ramey (b); Herbie Lovelle (d).
NYC, November 25, 1958:

CO61795	Sunday	*Col CL 1320*
CO61796	Swingin' Along on Broadway	*Col CL 1320*
CO61797	Night Train	*Col CL 1320*
CO61798	Buckini	*Col CL 1320*
CO61799	Moonglow	*Col CL 1320*
CO61800	Swinging at the Copper Rail	*Col CL 1320*
CO61801	Mean to Me	*Col CL 1320*
CO61802	Outer Drive	*Col CL 1320*

REX STEWART/DICKY WELLS QUINTET
Rex Stewart (ct); Wells (tb); John Bunch (p); Leonard Gaskin (b); Charles Master Paolo (d).
NYC, January 20, 1959:

K2PB0877	Ain't We Got Fun?	*Vic LPM-2024*
K2PB0878	Jeepers Creepers	*Vic LPM-2024*
K2PB0879	I May Be Wrong	*Vic LPM-2024*
K2PB0880	Little Sir Echo	*Vic LPM-2024*

NYC, January 21, 1959:

K2PB0882	Side by Side	*Vic LPM-2024*
K2PB0883	Thou Swell	*Vic LPM-2024*
K2PB0884	Let's Do It	*Vic LPM-2024*

NYC, January 22, 1959:

K2PB0881	Gimme a Little Kiss	*Vic LPM-2024*
K2PB0885	Frankie & Johnny	*Vic LPM-2024*
K2PB0886	Together	*Vic LPM-2024*
K2PB0887	Let's Call the Whole Thing Off	*Vic LPM-2024*

DICKY WELLS & HIS ORCHESTRA
Vic Dickenson, George Matthews, Benny Morton, Wells (tb); Skip Hall (p/org); Kenny Burrell (g); Everett Barksdale (b); Herbie Lovelle (d).
NYC, April 21, 1959:

	Blue Moon (-1)	unissued
	Blue Moon (-2)	unissued
	Blue Moon (-3)	unissued
	Blue Moon (-5)	*Fel FAJ 7009*
	It's All Over Now (-1)	unissued
	It's All Over Now (-5)	unissued
	It's All Over Now (-7)	*Fel FAJ 7009*
	Wine-O Junction (-3)	unissued
	Wine-O Junction (-7)	unissued
	Wine-O Junction (-8)	*Fel FAJ 7009*

Air Lift (-1)	unissued
Air Lift (-2)	unissued
Air Lift (-?)	*Fel FAJ 7009*

Omit Burrell. Everett Barksdale (g); Major Holley (b).
Same date:

Heavy Duty (-3)	unissued
Heavy Duty (-5)	unissued
Heavy Duty (-6)	*Fel FAJ 7009*
Girl Hunt (-7)	unissued
Girl Hunt (-9)	unissued
Girl Hunt (-11)	*Fel FAJ 7009*
Girl Hunt (insert for -11)	*Fel FAJ 7009*
Short, Lean, Fat & Small (-2)	unissued
Short, Lean, Fat & Small (-6)	*Fel FAJ 7009*

BUCK CLAYTON ALL-STARS

Emmett Berry, Buck Clayton (tp); Wells (tb); Earle Warren (cl/as); Buddy
Tate (ts); Al Williams (p); Gene Ramey (b); Herbie Lovelle (d); Jimmy Rush-
ing (vo).
Concert, Copenhagen, September 17, 1959:

Outer Drive	*Steep SCC-6006*
Swinging at the Copper Rail	*Steep SCC-6006*
Moonglow	*Steep SCC-6006*
Night Train	*Steep SCC-6006*
Swinging Along on Broadway	*Steep SCC-6006*
Exactly Like You (vJR)	*Steep SCC-6007*
I Want a Little Girl	*Steep SCC-6007*
Every Day I Have the Blues	*Steep SCC-6007*
'Deed I Do (vJR)	*Steep SCC-6007*
Goin' to Chicago (vJR)	*Steep SCC-6007*
Sent for You Yesterday (vJR)	*Steep SCC-6007*
Sent for You Yesterday (encore) (vJR)	*Steep SCC-6007*

Concert, Olympia Theatre, Paris, October 17, 1959:

Swingin' the Blues	*Palm Club 26*
Goin' to Chicago (vJR)	*Palm Club 26*
Sent for You Yesterday (vJR)	*Palm Club 26*
Sunny Side of the Street (vJR)	*Palm Club 26*
Night Train	*Palm Club 26*
Outer Drive	*Palm Club 26*
Moonglow	unissued
I Want a Little Girl	unissued

EMMETT BERRY SEXTET

Emmett Berry (tp); Wells (tb); Paul Gonsalves (ts); Skip Hall (p); Milt Hinton
(b); Panama Francis (d).
NYC, November 18, 1959:

Miss Chris	*Col(E) 33SX 1246*
Slow, Man, Slow	*Col(E) 33SX 1246*
Three Alarm	*Col(E) 33SX 1246*

| Baby, Won't You Please Come Home? | *Col(E) 33SX 1246* |
| Pee Gee | unissued |

ANDY GIBSON & HIS ORCHESTRA

Emmett Berry, Willie Cook, Jimmy Nottingham (tp); Vic Dickenson, Eli Robinson, Wells (tb); George Dorsey, Hilton Jefferson (as); Paul Gonsalves, Prince Robinson (ts); Leslie Johnakins (bs); Jimmy Jones (p); Kenny Burrell (g); Milt Hinton (b); Jimmy Crawford (d).
NYC, December 1, 1959:

| K3JB6345 | Blueprint | *Cam CAL-554* |

BUTTERBEANS & SUSIE

Butterbeans & Susie (Joe & Susie Edwards) (vo) acc. Dick Vance (tp); Wells (tb); Earle Warren (as); Eddie Heywood (p); Leonard Gaskin (b); Jimmy Crawford (d).
NYC, April 8, 1960:

Ballin' the Jack (vB&S)	*Fest LP 7000*
There'll Be Some Changes Made (vB&S)	*Fest LP 7000*
Until the Real Thing Comes Along (vB&S)	*Fest LP 7000*
A Married Man's a Fool (vB&S)	*Fest LP 7000*

LEROY PARKINS & HIS YAZOO RIVER JAZZBAND

Johnny Letman (tp); Wells* (tb); Leroy Parkins (cl/ts); Dick Wellstood (p); Danny Barker (g/vo); Ahmed Abdul-Malik (b); Manzie Johnson (d).
NYC, May 3, 1960:

B6590	Ham & Eggs (vDB)	Bethlehem 11098
B6591	Little Liza Jane (vDB)	Bethlehem 11098
	Louisiana	
	Tishomingo Blues	
	Careless Love (vDB)	
	Limehouse Blues	
	Baddest Man in Texas (vDB)	
	Struttin' with Some Barbecue	
	Royal Garden Blues	

NB: All titles on Bethlehem *BCP 6047*.
*Previously listed as Dick Rath, but identified as Wells by Bethlehem's then newly appointed A&R man, vibist Teddy Charles, in *Down Beat*, July 21, 1960, p. 14. This was the first Bethlehem record date Charles had supervised.

JIMMY RUSHING WITH BUCK CLAYTON'S ALL-STARS

Buck Clayton (tp); Benny Morton, Wells (tb); Buster Bailey (cl); Coleman Hawkins (ts); Claude Hopkins (p); Everett Barksdale (g); Gene Ramey (b); Jimmy Crawford (d).
NYC, July 7, 1960:

CO65017	Shipwrecked Blues (vJR)	*Col CL 1605*
CO65018	Muddy Water (Mississippi Moan) (vJR)	*Col CL 1605*
CO65019	Gulf Coast Blues (vJR)	*Col CL 1605*
CO65020	Everybody Loves My Baby (vJR)	*Col CL 1605*
CO65021	Trouble in Mind (vJR)	*Col CL 1605*

NYC, July 13, 1960:

CO65059	Downhearted Blues (vJR)	*Col CL 1605*
CO65060	Squeeze Me (vJR)	*Col CL 1605*
CO65061	How Come You Do Me Like	*Col CL 1605*
	You Do? (vJR)	
CO65062	Crazy Blues (vJR)	*Col CL 1605*
CO65063	Arkansas Blues (vJR)	*Col CL 1605*

TOMMY GWALTNEY'S KANSAS CITY NINE

Buck Clayton (tp); Bobby Zottola (tp/a-h); Wells (tb); Tommy Gwaltney (cl/as/vb/xyl); Tommy Newsome (cl/ts); John Bunch (p); Charlie Byrd (g); Whitey Mitchell (b); Buddy Schutz (d).
NYC, October 5–6, 1960:

Hello Babe	*Riv RLP 353*
Just an Old Manuscript	*Riv RLP 353*
Kansas City Ballad	*Riv RLP 353*
The Jumping Blues	*Riv RLP 353*
Walter Page	*Riv RLP 353*
Midnight Mama	*Riv RLP 353*
John's Idea	*Riv RLP 353*
Steppin' Pretty	*Riv RLP 353*
Dedicated to You	*Riv RLP 353*
The New Tulsa Blues	*Riv RLP 353*

NANCY HARROW WITH BUCK CLAYTON'S JAZZ STARS

Buck Clayton (tp); Wells (tb); Tommy Gwaltney (cl/as); Buddy Tate (ts); Danny Bank (as/bs); Dick Wellstood (p); Kenny Burrell (g*); Milt Hinton (b); Oliver Jackson (d); Nancy Harrow (vo).
NYC, November 2–3, 1960:

Can't We Be Friends?* (vNH)	*Candid CJM 8008*
Sunny Side of the Street* (vNH)	*Candid CJM 8008*
Take Me Back, Baby (vNH)	*Candid CJM 8008*
All Too Soon (vNH)	*Candid CJM 8008*
Wild Women Don't Have	*Candid CJM 8008*
the Blues (vNH)	
I've Got the World on a String (vNH)	*Candid CJM 8008*
I Don't Know What Kind of Blues	*Candid CJM 8008*
I've Got (vNH)	
Blues for Yesterday (vNH)	*Candid CJM 8008*

BOOTY WOOD OCTET

Vic Dickenson, Wells, Booty Wood (tb); Johnny Hodges (as); Paul Gonsalves (ts); Sir Charles Thompson (p); Aaron Bell (b); Oliver Jackson (d).
NYC, December 13, 1960:

Sunday	*Col(E) 33SX 1342*
Snowstorm	*Col(E) 33SX 1342*
Blues in Bones	*Col(E) 33SX 1342*
Our Delight	*Col(E) 33SX 1342*

214

BUCK CLAYTON ALL-STARS
Emmett Berry, Buck Clayton (tp); Wells (tb); Earle Warren (cl/as); Buddy
Tate (ts); Sir Charles Thompson (p/cel*); Gene Ramey (b); Oliver Jackson
(d).
NYC, April 10, 1961:

Night Ferry	*Col(E) 33SX 1390*
I Can't Give You Anything but Love	*Col(E) 33SX 1390*
One for Buck	*Col(E) 33SX 1390*
Mr. Melody Maker*	*Col(E) 33SX 1390*
Blue Mist	*Col(E) 33SX 1390*
Prince Eagle Head	*Col(E) 33SX 1390*

BUCK CLAYTON ALL-STARS WITH JIMMY WITHERSPOON
As last, add Jimmy Witherspoon (vo).
Olympia Theatre, Paris, April 22, 1961:

Swinging at the Copper Rail	*Vg LD-544*
Outer Drive	*Vg LD-544*
Robbins' Nest	*Vg LD-544*
Moonglow	*Vg LD-544*
Swinging the Blues	*Vg LD-544*
Night Train	
Stompin' at the Savoy	
I'll Always Be in Love with You (vJW)	*Vg LD-546*
Gee, Baby, Ain't I Good to You? (vJW)	*Vg LD-546*
See See Rider (vJW)	*Vg LD-546*
I Make a Lot of Money (vJW)	*Vg LD-546*
Blowin' the Blues (vJW)	*Vg LD-546*
'Tain't Nobody's Business If I Do (vJW)	*Vg LD-546*
Everything I Do Is Wrong (vJW)	*Vg LD-546*
Roll 'Em Pete (vJW)	*Vg LD-546*

NB: All instrumental performances also on *Vg 600160* (CD).

RAY CHARLES WITH GERALD WILSON'S ORCHESTRA
Martin Banks, Wallace Davenport, Phil Guilbeau, John Hunt (tp); Jim Her-
bert, George Matthews, Wells (tb); Keg Johnson (btb); Hank Crawford, Rudy
Powell (as); David Newman, Don Wilkerson (ts); Leroy Cooper (bs); Ray
Charles (p/vo); Sonny Forrest (g); Edgar Willis (b); Bruno Carr (d).
LA, February 5, 1962:

10747	Bye, Bye Love (vRC)	*ABC-Par ABC410*
10748	Careless Love (vRC)	*ABC-Par ABC410*
10749	Hey! Good Looking (vRC)	*ABC-Par ABC410*
10750	Just a Little Lovin' (vRC)	*ABC-Par ABC410*

RAY CHARLES WITH GIL FULLER'S ORCHESTRA
Personnel as last.
LA, February 7, 1962:

10755	Just a Little Lovin' (vRC)	*ABC-Par ABC410*
10756	Half as Much (vRC)	*ABC-Par ABC410*
10757	Move It on Over (vRC)	*ABC-Par ABC410*
10758	It Makes No Difference Now (vRC)	*ABC-Par ABC410*

LEONARD GASKIN ALL-STARS
Herman Autrey (tp); Wells (tb); Herb Hall (cl); Red Richards (p); Leonard
Gaskin (b); Herbie Lovelle (d).
Englewood Cliffs, NJ, August 23, 1962:
SA170   Ballin' the Jack   *Pr SVLP 2033*
SA171   Memphis Blues   *Pr SVLP 2033*

Add Pee Wee Erwin (tp), Big Chief Russell Moore (tb), & Bud Freeman (ts).
Same date:
SA173   Darktown Strutters' Ball   *Pr SVLP 2033*
NB: Wells absent from other performances recorded at this session.

JOHN LEE HOOKER BAND
Wells (tb); John Lee Hooker (g/vo); Barry Galbraith (g); Milt Hinton (d).
NYC, November 23, 1965:
               Money (That's What I Want) (vJLH)   *Imp AS 9103*
NB: Wells absent from other performances recorded at this session.

JIMMY RUSHING WITH OLIVER NELSON & HIS ORCHESTRA
Clark Terry, others u/k (tp); Wells, others u/k (tb); u/k (as); Bob Ashton,
u/k (ts); Hank Jones (p/org); Shirley Scott (org); Kenny Burrell (g); George
Duvivier (b); Grady Tate (d); Jimmy Rushing (vo).
NYC, February 9 & 10, 1967:
               Berkeley Campus Blues (vJR)   *Bway BLS 6005*
               Keep the Faith, Baby (vJR)   *Bway BLS 6005*
               You Can't Run Around (vJR)   *Bway BLS 6005*
               Blues in the Dark (vJR)   *Bway BLS 6005*
               Baby, Don't Tell on Me (vJR)   *Bway BLS 6005*
               Every Day I Have the Blues (vJR)   *Bway BLS 6005*
               I Left My Baby (vJR)   *Bway BLS 6005*
               Undecided Blues (vJR)   *Bway BLS 6005*
               Evil Blues (vJR)   *Bway BLS 6005*

JIMMY RUSHING ALL-STARS
Buck Clayton (tp); Wells (tb); Julian Dash (ts); Sir Charles Thompson (p);
Gene Ramey (b); Jo Jones (d); Jimmy Rushing (vo).
NYC, October 30, 1967:
               M. J. R. Blues   *MJR MJR-8104*
               Who's Sorry Now? (vJR)   *MJR MJR-8104*
               Broadway   unissued
               St. James Infirmary (vJR)   *MJR MJR-8104*
               C-Jam Blues   *MJR MJR-8120*
               Good Morning Blues (vJR)   unissued
               'Deed I Do (vJR)   unissued
               These Foolish Things   *MJR MJR-8104*
               You Can Depend on Me (vJR)   unissued
               The Sheik of Araby   unissued
               Gee, Baby, Ain't I Good To You? (vJR) *MJR MJR-8104*
               Moten Stomp   unissued
               Baby, Won't You Please   *MJR MJR-8120*
               Come Home? (vJR)
               All of Me (vJR)   *MJR MJR-8120*

216

Old Man River	unissued
Sunny Side of the Street (vJR)	unissued
Boogie Blues	unissued
I Ain't Got Nobody (vJR)	unissued
I Surrender Dear (vJR)	*MJR MJR-8120*
One O'Clock Jump	unissued
Outskirts of Town (vJR)	unissued
Stormy Monday Blues (vJR)	*MJR MJR-8120*
Jelly Jelly (vJR)	*MJR MJR-8120*
Perdido	unissued
Good Morning Blues (vJR)	*MJR MJR-8104*
Tin Roof Blues	unissued
I'm Gonna Sit Right Down & Write Myself a Letter (vJR)	unissued

NB: Wells absent from one other title from this session.

Wells (tb); Buddy Tate (ts); Dave Frishberg (p); Hugh McCracken, Wally Richardson (g); Bobby Bushnell (elb); Joe Marshall (d); Jimmy Rushing (vo). NYC, early 1968:

Sent for You Yesterday (vJR)	*Bway BLS 6017*
Bad Loser (vJR)	*Bway BLS 6017*
Sonny Boy Blues (vJR)	*Bway BLS 6017*
We Remember Prez	*Bway BLS 6017*
Cryin' Blues (vJR)	*Bway BLS 6017*
Take Me Back, Baby (vJR)	*Bway BLS 6017*
Tell Me I'm Not Too Late (vJR)	*Bway BLS 6017*

JAY McSHANN & HIS ORCHESTRA
Doc Cheatham (tp); Wells (tb); Earle Warren (as); Herbie Mann (ts); Jay McShann (p/vo); John Scofield (g); Eddie Gomez (b); Connie Kay (d); Janis Siegel (vo).
NYC, August 3, 8, & 10, 1978:

Blue Feeling	*Atl SD 8804*
Ain't Misbehavin' (vJS)	*Atl SD 8804*

Milt Hinton (b) replaces Gomez.
Same dates:

Dickie's Dream	*Atl SD 8804*
Jumpin' the Blues	*Atl SD 8804*

DICKY WELLS QUINTET
Wells (tb/vo); Buddy Tate (cl/ts); Dick Katz (p); George Duvivier (b); Oliver Jackson (d).
NYC, April 8–9, 1981:

Honeysuckle Rose	*Uptown UP 27.07*
Lonesome Road (vDW)	*Uptown UP 27.07*
Tweedledee Dee Dum	*Uptown UP 27.07*
Dicky's Famous Break	*Uptown UP 27.07*
She's Funny That Way (vDW)	*Uptown UP 27.07*

Omit Buddy Tate. Michael Moore (b) replaces George Duvivier.
NYC, April 29, 1981:

I Surrender Dear (vDW)	*Uptown UP 27.07*
Dicky Wells' New Blues (-1)	*Uptown UP 27.07*
Dicky Wells' New Blues (-2)	*Uptown UP 27.07*
Black & Blue	*Uptown UP 27.07*

.... glossary

Ann, n. White girl.
anything-goes, n. Very sexy girl.
Apple, n. Big city
apple-head, n. Apple shaped head
ax, n. Often an instrument

bad, adj. Often the reverse of literal
 meaning. Good, great.
ball, n. A good time.—v. To have
 fun.
ball-a-week, n. $100 a week.
ball-fifty, n. $150 a week.
barrelhouse, adj. lowdown and
 ornery.
b. b., n. (*See* biscuit butt; butter
 butt)
beans, n. pl. Dollars.
beat-shoes, n. pl. Socks.
B Flat, adj. Large.
big stockings, n. pl. Big legs.
big wheels, n. pl. Big legs.
birdlegs, n. The ability to sing well.
 (e.g. "She's got birdlegs.")
biscuit butt, n. A rounded
 bottom.
blanket, n. Overcoat.
blow, v. To play an instrument.
bone, n. Trombone.—pl.
 Trombones or dollars.
boon-koon buddy, n. Close friend.
bread, n. Money.
bubble eye, adj. Big-eyed.
bug, v. To annoy or handicap.
buns, n. Buttocks.
burn, v. To cook.
butter butt, n. Fat bottom.

carve, v. To excel in playing.
cat, n. A man.
Charlie, n. A white male.
chick, n. a girl.
chocolate malt, n. A colored girl.
chops, n. pl. Lips.
Claw, n. The other man, a rival
 lover.
cleanhead, n. A bald person.
cream, v. To smile or be happy.—n.
 The elite, the cream of the crop.
crumbcrushers, n. pl. Teeth.
cut, v. To excel in playing. Also, to
 leave.

d. a., n. Dog's ass.
Darby Hicks, n. The other man, a
 rival lover.
day people, n. pl. Those who work
 by day.
dig, v. Understand, appreciate, or
 give attention to.
dirty stockings, n. pl. Hairy legs.
dog, v. To hurt or distress.—n. An
 inferior tune.
dog-bed, n. Overcoat.
dog face, n. An ugly face.
domino, n. Dice or craps.
down, adj. Aware (*See also* hip).
drag, v. To depress.—n. A depressing person, performance or
 situation.

E Flat, adj. Small.
egghead, n. Egg-shaped head. Also,
 an intellectual.

every-day, n. A very sexy girl.
eyes, n. pl. Admiration or desire ("I have eyes for his kind of music.")

fade, v. To cover a bet in gambling.
fan, v. Mollify.
feet, n. A person with sore feet, bunions or corns.
fin, n. Five dollars.
flappers, n. pl. Arms.
flea-bed, n. A dog.
fly, adj. Slick.
four bars, n. pl. A short time. (See two bars.)
full, adj. Colored.
full-blooded, adj. Wholly white or Negro.
funky, adj. Earthy. Contemporary equivalent of barrelhouse and gutbucket. q.v.

gam, n. Leg.
ghost, n. A white person.
gig, n. A job or engagement. "Gigging" implies irregular engagements.
gold, n. Money.
goof, n. A mistake—v. To make a mistake.
grey, n. A white person.
ground-pad, n. A shoe.
gutbucket, adj. Lowdown & ornery (See also barrelhouse and funky.)

hand grenade, n. An amorous note.
hang, v. To outdo or exhaust.
head, n. An oral arrangement.
hemp, n. Marijuana.
hid, n. Drum.
high-pockets, n. A tall fellow.
high-sitting, adj. Sitting carelessly, legs apart.
hip, adj. Aware, understanding.
hog-head, n. A big head.
hole, n. A basement club.
Homes, n. A nickname for someone from your hometown.
honeydripper, n. A good-looking boy or girl.
horn, n. Instrument.

iron jaws, n. pl. Strong lips, particularly in the case of trumpet players.

jam, v. To improvise, usually after hours, hence "jam session."
Jane, n. A colored girl.
jaw, n. Jowls, hence "hog jaw," "big jaw," and "bubble jaw."
jive, n. Nonsense—adj. Sham.—v. To play around lightheartedly.
John, n. A colored male.
joint, n. Place, club, restaurant, house.
jug, n. A bottle of liquor.
juice, n. Liquor. Also, marijuana.
junkie, n. One addicted to such drugs as heroine or cocaine.

kisser, n. Lips.
knock-on-any-door, n. A very sexy person.
knowledge bump, n. Head.

later, adj. Good bye, abbreviation of "See you later."
line, n. Money. When borrowing, "line" doubles the amount actually required. Thus "line fifty soft" indicates a need for twenty-five cents and "line fifty hard" for twenty-five dollars.
little onions, n. Children.
Little Snow White, n. A white child.
loot, n. Money.
loving-cup ears, n. pl. Big ears.
lush, n. A drinker.

maulers, n. pl. Teeth.
moss, n. Hair.
mudlocks, n. pl. Shoes.

new girl, n. Either new lover or child.
night-fighter, n. A colored person.
night people, n. pl. Those who work by night.
no days, adv. Never.
not-tonight, n. A good girl.

ofay, n. A white person.
onion-head, n. Onion-shaped head.

outer vine, n. Overcoat (*See* vine.)
Oxford Grey, n. A colored person.

pad, n. House, room, apartment.
paddle-foot, n. A flat-footed person.
paint job, n. Color of skin.
peck, v. To eat.
pecker, n. A Southern white person
    (from red-necked woodpeckers).
pegs, n. pl. Legs.
peola, n. A very light-skinned
    colored person.
pieces, n. Money or musicians.
pink-toes, n. A white person.
pimpsteak, n. A hot dog.
pot, n. Marijuana.
potatoes, n. pl. Dollars.

rough, adj. Outstanding.
rub, v. Mollify.

sawbuck, n. Ten dollars.
scarf, v. To eat.
scratch, n. Money.
sharp, adj. Smart.
short, n. A car.
shorty, adj. Tall.
Shorty George, n. The other man, a
    rival lover.
slim, adj. Short.
slue-foot, adj. Bat-footed.
socks, n. pl. Thin shoes.
spareribs, n. A real skinny fellow.
split, v. To leave.

squashy, adj. Short and fat.
steeplehead, n. A high head.
stems, n. pl. Legs.
stretch, adj. Tall.
stumpy, adj. Short.
sugar hips, n. pl. Pretty hips.

tab, n. Credit.
taste, n. A drink, or a small
    quantity.
three-quarter, adj. Almost white.
tog, n. A suit.
toothpicks, n. pl. Thin legs.
Track, n. The Savoy ballroom.
trail-blazer, n. A fine girl with all
    the charms.
turf, n. The street.
turn on, v. To explain.
two bars, n. pl. A very short time
    (*See* four bars.)

vanilla malt, n. A white girl.
vine, n. A suit. Also rumor, as from
    the grapevine.

wayback, n. Too old.
whimpy, adj. Short, half a man.
Whitey, n. A white person.
wig, n. Head. To have a "tight wig"
    is to be high or drunk.
windshield, n. Thin overcoat.
wings, n. pl. Arms.
wingy, adj. one-armed.
woodshed, v. To practice.

. . . . *index*

227